OPERATION ORCA

OPERATION ORCA

Springer, Luna and the Struggle to Save

West Coast Killer Whales

Daniel Francis & Gil Hewlett

HARBOUR PUBLISHING

Harbour Publishing Co. Ltd.
P.O. Box 219, Madeira Park, BC, V0N 2H0
www.harbourpublishing.com

Printed and bound in Canada

Text Design by Nancy de Brouwer, Alofii Graphic Design
Front cover photo by David Fleetham
Maps by Roger Handling, information courtesy of Doug Sandilands,
Vancouver Aquarium

Harbour Publishing acknowledges financial support from the Government
of Canada through the Book Publishing Industry Development Program
and the Canada Council for the Arts, and from the Province of British
Columbia through the British Columbia Arts Council and the Book
Publisher's Tax Credit through the Ministry of Provincial Revenue.

THE CANADA COUNCIL | LE CONSEIL DES ARTS
FOR THE ARTS | DU CANADA
SINCE 1957 | DEPUIS 1957

BRITISH
COLUMBIA
ARTS COUNCIL
Supported by the Province of British Columbia

LIBRARY AND ARCHIVES CANADA CATALOGUING IN PUBLICATION

Francis, Daniel
    Operation orca : Springer, Luna and the struggle to save west coast
killer whales / Daniel Francis and Gil Hewlett.

Includes index.
ISBN 978-1-55017-426-7
    1. Springer (Whale)
    2. Luna (Whale)
    3. Killer whale — British Columbia.
    4. Killer whale — Washington (State)
    5. Wildlife rescue.
I. Hewlett, Gil, 1947- II. Title.

QL737.C432F72 2007   599.53'617743   C2007-903866-2

This book is dedicated to the memory of Dr. Michael A. Bigg (1939–1990). Mike spent his working career as head of marine mammal research with Fisheries and Oceans Canada, based in Nanaimo, BC. He was best known for his pioneering research on killer whales, which included key photo-identification techniques that enabled Mike to systematically catalogue all of the killer whales frequenting British Columbian waters. His research confirmed that killer whales maintain group-specific traditions that persist for generations, that two fundamentally different types of killer whales (fish-eating residents and mammal-eating transients) share the same waters and that resident killer whales of both sexes spend their entire lives with their mothers and close maternal kin. Mike mentored students from around the world, including a number of key figures in this book, and produced collaborative, long-term killer whale research that made this project possible. Mike is missed by all who knew him personally; those who didn't are well acquainted with his work and continue to work within the traditions he established.

▪ CONTENTS

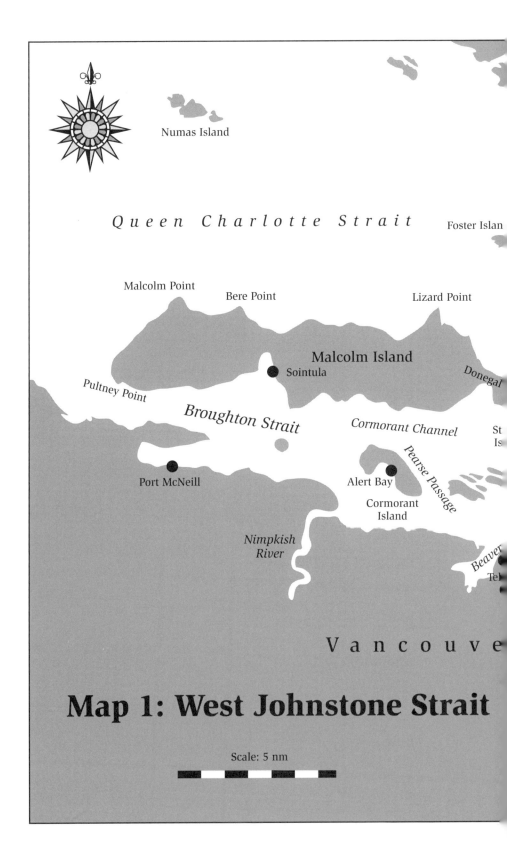

Numas Island

Queen Charlotte Strait

Foster Islan

Malcolm Point

Bere Point

Lizard Point

Malcolm Island
Sointula

Donegal

Pultney Point

Broughton Strait

Cormorant Channel

St
Is

Port McNeill

Pearse Passage

Alert Bay

Cormorant
Island

Nimpkish
River

Beaver

Tel

Vancouve

Map 1: West Johnstone Strait

Scale: 5 nm

Fife Sound

Eden
Island

Baker
Island

Bonwick
Island

Gilford Island

Spring Passage

Swanson
Island

Knight Inlet

Village Island

Dong
Chong
Bay

Turnour Island

Hanson
Island

Orcalab

Blackney Passage

Harbledown Island

West Cracroft Island

Boat Bay

sland

Johnstone Strait

Robson Bight
(Michael Bigg)
Ecological Reserve

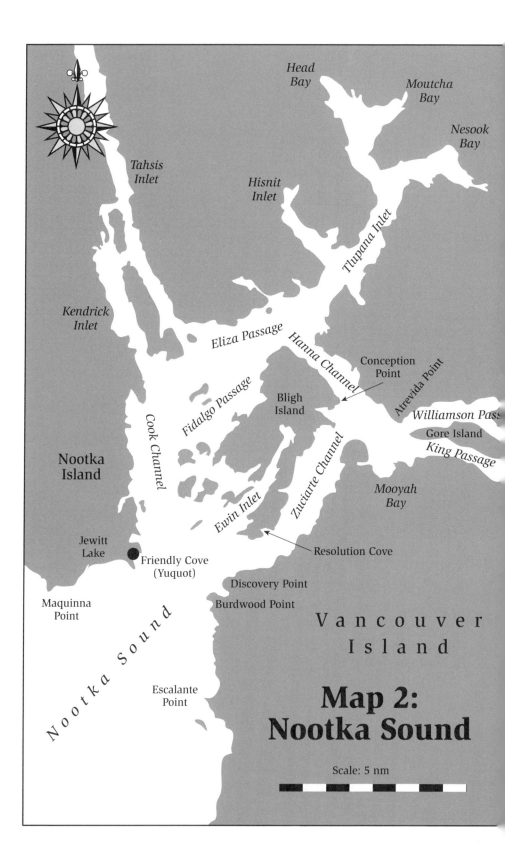

Head
Bay

Moutcha
Bay

Nesook
Bay

Tahsis
Inlet

Hisnit
Inlet

Tlupana Inlet

Kendrick
Inlet

Eliza Passage

Hanna Channel

Conception
Point

Atrevida Point

Fidalgo Passage

Bligh
Island

Williamson Pass

Gore Island

King Passage

Cook Channel

Nootka
Island

Zuciarte Channel

Mooyah
Bay

Jewitt
Lake

Ewin Inlet

Friendly Cove
(Yuquot)

Resolution Cove

Discovery Point

Maquinna
Point

Burdwood Point

Vancouver
Island

N o o t k a   S o u n d

Escalante
Point

**Map 2:
Nootka Sound**

Scale: 5 nm

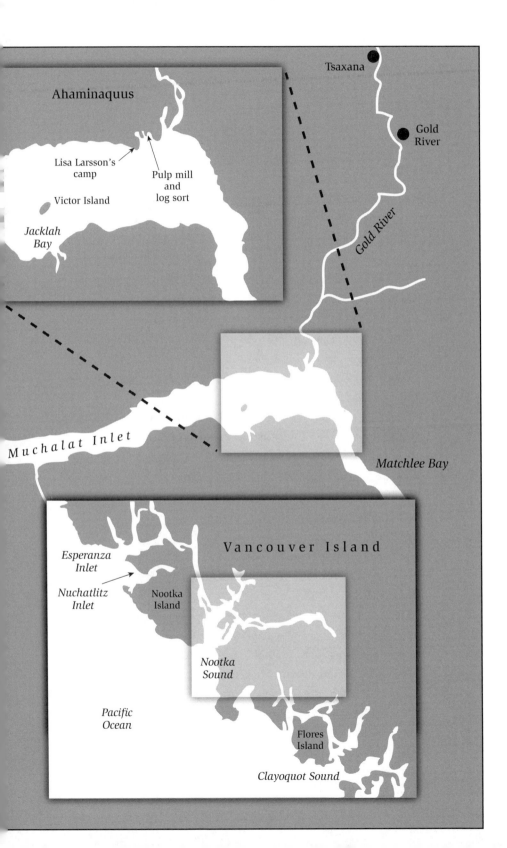

■ CHRONOLOGIES

Springer (A73) Chronology

1999/2000 Winter — Springer born to Sutlej (A45), a member of the A24 matriline in A4 pod. Sutlej died during the subsequent winter.

2000   June 9 — Springer sighted in Whale Channel on the north coast by Graeme Ellis and John Ford.

September 18 — Springer sighted in Alaska by Marilyn Dalheim of the US National Marine Mammal Laboratory.

2001   August — Springer spotted in Queen Charlotte Strait in the company of an adolescent female, G50. G50's pod is seen in the autumn near the entrance to the Strait of Juan de Fuca.

November 1 — First sighting in Puget Sound of a lone whale that might have been Springer.

December — Washington State Ferries employee sees a lone killer whale around the Vashon Island ferry terminal.

2002   January 12 — Mark Sears makes the first confirmed sighting of the calf that was later identified as Springer off the north end of Vashon Island.

February 13 — Delegation from the Vancouver Aquarium visits Springer to assess her health.

February 14 — Vancouver Aquarium proposes a rescue plan to the US National Marine Fisheries Service.

February 22 — Scientific panel convened by the NMFS has its first conference call.

March 4 — Public meeting held in Seattle to discuss Springer.

May 24 — NMFS announces that it will intervene to capture Springer.

June 13 — Springer is captured and transported to a netpen at Manchester, Washington, for assessment.

July 13 — Springer is transported by boat from Manchester to a netpen in Dong Chong Bay on Hanson Island near Johnstone Strait.

July 14 — Springer is released from the netpen back into the wild.

July 15 — Springer briefly joins other whales at the rubbing beach in Robson Bight.

July 18 — Springer seen for the first time closely associating with another whale, Nodales (A51). From this point she is spotted regularly with other whales.

October 6 — Springer seen leaving the Johnstone Strait area.

2003   June 9 — A young whale photographed in Fisher Channel is identified as Springer.

July 9 — Whale watcher Bill Mackay spots Springer in Johnstone Strait in company with her family pod. She has survived her first winter up the coast and her relocation is considered a success.

Luna (L98) Chronology

1999   September 19 — Luna is born near San Juan Island to Splash (L67).

2000   Spring — Luna returns to Puget Sound with his mother.

September 23 — Luna seen in Haro Strait swimming in the company of his uncle, Orcan (L39). This is the last time Orcan is seen, and the last time Luna is seen until he appears in Nootka Sound.

2001   May 20 — Luna's family pod appears in Haro Strait but Luna is absent and presumed dead.

July 6 — Fred and Darlene Lazuk sight a lone killer whale calf in Mooyah Bay, Nootka Sound.

October — The Nootka Sound calf is identified as Luna.

December — At an international marine mammal conference hosted by the Vancouver Aquarium, Luna's presence in Nootka Sound is revealed to a small number of researchers.

2002   August — The Marine Mammal Monitoring Project (later the Luna Stewardship Project) begins monitoring Luna's interactions with boats in Nootka Sound.

September — Luna has strayed outside his "box" in Mooyah Bay and begun visiting the Gold River dock.

2003   February — The federal department of Fisheries and Oceans Canada, or DFO, convenes the first meeting of a scientific advisory panel to discuss Luna. The panel reaches no consensus about what to do, but a Springer-like relocation seems probable.

March 2—A delegation from the Vancouver Aquarium arrives in Gold River to try, unsuccessfully, to obtain a blood sample from Luna.

May 29—DFO announces that it is not prepared to intervene with Luna but will continue monitoring the situation through the Luna Stewardship Project.

September 10—DFO reconvenes its scientific panel. During the summer, interactions between Luna and boats became more frequent and serious. DFO tells the scientists it is now ready to move Luna and wants a plan.

October—DFO announces that it will relocate Luna to southern Vancouver Island the following spring.

2004   March—The Luna Research Project begins, sponsored by OrcaLab.

April—DFO announces details of the plan to relocate Luna, to be carried out by the Vancouver Aquarium. The local Mowachaht-Muchalaht First Nations are opposed.

June 1—The Aquarium is told to start preparations for the capture and relocation.

June 9—DFO gives final authorization for the plan.

June 22—The first attempt to lure Luna into a netpen is thwarted by the arrival of canoes paddled by the Mowachaht-Muchalaht.

June 24—DFO suspends the attempt to capture Luna pending further consultations.

September—The Mowachaht-Muchalaht launch their own stewardship plan, the Tsux'iit Guardians.

2005   March—The Luna Research Project continues.

2006   March 10—Luna is killed when he is sucked into the propeller blades of a large tugboat near Mooyah Bay.

▪ INTRODUCTION

*"The greatness of a nation and its moral progress
can be judged by the way its animals are treated."*
— MAHATMA GANDHI

THE STORY TOLD IN *OPERATION ORCA* begins in 2001 with the discovery of two killer whales along the coast of British Columbia
and Washington State. These two whales became the focus of
an unprecedented scientific adventure that attracted worldwide
attention, ending in rescue for one and tragedy for the other.

But really this book begins much earlier, with the discovery
by its two authors of a fascination with whales that would last a
lifetime. One of Gil Hewlett's earliest memories is of walking on
the beach at Sidney near Victoria with his father and finding a
stranded gray whale lying in the sand. Two boys were carving their
initials into the flesh of the still-living animal. The huge whale died
and Gil watched the next day as the carcass was towed back out
to sea. As a youngster growing up on Vancouver Island, Gil recalls
hearing the killer whales as they swam through Sansum Narrows
near Maple Bay. The sound of their breathing and the sight of them
moving effortlessly through the water, so powerful and confident,
had a profound impact on the young boy. In 1964 Gil was hired
to work at the Vancouver Public Aquarium, as it was then called,
when he was still a graduate student in biology at the University
of British Columbia. This was a time when killer whales were

shot at and generally reviled by fishers and terrified boaters. The Aquarium's director, Murray Newman, was determined to capture a specimen, and shortly after Gil joined the staff he was dispatched to Sointula on Malcolm Island in Queen Charlotte Strait to assist a pair of American whale catchers, Frank Brocato and "Boots" Calandrino, who were trying to obtain an animal for a California oceanarium. Nothing came of this expedition, but in 1965 Gil was a member of the team that accompanied the captured killer whale Namu down the coast to Seattle, an adventure that is described in chapter 2 of *Operation Orca*. Thus began his long professional involvement with these fascinating marine mammals.

So little was known about killer whales at the time that it was widely, and wrongly, assumed there were thousands of them and they could be killed and captured without heed. Gil recalls talking to the esteemed Campbell River naturalist and author Roderick Haig-Brown, who told him that "thousands" of orcas swam through Seymour Narrows every year. We now know that the entire coastal population has never numbered much more than 350. In 1967 the Vancouver Aquarium obtained its first resident killer whale, named Skana, and Gil helped to train her. Since no one had any experience with cetaceans, they had to ask a local dog trainer for advice! For the entire thirty-year period that the Aquarium kept killer whales, Gil, as general curator of the marine mammal, BC fishes, tropical fishes, Amazon gallery and engineering departments, participated in their care and in research into their behaviour.

Dan Francis is a historian who discovered whales in the archives, not in the ocean. While researching the history of the Hudson's Bay Company, Dan became interested in a whaling operation the company ran in northern Quebec in the mid-nineteenth century. One thing led to another and Dan ended up writing two books about the history of commercial whaling. He experienced his first encounter with the animals in the wild in the early 1970s. It was long before whale watching had become the multimillion-dollar industry it is today—just a few shivering enthusiasts out on the St. Lawrence River in a battered old fisheries department vessel searching for belugas to look at — but the experience kindled an interest in whales that has never left him.

In 2001, Gil realized the Aquarium's involvement in the rescue of the lost whale Springer and the attempted rescue of Luna in Nootka Sound represented the culmination of the facility's long years of experience working with stranded marine mammals (see Afterword). The episode also seemed to sum up the complete transformation of the image of the killer whale, from just a few decades ago when it was official government policy to shoot them on sight, to today when thousands of people can be mobilized to work together to rescue a single animal. As he watched the intense public interest surrounding these "orphan" whales, Gil felt that it was a story that must be told. And who better than himself to tell it? He had been involved with killer whales his entire career, he had met and worked with all the major figures involved, and he possessed hands-on experience with many of the stranded animals the Aquarium has rescued over the years.

Gil spent four years conducting interviews with all the participants in the Springer/Luna saga: marine mammal scientists, animal rights activists, Aboriginal leaders, government officials, Aquarium staff and volunteers, and ordinary folks who found themselves swept up in the story. Then he and Dan shaped the research into this compelling story of rescue and return set in the context of our evolving ideas about the nature of killer whales.

■

DURING THE SEVERAL YEARS that we have been researching and writing this book, the authors have acquired many debts. First and foremost, Lance Barrett-Lennard, senior marine mammal scientist at the Vancouver Aquarium, has been a constant source of information and encouragement. Lance played a key role in both the relocation of Springer and the attempted relocation of Luna. His perspective on these events and his extensive knowledge of killer whales have helped us tremendously. Janet

Landucci, who in 2002 was the chair of the conservation and research committee of the Aquarium's board of directors, convinced the board that the Aquarium had to get involved in rescuing Springer and later recognized how important it was to write about this remarkable story. *Operation Orca* would not have come into being without her commitment to the project.

Members of the book committee made many useful comments on the manuscript as it evolved. Thanks to each of them: Janet Landucci, Hal Nelson, David Hoar, Bernie Hanby, Lance Barrett-Lennard and Margot Spence. Lisa Baskett, a volunteer at the Aquarium, contributed over two thousand hours of her time during the past five years organizing the taped interviews, transcribing many of the lengthy ones and doing much of the background research for the book. Hal Nelson, a retired marine biologist on the BC coast, carried out a variety of literature searches and organized the photographic archive. Doug Sandilands, coordinator of the Aquarium's Cetacean Sightings Network, spends his summers in Johnstone Strait as head of the Robson Bight Warden Program. Doug prepared the maps for the book and conducted much of the background research. Cara Lachmuth, a graduate student who worked with Lance Barrett-Lennard, proved to be a wizard at internet and library research. A number of Aquarium volunteers assisted with research, interview transcription, proofreading and cataloguing. They are: Amanda Maxwell, Judy Brown, Stephanie Kulferst, Sharon Hobbs, Tomiko Johnson, Doreen Guthrie, Lee Taylor, the late Norman Filmer, Monique Gardiner, Charissa Fung, Hans del Rosario, Jason Grafstrom, Kari Berdahl, Naomi Trepanier, Stephanie Chong, Suzanne Fearn, Daniel Amaya, Robert Visscher, Robynn Chan, Kathryn Morrisey and Cathy Wong. At the Aquarium, Lindsay Bradshaw, Rachelle Davidson, Ali Gomez, Brett Vo, Sarah Atherton, Sheryl Barber and Judy McVeigh helped us in so many ways. We extend special thanks to our wives, Robyn Hewlett and Quita Francis, who coped with the many weekend and evening hours "the book" intruded on our home lives.

1 ▪ FINDING SPRINGER

AS THE LATE AUTUMN OF 2001 turned to winter, scattered reports began filtering in to Ken Balcomb at the Center for Whale Research in Washington State's San Juan Islands. An unidentified killer whale had been seen swimming alone in southern Puget Sound. Balcomb was the clearing house for information about whale movements in northwest Washington. He was on a first-name basis with every killer whale in the sound and not much happened in local waters that he didn't hear about. On November 1, Tom McMillen, a com-

▪ This photograph of young Springer and his mother Sutlej (A45) was taken by Graeme Ellis on June 9, 2000, in Whale Channel on the north coast. *Graeme Ellis*

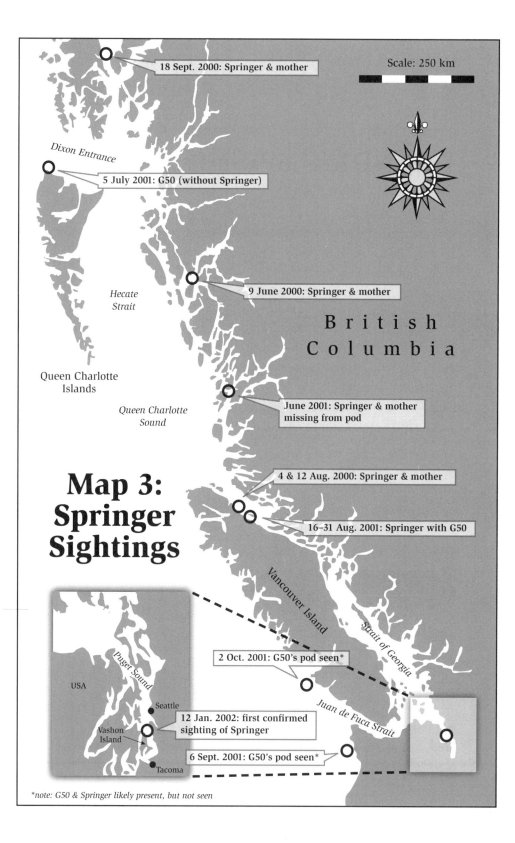

18 Sept. 2000: Springer & mother

Scale: 250 km

Dixon Entrance

5 July 2001: G50 (without Springer)

Hecate
Strait

9 June 2000: Springer & mother

B r i t i s h
C o l u m b i a

Queen Charlotte
Islands

Queen Charlotte
Sound

June 2001: Springer & mother
missing from pod

4 & 12 Aug. 2000: Springer & mother

Map 3:
Springer
Sightings

16–31 Aug. 2001: Springer with G50

Vancouver Island

Strait of Georgia

Puget Sound

USA

Seattle

2 Oct. 2001: G50's pod seen*

Juan de Fuca Strait

Vashon
Island

12 Jan. 2002: first confirmed
sighting of Springer

6 Sept. 2001: G50's pod seen*

Tacoma

*note: G50 & Springer likely present, but not seen

mercial whale watcher working out of Seattle, reported to Balcomb that he had been out in his boat between the mainland and Vashon Island when a little whale had popped up in front of him, then disappeared. A few weeks later, in the days before Christmas, Kim Shride, an employee on the Washington State ferry between Seattle and Vashon, began seeing a small whale off the ferry dock at the north end of the island. When Shride reported for work early in the morning, before the first ferry of the day, the whale would often be there, hanging around the bow of the vessel as it lay in its overnight slip. The whale would disappear when the ferry started its engines but it always came back. Shride called the whale Boo, for Baby Orphaned Orca.

On January 2, a female killer whale became stranded on the Dungeness Spit, near the entrance to Puget Sound, and died. She was accompanied by a male, possibly her son; he was rescued and released in the Strait of Juan de Fuca. Following this incident, reports began coming in more regularly of a lone whale appearing in the sound. Researchers wondered whether the two stranded whales might have had a calf that swam away from the spit and got lost. Or was it the animal that had been spotted earlier around Vashon Island? Then, on January 12, Mark Sears, an employee of Seattle Parks and Recreation and a veteran whale watcher with a network of informants around the sound, received a phone call from a friend working on the ferry: there was a small whale off the north end of the Island. Sears hopped into his small runabout. As he approached the spot where the whale had been seen, it suddenly broke the surface beside him. As soon as he returned home from this encounter, Sears phoned Balcomb with the news. The next day Balcomb went down to Seattle and the two men went out to have a look. They estimated that the whale was about two and a half years old. It appeared healthy, and Balcomb took some photographs but its origins remained a mystery. One possibility was that it was the same whale that had turned up in Nootka Sound on the west coast of Vancouver Island the previous summer. The odds against two lone killer whales appearing on the coast at almost the same time seemed huge. But on February 7, the other whale, by this time known as Luna, was spotted once again in Nootka Sound, leaving the identity of the Puget Sound animal still unknown.

What made the appearance of the Vashon Island calf both unusual and worrisome was that killer whales are extremely social animals. In the wild they are almost never alone. "More than mating, more than food, more than home territories," writes the researcher Alexandra Morton, "it's family around which a killer whale's world revolves."[1] Killer whales organize themselves into extended family groupings known as pods. After a calf is born and for as long as it is nursing, it does not wander far from its mother. The baby even learns to breathe in unison with its mother, a habit that may persist into adulthood: members of family groups have been observed breathing within a few seconds of each other while resting or travelling.[2] As a juvenile, the whale does not cut the maternal apron strings. In fact, as long as the mother is alive, her offspring will remain her almost constant companions. The technical term for this form of social organization is *matrilineal,* and a group of closely related whales linked by descent from a common mother is known as a *matriline.* In almost all other animal species that live in matrilineal societies, male offspring will leave the family group on reaching maturity and join or form new groups. Not the killer whale. So what was the calf doing on its own in Puget Sound?

Before they could answer that question, the scientists who were drawn into the mystery had to find out where the whale came from. To the unpractised eye, all killer whales in the Pacific Northwest look the same. But in fact, there is no single type of killer whale. Instead there are three types, each with its own diet, its own social structure, its own physical and behavioural characteristics.[3] Even the DNA of the different types is genetically distinct. One type is known as resident killer whales. Commonly, residents associate in pods of 10 to 25 animals, which move along the coast in fairly predictable patterns. Though their winter range remains uncertain, they tend to turn up most summers in the same geographic areas. Some of them, known as northern residents, visit the waters of Johnstone Strait and the neighbouring passages between northern Vancouver Island and the mainland. Members of this group seldom venture south of Seymour Narrows near Campbell River, and they range north to the Queen Charlotte Islands and southern Alaska. They are estimated to number about 215 individuals. A second, southern community of residents, about 85 strong, exists off southern Vancouver Island and in Puget Sound, while a third resident community (at least 360 whales) resides in Alaskan waters.

Resident whales eat fish, mainly salmon. This is the characteristic that most strongly differentiates them from the second type of killer whale, known as transients. Transient whales prey on marine mammals: seals, sea lions, porpoises, even larger whale species. They are more restless than their resident cousins, roaming the coast in search of their prey. They tend to travel in small groups of six or fewer. Unlike the residents, transients do not necessarily remain with their maternal group for life. They are known sometimes to disperse into social groups of their own or to strike off by themselves. As a result, their groups do not attain the same size and stability as resident groups, and researchers prefer not to refer to them as pods. Transients, about 220 of which have been identified off British Columbia, are also much quieter than residents, probably maintaining silence so as not to disturb their prey. It has been determined, for example, that harbour seals can distinguish between the sounds made by resident and transient whales and will disperse in a panic only when they hear the latter. Residents and transients often occupy the same territory, but they seldom interact and are not known to interbreed.

The third type of killer whale is known as offshores. They seldom appear in protected coastal waters, preferring to spend their time on the continental shelf at some distance from shore.

They appear to congregate in quite large groups, they do not mix with the other types and their population numbers are not known. They were only recognized in the late 1980s and much less is known about them than about the residents and transients of the inner coast.

Because the resident population is more predictable in its behaviour, researchers know much more about it than about the transients. The pioneer of this research was Dr. Michael Bigg, a marine mammalogist attached to the Pacific Biological Station at Nanaimo on Vancouver Island. When Bigg died in 1990, the mantle fell to his younger associate, Graeme Ellis, who had worked with him for over twenty years. Ellis, who first became involved with the whales in 1968 when the Vancouver Aquarium hired him to work at its temporary facility in Pender Harbour, is a self-described "killer whale accountant." No one has spent more time observing the animals in their natural habitat. He is the keeper of a vast archive of photographs accumulated over the years that documents the identity of every whale that

■   A group of transient killer whales. *Lance Barrett-Lennard*

visits the Pacific Northwest. Visible in the photographs — many of them taken by Bigg and Ellis, many contributed by a network of volunteer spotters — are the telltale marks and scars that a practised researcher like Ellis can use to identify individual whales in the wild. So Ken Balcomb and Mark Sears turned to Ellis when they wanted to identify the young whale that turned up in Puget Sound.

According to a system worked out by Bigg and elaborated by his colleagues, each resident killer whale on the coast is assigned a number and a letter as it is identified. Initially, the system was based on the pod structure. Each pod received a letter and each member of the pod was numbered, so that whales became A1, G2, B3 and so on. Some of the groups to which Bigg gave pod names early in his study turned out, on closer examination, to contain two or more pods, and he adjusted the system accordingly, naming pods after a readily identifiable adult member. Thus, A-pod was split into A1, A4 and A5 pods. Bigg initially used the resident naming system for transients as well, but when he observed that they had less loyalty to a particular social group he realized that they needed individual rather than group names. Shortly after Bigg's death, Ellis devised a simple and foolproof naming system. To start with, he assigned each known adult a unique number preceded by the letter *T*. Every calf and juvenile then received the same number as its mother, plus another letter signifying birth order. For instance, if T28, a female, has two calves, they are designated T28A and T28B, and when T28A matures and has offspring of her own, they become T28A1, and so on. Perhaps to simplify matters for the uninitiated, researchers also give the animals more familiar names, usually associated with some physical feature or behaviour, or a landmark near which the whale is seen swimming. For example, A1, the first whale to be named using the system, a female, was christened Stubbs because her dorsal fin had been badly mangled, probably by a ship's propeller. Other examples are Saddle (A14), named for her distinctive saddle patch, Top Notch (A5), a male with a nick in his fin, Kwatsi (T20), a transient spotted at Kwatsi Bay at the top end of Tribune Channel, and so on.

When Ellis first examined the photographs of the wayward Puget Sound whale, he thought he recognized it as a young female calf he had seen the previous summer (2001) in Queen Charlotte Strait. At that time the youngster was travelling in the company of an older female, G50, who Ellis naturally assumed was her mother, even though the calf seemed a bit large for a mother that he knew was only ten or eleven years old. Ellis named the calf G53. However, killer whales engage in an activity known as *alloparenting*. This means that adolescent whales will sometimes care for a related whale's offspring while the other, older whale is away hunting or is otherwise absent. It may be a way for young females to gain mothering experience, just as teenage girls babysit in human society, although adolescent male whales also alloparent related male calves. This was apparently the case with G50 and the calf when Ellis saw them in 2001; as more evidence came in over the next few days it became clear the Vashon calf was not a G pod whale at all.

Back in Puget Sound, researchers had employed another technique for identifying the calf. Killer whales are enthusiastic vocalizers. Like other cetaceans, they produce a wide variety of acoustic signals ranging from high-pitched whistles, squeals and squawks to rapid-fire bursts of clicking sounds. Some of these sounds are used to navigate and locate objects underwater; others are used to communicate with members of the group. Astonishingly, each pod of resident killer whales has its own dialect or collection of discrete calls that members of the pod learn as youngsters, in much the same way as human children learn to speak. (Transients use discrete calls that are easily distinguished from those of residents but do not appear to have group-specific dialects, a reflection of their social fluidity.) As a result, researchers have been able to associate dialects with particular resident pods. By listening to a whale, they are able to determine to which pod it belongs.

David Bain, a marine mammal expert from the University of Washington, made the first recordings of the Puget Sound calf with an underwater microphone. Bain, who had studied with the legendary California cetologist Ken Norris, traced her calls to one of the A-clan pods of northern residents. He shared his tape with Helena Symonds, an acoustics expert based at OrcaLab, a land-based whale research station on Hanson Island in Johnstone Strait. Symonds had arrived in Alert Bay in 1978 to teach at the local primary school. Two years later she met Dr. Paul Spong, the founder of OrcaLab, and eventually joined him at the station, which is about twenty-five kilometres from Alert Bay. OrcaLab monitors the northern resident community of whales year-round using video cameras and a network of remote hydrophones. From years of listening to the recorded "voices," Symonds had developed the sharpest pair of ears for whale dialects on the coast. When she heard Bain's recording of the mystery whale, she recognized a distinctive sound that she had recorded herself in 1985, when a young female known as A45 had stopped in front of OrcaLab and emitted a "wee ah wooh" call into a hydrophone over and over again. Now, Symonds was hearing that call again and knew at once that the calf must be A73, the offspring of A45.

Meanwhile, Graeme Ellis had gone back to his catalogue of photographs. "I started to think about it," he said, "and thought, 'Who's missing in A clan? Who might it be?' I started looking at that and I started to wonder. So I went back and found the early calf pictures, and matched the eye patch and said, 'Shit, it's A73'." Ellis's tentative photo identification was confirmed by Marilyn Dalheim, a wildlife biologist with the US National Marine Mammal Laboratory in Seattle. Dalheim travelled to southern Alaska each summer to carry out field research on the resident population of killer whales there. It turned out that she had seen and photographed A73 in September 2000 in Clarence Strait, a long passage leading north out of Dixon Entrance. In Dalheim's photographs, there were white scratches evident on the calf's saddle that matched perfectly to scratches on the back of the little whale that was swimming around Vashon Island.

Based on these discoveries, Ellis plotted a plausible scenario for the young whale's appearance in Puget Sound, far south of the usual range of a northern resident. Ellis had first seen the youngster A73, subsequently named Springer, in June 2000, the year she was born, on the northern coast of British Columbia, then again later that summer off northern Vancouver Island. He imagined that her mother, A45, Sutlej, may have become sick and lagged behind the rest of the group. Her calf would have stayed with her, and when Sutlej died, the young animal would have found itself alone and eager to attach herself to any other pod that passed by. "When her mom died, she was just bouncing around, probably from group to group," Ellis speculated, and this is why she was seen in the company of G50 in the summer of 2001. However, when winter comes, the whales tend to travel in smaller groups of closely associated animals and are less tolerant of "outsiders." "Maybe they just outdistanced her or maybe they physically chased her away, 'go back to your family' kind of thing. I don't know how they work that out when they're splitting off. It may be natural instinct for her not to go with them at a certain point when they start taking off in a direction that they are not familiar with." What happened next is unclear, but in September–October 2001, a group of northern residents to which G50 belonged was seen feeding off the entrance to the Strait of Juan de Fuca, south of their normal range. The calf may have been with them before becoming separated and wandering off on her own into Puget Sound.

Even though the experts were fairly certain they had found Springer, they used one last tool to confirm her identity, the modern science of genetic testing. Brad Hanson, a colleague of Dalheim's at the Marine Mammal Lab, took a skin sample from the whale. When tested and compared to the DNA of other whales that had been collected by the Vancouver Aquarium's senior marine mammal scientist Lance Barrett-Lennard in the course of his PhD research, the sample showed that the calf was indeed a northern resident. Barrett-Lennard later conducted a much more complete analysis, which showed that the calf belonged to A45. There could be no doubt that it was Springer.

In the end, an amazing process of scientific detective work that combined the efforts of researchers from Alaska to Seattle and took advantage of photographic, acoustical and genetic evidence gathered over two decades, had solved the mystery of who Springer was. Now the experts faced the larger question: what to do about her.

■

KILLER WHALES *(ORCINUS ORCA)* are the largest of the dolphin family of marine mammals. Also known as orcas and once disparaged as "blackfish," they range widely across the world's oceans from the North Atlantic to the South Pacific. The Pacific Northwest is one of the few locations where they are found in protected waters and can easily be studied. The killer whale is an attractive animal with glossy black back and sides, white front, white eye patches and a grey saddle patch that spreads across the back like a large birthmark. The wedge-shaped dorsal fin is the animal's most conspicuous feature. Towering as much as two metres in height on mature males, slightly less on females, it slices the surface of the water like a large blade. Male killer whales average about seven metres in length (females are smaller) and weigh as much as nine tonnes.

Female whales have their first calf when they are between eleven and fifteen years of age. The gestation period lasts about sixteen months, and at birth calves are 2.5 metres long and weigh about two hundred kilograms. Females may give birth every three years or so until their reproductivity ends at about age forty. Though they have no known enemies in the wild, killer whales have a high mortality rate; an estimated forty percent of calves die during their first year. For those that survive their first six months, the average life expectancy for females is

■ One-year-old Springer was photographed by Graeme Ellis in August 2001 off northern Vancouver Island. Four months later she was discovered, sick and alone, near Seattle. *Graeme Ellis*

about fifty years and for males about thirty, though there have been documented cases of individuals who became septuagenarians.

Killer whales usually swim near the ocean surface, where their prey is. They do not, and presumably cannot, dive as deep as other marine mammals, some species of which can reach depths of more than one thousand metres. The record for a killer whale is around three hundred metres. They are very swift, capable of speeds up to forty-five kilometres an hour. They spend much of their time foraging for food. Their mouths contain two rows of large, inward-curving teeth and they are skilled predators, a fact that is often forgotten by spectators who see them only in captivity. While residents subsist on fish, their transient cousins hunt other marine mammals and have been known to attack the larger whale species. Which raises the question: would they attack a human? There has been no recorded case of a killer whale attacking and killing a human in the wild. Their reputation for ferocity has abated during the past forty years but most researchers believe it is wise to give them a wide berth.

After foraging, killer whales will often rest. If they are alone they will simply float quietly on the surface for several minutes, taking the equivalent of a catnap. Resting also occurs communally. The animals bunch themselves within less than a body length of each other, slow their pace greatly, and surface synchronously after very shallow, short dives. Resting in this fashion may last from less than an hour to several hours.

When not foraging, resting or travelling from point A to point B, killer whales will engage in a variety of social behaviours. They will leap almost completely out of the water in a full breach, landing on their sides and throwing up a huge and noisy splash. They will spyhop, poking their head and upper body vertically out of the water to take a look around. Their vision is excellent, and spyhopping presumably allows them to orient themselves and investigate what is going on around them on the surface. They will lobtail, loudly slapping their tail flukes on the surface. And they will roll over on their sides and slap the water with a flipper.

Another communal activity, carried on by northern resident whales only, is beach rubbing. At particular beaches along the coast, a group of whales will enter shallow water and rub their bodies on the pebbly bottom. They arch and twist as they skid back and forth, obviously enjoying themselves, and the activity may have no other purpose than simple pleasure. Or the rubbing may be a way of sloughing dead skin or parasites. During the 1970s it was discovered that a favourite site for rubbing was at beaches in Robson Bight, a small nick in Vancouver Island's east coast about twenty kilometres east of Telegraph Cove in Johnstone Strait. When this site at the mouth of the Tsitika River was threatened by logging, whale researchers lobbied the government to protect the beaches, and in 1982 the Robson Bight (Michael Bigg) Ecological Reserve was created. The public is not allowed to enter the reserve so that the whales are undisturbed during their visits.

During the heyday of commercial whaling, killer whales were killed in substantial numbers although they were never specifically targeted. A toothed species, they did not possess the baleen that was so valued by whalers in the nineteenth century; smaller than deep-sea behemoths like the blue, sperm and right whales, they did not produce enough oil from their blubber to be considered a worthwhile catch. Their speed and agility made them more difficult to chase down than they were worth to the whalers. But what they lacked in commercial value, they made up for in personality, and killer whales have been a favourite display item in public aquariums and oceanariums worldwide. The Vancouver Aquarium put the first captive killer whale on public display, albeit briefly, in 1964, and today more than forty of them

■ Killer whale carcass at Coal Harbour in 1955. Located in Quatsino Sound on northern Vancouver Island, Coal Harbour was the site of a commercial whaling station from 1947 to 1967. Killer whales were never an important commercial species. *Department of Fisheries and Oceans*

arc living in captivity. As word of her presence spread, people began to wonder whether this was the fate that awaited Springer, the orphaned whale calf in Puget Sound.

∎

FOLLOWING THE INITIAL VISIT BY MARK SEARS and Ken Balcomb, Sears continued to pay regular visits to the whale to check on her. He counted her breaths and tracked the length of her dives and how long she remained on the surface, factors that might indicate how the animal was doing. She appeared to be chasing fish though it was not clear how well she was feeding. She also was rubbing on floating logs and branches, a worrisome practice because it might lead to rubbing on boats. On February 5, a delegation from the Vancouver Aquarium — scientist Lance Barrett-Lennard, veterinarian David Huff and vice-president of operations Clint Wright — travelled to Seattle to take a look at the whale. The Aquarium had assisted at the Dungeness stranding and was prepared to make its expertise in animal rescue available again.

These three men were destined to play crucial roles in the dramatic events that were set to unfold. Wright, who was a dolphin trainer in his native England before joining the Aquarium as a senior trainer in 1990, had worldwide experience in marine animal transportation, from whales to crocodiles. As the Aquarium's point man on the Springer project, he would require the organizing skills of a five-star general combined with the patience and tact of a marriage counsellor. Dave Huff, a graduate of the University of Guelph veterinary program, had practiced for more than thirty years and been a consultant to the Aquarium for more than twenty. He had rehabilitated many ailing sea mammals and routinely worked with the facility's whales, dolphins and sea lions. The affable "Doctor Dave" was well known to Vancouver-area animal lovers as a lecturer and regular pet specialist on local radio and television programs. Lance Barrett-Lennard took a more circuitous path to the Aquarium. Also a graduate of the University of Guelph, Barrett-Lennard moved out to the Pacific coast with his wife Kathy in 1980 and they became lighthouse keepers at Lawyer Island south of Prince Rupert. Lance had planned to return to graduate school after a year but the couple fell in love with the coast and the job. Three years later they moved to a light at the southern end of Johnstone Strait, at Chatham Point. There they joined Mike Bigg's network of amateur killer whale informants, installing a hydrophone to record vocalizations and photographing the animals as they travelled past the light. Lance and Kathy eventually returned to university, Lance to study the echolocation behaviour of the whales and later their population genetics. He obtained his PhD and worked as a research scientist for Fisheries and Oceans Canada before joining the Aquarium as the senior marine mammal scientist in 2001, just a few months before Springer's appearance.

The little whale would soon become a celebrity, but for the time being no one was taking much interest in her. The National Marine Mammal Lab in Seattle was the world's largest laboratory dedicated to these animals, but Brad Hanson and his colleague Sally Mizroch were the only staff members to pay any attention to the unusual visitor. The research boat Hanson had available was virtually derelict — when he went to ferry the delegation from the Vancouver Aquarium out to have a look at Springer he could hardly get the engine started. Once they did get going, weather conditions were so poor that they couldn't get a good look. When they returned to the lab to watch film footage of the whale, there was no working video player available so they trooped over to Mizroch's house to watch on her television. It was a far cry from the non-stop whirl of high-tech activity that would surround the whale once the world discovered her plight.

A week later, Barrett-Lennard, Huff and Jeremy Fitz-Gibbon, the manager of the Vancouver Aquarium's marine mammal rescue program, returned. This time they got a better look at the animal. They observed that her skin was covered in lesions and that she was lethargic and possibly underweight. Her obsessive rubbing on objects suggested she was missing contact with her mother. Barrett-Lennard noticed a strong acetone smell. At first he thought that something in the beaten up boat was leaking. It took a while for them to trace the smell to Springer's breath, an indication that she was metabolizing her own fat reserves because she was not getting enough food, a condition known as ketosis. In other words, she was slowly starving. "I was sure it was ketosis," David Huff recalled, "it was so dramatic. I remember phoning Dr. Ron Lewis with the Animal Health Centre in Abbotsford on the cellphone from the middle of Puget Sound because that's a cow disease and I'm not a dairy cow person. So I told Ron what was happening and asked if this could be anything other than ketosis? He replied, 'No'. That was the start of the whole investigation into her health. It's not an understatement to say that most of us at that time thought that she was never going to make it."

Hanson later called in Bets Rasmussen, a biochemist from Oregon who had developed techniques for learning about an animal's health by analyzing its breath. She had already designed a system for collecting exhalations from whales in specially designed stainless steel canisters using a length of tube that ended in an aluminum funnel. The tubing was duct-taped to a long broom handle and extended out near the whale's blow-hole so that when the animal exhaled, some of the mist flowed through the tube into the canister, where it was captured for analysis. Springer was the first animal from which Rasmussen had gathered a sample in the wild—her other experiences had been with captive animals—and it took a lot longer than she anticipated. She went out in the boat at nine in the morning and it wasn't until four in the afternoon that Springer came close enough to allow her to collect a sample. Rasmussen knew as soon as she smelled the breath, which she compared to "sweet-ened nail polish remover," that something was wrong with the animal, perhaps something as serious as a genetic disorder, and her analysis later confirmed the diagnosis of ketosis. There was something going on with Springer's metabolism, but what exactly?

By this time observers had confirmed that the animal had created an "imaginary box," an area about a kilometre and a half square lying between Vashon Island and Fauntleroy, south of Seattle, site of the mainland ferry terminal. She rarely wandered outside the box, which was situated in a heavily trafficked boating lane and was not well stocked with fish. As a result, her prospects for survival looked poor. Because she was so young, nobody knew whether she had even acquired the skills necessary to hunt for food.

The day after his second visit to Seattle, Lance Barrett-Lennard drafted a letter to Brent Norberg, a senior official with the National Marine Fisheries Service (NMFS), the responsible US government agency, expressing concern about Springer's situation. The letter, which was endorsed by Dave Huff, recommended immediate intervention. "We knew that we were breaching protocol in a way," Barrett-Lennard admitted. "Government people hate to get letters like that because it creates a paper trail that they ignore at their peril, and pressure from foreigners was likely to raise hackles. On the other hand, we already had the impression from talking to Brad Hanson and others that the US government would be slow to react, and we knew that the Canadian government would not intercede without pressure. We thought the Aquarium board would probably support us, but we also knew if we sent it up for approval it could get delayed for days and weeks…so we decided to just send it off and beg for forgiveness later if necessary." The letter contained an action plan for capturing the whale—which by now had pretty well been confirmed as a "Canadian"—and placing her in a netpen so that her health could be properly assessed.

After receiving this letter from the Aquarium, the NMFS, which to that point had appeared content to let nature run its course, convened a panel of scientists to advise it on what to do. On February 22, the same day Springer was identified with certainty, this group held a conference call to discuss the situation. Members agreed that the little whale was in poor health and getting worse. They considered it unlikely that she would reunite with her pod or attach to a surrogate if she remained where she was, pointing out that they had never known a resident calf who had strayed away from its family to rejoin it or to join a new pod. As a result, they believed Springer's chances for long-term survival were minimal if she was left alone. They all worried that attempts to feed the whale in situ might make her so dependent that she would never return completely to the wild. Given Springer's poor condition, members of the panel thought that it might make sense to capture and try to rehabilitate her. The scientists had no great confidence that Springer could be saved, even with rehabilitation, but they did agree that something should be done.

Despite the apparent urgency of Springer's situation, at least in the opinion of the advisory panel, this meeting was only the beginning of a lengthy process by which the administrators at the NMFS, which had ultimate authority, tried to make a decision. On March 2, Brian Gorman, an official with the NMFS, told the *Vancouver Sun* that something would be done "within the week."[4] In fact, it was almost three months before the NMFS put a plan into action.

Meanwhile, the Seattle media glare fell on Springer. Initially the media, preoccupied with the Winter Olympics taking place in Salt Lake City, had not paid much attention to the story. When the Games concluded at the end of February, the press and the public began taking more of an interest. Passengers on the ferries crowded the railings to catch a glimpse of the little whale, and more and more recreational boaters went out to visit. One ferry, the *Evergreen State*, seemed to hold a particular attraction for Springer, who continued to visit it during its overnight layovers at the Vashon Island dock. Floyd Fulmer worked the graveyard shift carrying out maintenance on the vessel. During the night, he would hear Springer's underwater calls echoing through the hull. Fulmer, whose mother was a member of the Tlingit First Nation from Alaska, would go up onto the deck to watch the whale as she raised her flukes in the air, seeming to wave at him. He was touched emotionally by her situation, orphaned and apart from her family. Killer whales play a significant role in the spiritual lives of many First Nations groups, including the Tlingit, and Floyd became convinced that Springer's appearance was intended to strengthen his Aboriginal identity. Kim Shride, the ferry employee who had been among the first to spot the calf, also felt a growing emotional connection to Springer. She took to staying late after work just to watch the whale swimming beside the ferry dock. She was convinced that Springer recognized her and performed tricks for her. At the same time, ferry company officials were frantic that one of their vessels might hit Springer, even kill her. Toward the end of March, she began swimming ever closer to the *Evergreen State* as it made its crossings, forcing the captain to slow down and change direction. So strong did the attachment appear to be that at one point the ferry company volunteered to allow the vessel to be used as "bait" to lure Springer back north to Johnstone Strait, an offer that the NMFS did not accept.

The NMFS asked an environmental group, People for Puget Sound, to organize a public meeting in Seattle. It took place on March 4 and was attended by about 150 people who came to hear about Springer's condition and debate her future. When it came to the killer whales in Puget Sound, many members of the public felt that they "owned" the animals, and government officials wanted to be sure the public felt they had input into whatever decision was taken. Opinion at the meeting was divided. Some people advocated doing nothing, either because they thought "nature should take its course" or because they suspected the scientists and the aquarium community of secretly planning to put Springer into captivity. On the other hand, many argued that Springer had to be rescued given the alternative, which they believed was certain death. There was definitely a strong feeling in the audience that Springer should not end up in a captive setting. Ellen Hartlmeier, a long-time volunteer with the Vancouver Aquarium, made the trip down to Seattle for the meeting. Hartlmeier had been going to Johnstone Strait to watch killer whales since 1990 and had gotten to know the northern residents very well. She had actually seen Springer in the wild not long after the calf was born. When she heard about the March 4 meeting in Seattle, she felt that she had to make an appearance, despite her fear of public speaking. Because of her experience with the whales, she was convinced that Springer could be reunited with her family. When she stood to defend the Aquarium's motives and explain how she thought reunification would work, she received a sustained round of applause. But she noted a strong bias at the meeting toward the "better dead than fed" philosophy, meaning that many people in attendance thought that Springer was better off dying in the wild than living in captivity.

Dave Huff, the Vancouver Aquarium veterinarian, attended a second packed public meeting in an elementary school auditorium on Vashon Island in mid-April. He observed what he called a growing "paranoia" about the intentions of the Aquarium. "Everyone was negative with the thought that this was just another ploy to get another whale into an aquarium," he said. "People were very skeptical about people's motives. They couldn't trust the fact that we [the Vancouver Aquarium] were involved." One of those who spoke up from the audience was a woman who introduced herself as an animal communicator. The woman said, "I have talked to Springer and she does not want to go anywhere. Springer sees herself as something like a harbinger for bringing new life into Puget Sound." The woman implied that it would not just be killer whales but that other animals would be coming back as well. "Springer does not want to go back because there are too many rules there. Springer refers to herself as 'the calling one'. Springer sees herself as calling all these other animals back to Puget Sound."

This suspicion of the scientists and government ran deep in public opinion, and decision-makers in the NMFS felt they could not ignore it. However, Paul Spong, the founder of OrcaLab and a noted anti-captivity activist as well as an independent researcher, sent a written message that was read to the meeting and expressed the viewpoint of the whale research community. "I feel I need to say that I'm still quite worried about Springer and the outcome of this episode," Spong wrote. "If she remains in her present circumstances she will clearly face increasing jeopardy, and if the worst happens, she and we will have lost a great chance. Even if she is not inadvertently injured or killed by boat traffic, A73 faces the risk of becoming a human plaything, a toy, if she remains where she is. So I see leaving her where she is as a very poor option. My preference, by far, is for a carefully thought out plan to be put in place which will see Springer returned to her home waters and her community."

■

FIVE YEARS BEFORE SPRINGER APPEARED in Puget Sound, another killer whale had turned up unexpectedly in the Pacific Northwest. Keiko was the most famous whale in the world, thanks to his starring role in the *Free Willy* movies.[5] He had been captured as a calf near Iceland in 1979 and had been living in amusement parks ever since, most recently in a shabby facility in Mexico City, but it was his good fortune to be discovered by Hollywood and turned into a movie star. The first *Free Willy* film, released in 1993, was followed by two sequels and launched a worldwide movement to turn fiction into fact and "save" Keiko by putting him back in the ocean. The Mexican park agreed to give him to a charitable foundation that was created to manage his release. Money flowed from many different sources, including Craig McCaw, the Seattle cellphone tycoon, who donated several million dollars, part of which was earmarked for the construction of a new home for Keiko at the Oregon Coast Aquarium.

In January 1996, Keiko flew from Mexico to a state-of-the-art tank in Newport, Oregon, where his new minders, some of whom would be involved with Springer a few years later, planned to restore him to health and prepare him for life in the wild. Keiko turned out to be a windfall for the Oregon facility, where attendance soon reached record highs. Indeed, he was so popular that the aquarium took the foundation to court in an attempt to keep him in captivity. But the "Free Keiko" movement could not be stopped, even though many observers wondered how a whale who had lived in captivity all his life could possibly know enough to survive in the wild.

In September 1998, Keiko got on another plane that carried him to Iceland and a small harbour on Surtsey, one of the Westman Islands, a ferry ride southeast of Reykjavik, where he took up residence inside a net pen. It took another two years but finally, in the summer of 2000, Keiko began to venture outside the pen, accompanied by a boat to which he remained attached, mentally if not physically. Gradually he wandered farther from his minders and stayed away longer until one day in July 2002 Keiko joined a passing group of killer whales and never came back to Surtsey. All of this happened during the time that Springer made her appearance in Puget Sound and Keiko's example naturally encouraged those who believed that Springer too could be returned to the wild. (They could not know that later that summer Keiko would reappear in a fjord in Norway, sixteen hundred kilometres from Iceland, in apparent good health but a little over-dependent on human attention. He was interned in a remote bay in Norway to be prepared for another release but he died there of pneumonia in December 2003, aged about twenty-six.)

Much closer to home, another solitary cetacean had recently been attracting public attention in Vancouver and Puget Sound.

This was Rufus, a pseudorca who first appeared in the Vancouver Harbour in May 1990. Pseudorcas *(Pseudorca crassidens)*, also known as False Killer Whales, resemble killer whales in appearance but they are usually smaller, lack the white markings and the dramatic dorsal fin and, in the eastern Pacific, seldom stray north of Mexico. Indeed, the first group of pseudorcas ever seen in the Pacific Northwest had appeared just three years earlier and Rufus may have been the sole member of that group to remain "up north." For the previous three years, this animal had lived in Barkley Sound on the west coast of Vancouver Island where it had formed an attachment to a former Union Steamship vessel, the MV *Lady Rose*. The *Lady Rose* operates a scheduled ferry service in Barkley Sound and Rufus had taken to accompanying it. In the spring of 1990, the vessel had travelled three hundred kilometres to Vancouver to attend a reunion of historic ships at the Vancouver Maritime Museum. It seems likely that Rufus, unbeknownst to the crew, followed. Making Vancouver its new home, the whale, which now became known as Willy (this was years before the *Free Willy* movies), became a common sight around the city's waterfront. But apparently Willy had been bitten by the wanderlust. The next summer an animal that was believed to be Willy turned up in Puget Sound near Tacoma, playing with the ferries coming and going at the Point Defiance terminal. Early in 1992 he returned to Canada briefly, then spent the spring and summer near the ferry landing on Lummi Island in northern Puget Sound. Passengers on the ferries for some reason began calling the animal Foster. (Willy/Foster was assumed to be a male, even though his sex was never determined for certain.) He was active in the water and seemed to interact with boaters and ferry passengers, who enjoyed watching him and feeding him junk food. In time he wandered back north of the border, where he became a fixture near the Roberts Bank freighter terminal and where he was once again known as Willy.

The relevance of this lone pseudorca to the story of Springer is that some of the first people to see Springer in Puget Sound may have surmised that it was wandering Willy they were seeing, back for another visit, and paid little attention. (In 2003, Willy/Foster apparently left his familiar haunts around Vancouver and travelled all the way north to Alaska, where he was photographed near Juneau.)

■

ALL THIS PUBLICITY AND SPECULATION about killer whales and false killer whales meant the public's interest in Springer's fate remained intense. During March and April, several non-governmental organizations (NGOs) became involved in discussions about the orphan, including People for Puget Sound, the American Cetacean Society, the Orca Conservancy and the Center for Whale Research. None were as active on the water as Project Sea Wolf and the "Two Bobs." Project Sea Wolf was led by Michael Kundu, a veteran anti-whaling campaigner. Kundu had been to Siberia with a film crew to document illegal commercial whaling there, and in the fall of 1998 he and the Sea Shepherd Society, for whom he was the local coordinator, had opposed the gray whale hunt mounted by the Makah Nation at Neah Bay. About the same time he formed his own organization, Project Sea Wolf, to focus more directly on marine environmental issues in the Pacific Northwest. The "Two Bobs" were his closest collaborators. Bob McLaughlin made documentaries for both radio and television, usually on the subject of marine mammals. He interviewed Kundu on his radio program and the two began working together on projects. McLaughlin provided the media experience while Kundu had the scientific background and a track record in the environmental movement. Bob Wood, a former broadcaster, got interested in the Puget Sound killer whales as a recreational boater and became involved with the American Cetacean Society. When he met McLaughlin, the two began experimenting with filming whales using underwater cameras.

With the arrival of Springer, McLaughlin and Wood began going out in Wood's boat, the *Shelmar*, to film her. They became her self-appointed guardians, believing that no one else was keeping an eye on her. They were on the water several days a week for hours at a time, filming and observing the whale and her interactions with boaters. (Of course, in the eyes of some of the scientists, who did not want Springer interacting with people, this made the Bobs part of the problem. They were so concerned about the whale that they wouldn't leave her alone, and all anyone looking for her had to do was find the *Shelmar*.) Much of the information supplied to the media about the condition of the little whale came from the Bobs, including her interactions with boaters. (At one point they actually filmed a boater feeding Springer french fries.) They kept the ferries informed about Springer's location and they were the first people to recognize that she was staying within a self-defined "box." It is possible that without their persistent lobbying, the NMFS might not have felt pressured to intervene with Springer. As it was, they also developed an antagonistic relationship with the NMFS by setting themselves up as advocates for the whale, demanding that somebody do something and feeding the media information. They thought that the NMFS was using Springer's health as a red herring. To them, the real issue was not the animal's health but her presence in a busy shipping lane where she posed a danger to herself and others.

Brent Norberg, the NMFS coordinator, was concerned about Springer becoming too attached to people and preferred that boaters, including the Bobs, leave the whale alone. As a public official, he felt he could not be seen to favour one NGO over another, whether it was providing valuable information or not. Norberg already had a history of antagonism with Sea Wolf and Michael Kundu over other issues. During the 1990s Kundu had opposed what the NMFS was doing to remove sea lions from the Ballard Locks and he had been a vocal critic of the agency's handling of the Makah whale hunt. As a result, Kundu was convinced that Norberg had it in for Sea Wolf and his partners, the "Two Bobs." In mid-April, for example, the NMFS hired educators from Soundwatch, a program operating out of the Whale Museum at Friday Harbor on San Juan

Island, to warn boaters to keep their distance from Springer. Kundu interpreted this as one more attempt to keep Project Sea Wolf away from the whale. He was convinced that the federal government, through the NMFS, did not want to get involved with Springer. The issue of whether to declare the southern resident population of killer whales an endangered species was pending. Kundu believed the government did not want the whales designated, "because if they do list the southern resident orca," he argued, "so much money will be needed to be spent on protection measures and reclamation and building stocks." In Kundu's mind, the NMFS would put off making a decision about Springer forever, unless they were forced by public pressure to do something. But as a public official, Brent Norberg did not have the freedom of an NGO. He had to be sure that any steps taken were in compliance with the law and took into account the points of view of all the interested parties.

The longer the NMFS delayed making a decision about Springer, the more confused and recriminatory the situation became. Nonetheless, to the frustration of all parties, the NMFS would not act. Early in March, Brian Gorman told a newspaper that "we [the NMFS] are not going to stand by and let the whale die. What we end up doing is the big question."[6] During the month discussions continued with the Vancouver Aquarium to develop a capture scenario. On March 8, Clint Wright had a long telephone conversation with Brent Norberg about capturing and moving Springer back to Canada for rehabilitation, something that had never been attempted with a wild whale before. Wright was left in little doubt that "we would actually be doing something very soon." Planning continued and the Aquarium staff at least were under the impression that they would be undertaking a transfer, probably by truck to a temporary rehabilitation facility near Vancouver. Wright explained that "the reason for doing that was that we have the medical expertise nearby and the staff resources. We had people nearby who could get there very quickly...If it's got to come to Canada in the end, why not do it at this step and move it up." The logistical challenges were enormous. Arrangements had to be made to build or obtain a netpen, obtain the proper licences and permits, devise techniques for capturing the whale and transporting her over a long distance, set up a program to feed her and assess and treat any health problems, and monitor the success of Springer's anticipated reattachment to a pod in the wild.

Springer's appearance came at a particularly awkward time for the Vancouver Aquarium and its board of directors. The wayward whale was only one item on the facility's lengthy agenda. Jim Kershaw, who was chair of the board at the time, admitted that involvement with Springer "was the last thing that any of us wanted financially." In the wake of the September 11, 2001, terror attacks in the United States and the earlier departure of Bjossa, the last killer whale to reside at the Aquarium, the Aquarium's attendance was down and it was reeling financially. There were other important projects underway. Construction was due to begin on a new research facility for the Steller sea lions, the seal rehabilitation site on the waterfront needed a new home, and senior staff were preoccupied with the impending birth of a beluga calf, due in July. The last thing many board members wanted was to take on an expensive rescue project that was outside the day-to-day operations of the facility, especially when it had no guarantee of success and lots of potential to become a public relations disaster should Springer not survive. A rescue was certainly within the mandate of the Aquarium but it was not part of the core operations, so there was room for disagreement about whether to proceed. At a mid-March meeting, several members of the board forcefully expressed their reservations. But Janet Landucci had other ideas.

Landucci was a professional biologist turned management consultant who had worked for the federal department of the environment for many years before joining the Aquarium's board. A scientist herself, she had a broader understanding of marine issues and had spent more time around the Aquarium than many of her colleagues on the board. Landucci acknowledged at the meeting that the Springer project presented risks. "Yes, it could all go wrong," she said. "We could accept the responsibility of taking care of the whale, it could get too sick and die in our care. Then we're the bad guys and we have more bad publicity. That would be tragic." But, she said, it also presented an enormous opportunity for the Aquarium to do something extremely worthwhile. Given that the whale would be looked after by a staff who knew what they were doing, she argued that the risks were not as great as they seemed. "This is an amazing opportunity for the Aquarium to do something that has never been done before," she said, meaning the rescue of a whale and reuniting it with its family in the wild. After Landucci sat down there was a long silence. Then the others began reassessing the project and, one by one, considering its upside. It was a critical moment in the history of the Springer project. Landucci carried the day and the board agreed to back the plan its staff had developed. The Aquarium's director, John Nightingale, was now way out on a limb. With Landucci's support, he had persuaded the board to back the rescue. If anything went wrong, he would be blamed. If for some reason Springer was captured and died, or for some medical reason she could not be returned to her pod and had to be retained, public opinion might well conclude that right from the beginning the whole thing had been a ploy by the government and the Vancouver Aquarium to get a whale into captivity.

Despite all this preliminary work, by the end of March, non-intervention had become official NMFS policy. Springer's health did not appear to be deteriorating, perhaps had even improved slightly, so the agency decided to hold a watching brief. Brent Norberg was in a difficult position. The scientists were advising him to move quickly and he had the Vancouver Aquarium's relocation plan. On the other hand, he had proposals from other US facilities, such as the Oregon Coast Aquarium and San Diego's Sea World, and he could not be seen to favour one over another. If he authorized a capture, he had to be able to justify it according to the law and he was not sure that he could. The whale was not stranded; she was not making a nuisance of herself, though the people from Project Sea Wolf argued that her attachment to the ferry was a form of nuisance; nobody was trying to capture her for display. There seemed to be no basis in policy that justified the government's involvement. Norberg was also faced with public opinion that was growing increasingly suspicious of any capture plan, and he wanted to be very sure not to make the wrong decision, knowing that if Springer was captured and then died he would face enormous criticism.

In the face of these pressures (one observer referred to him as "the ham in the sandwich"), Norberg decided simply to continue to monitor the whale by observing her behaviour and gathering blood and fecal samples for analysis. Complicating Norberg's position were the remarks of his associate Brian Gorman, who infuriated the scientists with his contradictory statements to the press. At one point he seemed to suggest that if Springer died, it was no worse than a life in captivity. Naturally, personnel from the American aquariums that were involved in the situation took offence, and Sea World even considered pulling one of its vets off the project. On another occasion Gorman was quoted as saying, "I think we'd be hard-pressed to rationalize swooping down and snatching this whale up and taking her to her pod in Canada," an inflammatory comment guaranteed to rile the Vancouver Aquarium, which was advocating just such a plan.

In April, another health concern suddenly appeared. The issue of Springer's ketosis had never been resolved. It was hard to tell if she was eating properly. She was seen to catch fish from time to time but she seemed to play with them rather than eat them, and there was no way of knowing if she was consuming enough. She continued to exhale a metallic odour, evidence that she was catabolic: she was breaking down the stores of fat and protein in her body. The presence of ketosis indicated that Springer was either starving, infected by certain pathogens or had an inborn metabolic abnormality that affected the way she turned nutrients into energy. Starvation would be easy to correct and an infection could likely be treated, but an inborn metabolic abnormality would mean that her prospects for survival in the wild, or anywhere for that matter, were dim. The veterinarians turned for help to Dr. Hilary Vallance, a pathologist and specialist in biochemical genetics at the BC Children and Women's Health Centre in Vancouver. After testing Springer's blood and urine, Dr. Vallance concluded that there was no inborn metabolic problem and that her ketosis likely resulted from underfeeding or a bacterial infection. Either way, this diagnosis brought relief to the scientific team, who now believed that whatever happened, Springer had a future.

Early in May, Brian Gorman had reiterated his agency's wait-and-see policy. "I don't anticipate anything happening soon," he told the press, "even though there is a contingent of people that think we're temporizing and dithering. We're not."[7] When news that Springer had been cleared of an inborn metabolic problem arrived a week later, it seemed to open the door to action. Certainly the Vancouver Aquarium thought so. Aquarium personnel had grown increasingly impatient at the failure of the NMFS to make a decision. Time was becoming a factor. If Springer was going to be reintroduced to her pod, she had to be in Johnstone Strait before the end of the summer, when the other whales were likely to be there. Before that time, she had to be captured, monitored and completely restored to health. And post-release, there had to be time for at least some monitoring before her pod left the area in the fall. Early in May Lance Barrett-Lennard, who had been working feverishly behind the scenes trying to get the Americans to act sooner rather than later, proposed setting a deadline of May 17 as the latest date at which the Aquarium would continue to commit to the project. Along with the scientific urgency, there was a financial one. The Aquarium could not start raising money from the public for the project until the NMFS declared itself ready to proceed. Barrett-Lennard hoped that giving the Americans a deadline would prompt them to act.

After some discussion, Aquarium president John Nightingale wrote to the NMFS on May 10 advising that "our plan cannot be implemented unless the plan is approved by Wednesday May 15, and the whale captured by Tuesday May 21." After that time, Nightingale said, the Aquarium might be involved in some capacity but could not undertake the fundraising necessary to finance its initial plan. In effect, he had thrown down the gauntlet. The NMFS must act or lose its main partner in the Springer rescue. "We hate to see A73 sentenced to death because of bureaucratic indecision and an inflexible and unrealistic position," a frustrated Nightingale wrote in a memo to senior personnel a few days later. But he feared that was how the story was going to end.

Or maybe not. The pressure on the NMFS was clearly building. On May 16, Maria Cantwell, a Democratic senator for Washington State, wrote a letter acknowledging the Aquarium's deadline and urging the NMFS to intervene. Before she sent the letter she showed it to Bob McLaughlin to ask for his input. "We cannot afford to let indecision on timing determine this orphaned orca's fate," Senator Cantwell wrote.[8] On May 19, the scientific panel was polled again, and again concluded that Springer should be taken into custody according to the plan devised by the Vancouver Aquarium, a plan that might expire within a week if the agency did not make a decision. For several weeks, signs had been posted at area marinas warning boaters to stay away from the whale, and as summer approached, boating activity in Puget Sound was increasing, raising acute safety concerns for both boaters and whale. Apparently the NMFS had run out of time.

On May 24 the agency held a news conference to announce that Springer would be taken into custody and prepared for reintegration with her pod in a rescue effort led by the Vancouver Aquarium. It was typical of the ongoing turmoil within the NMFS that the agency neglected to inform the Aquarium—which would play such a vital role in the operation on both sides of the border—until an hour before the announcement was made public in Seattle. But at least a decision had finally been taken and everyone now turned their attentions to the challenge of accomplishing the unprecedented: reuniting a killer whale with its family in the wild.

2 ▪ THE GOLD RUSH

THE FACT THAT ANYONE WAS EVEN CONTEMPLATING a rescue attempt in Puget Sound illustrates how profoundly attitudes about killer whales have changed in just a few decades. In the 1960s Springer most likely would have been shot for sport and no one would have given it a second thought. During the 1970s she'd almost certainly have been captured and lived out the rest of her days in an oceanarium. Instead, she was the object of solicitous attention from the media, the bureaucrats, the scientific community and the public. How did this remarkable shift in attitudes come about?

The beginning of the change can be traced back to 1964 and the accidental capture of a whale dubbed Moby Doll. The Vancouver Aquarium was planning its first major expansion and director Murray Newman decided that a life-sized sculpture of a killer whale hanging from the ceiling in the entrance hall would make a dramatic welcome for visitors. There were no killer whales in any aquariums anywhere in the world at the time. The animal was thought to be far too dangerous to capture and put on display. Today we know so much about this fascinating marine mammal we forget that fifty years ago even an expert such as Murray Newman would have known almost nothing about its biology or its habits. And because so little was known, much was imagined. Most fishermen hated killer whales, or blackfish as they called them, considering them rivals for the precious salmon on which they both depended for a living. Whenever possible, whales were shot on sight. The general public feared them as vicious man-eaters. The animal's easy sociability was interpreted as frightening aggression. The sight of a tall dorsal fin slicing through the water conjured up alarming images of man-eating sharks and other sinister "monsters" of the deep. The fact that the whales travelled in groups brought comparisons to wolves and other predators that hunted in packs. As Murray Newman remarks in his memoirs, the killer whale was considered "the marine world's Public Enemy Number One."[9]

Fishermen, sport and commercial, were confident that the number of killer whales on the Pacific coast was growing and had to be controlled. In 1960, representatives of fishing organizations in the Campbell River area met with officials from the federal department of fisheries to discuss the prevalence of "blackfish" in Discovery Passage. Various remedies were proposed, including bombing the animals from the air. In the end, the fishermen con-

■ The harpoon gun on Saturna Island, used to capture Moby Doll in 1964. Sculptor Sam Burich is at right; Ronald Sparrow is seated behind the gun. *Fisheries and Oceans Canada*

vinced the government to install a Browning machine gun on a lookout on Quadra Island overlooking Seymour Narrows, northwest of Campbell River. The narrows were much used for coastal shipping and by killer whales on their travels along the coast. (In 1958 the government had planted 1,250 tonnes of explosives and blown up Ripple Rock, a dangerous obstacle to navigation in the passage that had ripped open the hulls of dozens of vessels over the years.) It was expected that a gunner would kill as many whales as he could from his perch above the Narrows and stop others from coming south into the Campbell River area. But as it turned out there was no shooting. Worried that a bullet might ricochet off the water and strike someone, the fisheries official responsible for the gun told the local people that the weapon was a potential forest fire hazard. Though it was mounted in June 1961, the gun was never fired. Still, the plan illustrates the degree to which killer whales were feared and hated along the coast.

Unhappily, the whales were not unique in this regard. British Columbia has a long history of intolerance and waste when it comes to marine animals. With the arrival of the earliest explorers on the coast in the late eighteenth century, sea otters began to be harvested for their luxurious pelts. Vessels from Britain and the United States visited the coast each summer, trading otter furs from the local First Nations and carrying them across the Pacific for sale in China. As a result, the animal was exterminated from the BC coast and was only reintroduced in the late 1960s. Large whale species such as humpback, minke and gray were hunted from shore-based whaling operations starting in the 1860s. Industrial whaling was practised from whaling stations on Vancouver Island and the Queen Charlottes between 1905 and 1967, when the last station at Coal Harbour closed. Humpbacks are a case in point. "Used to be humpbacks all over the place here," one old-timer told the researcher Alexandra Morton, referring to the inner coastal waters of the Broughton Archipelago. In the summer of 1952 a catcher boat came around from the station at Coal Harbour and wiped them out.[10] Seals and sea lions also fell victim to human predators, shot as pests that threatened the commercial fishery and, in the case of seals during the 1960s, for their skins. Between 1913 and 1969, more than 200,000 harbour seals were killed in British Columbia for pelts and bounties, and sea lions were systematically slaughtered in the name of predator control.

A particularly gruesome hunt targeted the basking shark, the second-largest fish in the world. At one time these creatures, which may reach fifteen metres in length, were abundant along the coast. For all their size they are peaceable giants, feeding on zooplankton in the nutrient-rich ocean waters close to the surface. They do not eat salmon or any other fish, but fishermen considered them a nuisance because they often became entangled in fishing gear. In 1949 the department of fisheries labelled them a "destructive pest" and in 1955 the department was persuaded to take aggressive action against the sharks in Barkley Sound, on the west coast of Vancouver Island, where they were especially prevalent.[11] A large triangular cutting blade was mounted on the bow of a fisheries patrol vessel, the *Comox Post*. This knife could be lowered just below the surface of the water. When the vessel drove straight into a lounging shark, the blade sliced the animal in half. Between 1955 and 1969, when the blade was in use, hundreds of sharks were slaughtered in the sound. "The great shark slaughter began at noon and continued for hours," wrote a reporter who witnessed one of these excursions in 1956. "We littered the beaches with their livers and the bottom with their carcasses."[12] Other fisheries vessels that were not equipped with the knife had orders to simply ram any sharks they encountered in the hope of killing them. Basking sharks are today almost never encountered in Barkley Sound or anywhere else on the coast.

Basically, it was open season on any marine animal that seemed to interfere with the fishery or had some commercial value of its own, including the killer whale. Nonetheless, Murray Newman wanted to catch one so enough information could be gathered about its physical features to allow an artist to make an accurate sculpture. The Aquarium director had one precedent on which to draw. Two years earlier, in the summer of 1962, two marine mammal collectors from California had arrived in BC with their twelve-metre boat, intending to lasso themselves a killer whale. The idea seemed absurd to most locals, but Frank Brocato and "Boots" Calandrino had a lot of experience wrangling marine animals in the wild, principally for Marineland of the Pacific outside Los Angeles. Their boat was equipped with a long boom extending from its bow, at the end of which was a pulpit where one of the collectors positioned himself to drop a net over the animal and get a rope around its tail. Brocato and Calandrino managed to find and lasso a female killer whale off Point Roberts, but as the animal attempted to escape she wrapped the line around the boat's propeller. The female's distress call was answered by a large bull and the two whales charged the boat in tandem, veering aside only at the last moment. The collectors, thinking they were under attack, killed the female with a high-powered rifle and drove the male away.[13] Discouraged and not a little rattled from their adventure, they returned to California empty-handed.

The example of Brocato and Calandrino showed how difficult it was to capture a killer whale alive, and initially Newman expected that he would have to kill one.[14] He was advised that the best place to go looking for whales was at the eastern end of Saturna Island, where they often passed close to the sandstone bluffs. There the Aquarium director installed his team, including Sam Burich, a sculptor who also happened to be a commercial fisherman, Ronald Sparrow, another commercial fisherman from the Musqueam First Nation who had experience with a harpoon, a team of volunteer watchers and a patrol vessel on loan from the department of fisheries. They arrived on Saturna on May 22 and set up a camp on the bluff near East Point, opposite Tumbo Island. While they waited for the whales to appear, Sparrow and Burich practised with the muzzle-loading harpoon gun, shooting at a raft the patrol boat towed past. As the days lengthened into months, members of the team drifted away. When Ronald Sparrow left to go halibut fishing, he was replaced at the harpoon by Josef Bauer, another commercial fisherman who had a long association with the Vancouver Aquarium. So Burich and Bauer were alone and more than a little bored on July 16, when a pod of killer whales entered the channel. As one of the animals cruised close to shore Burich took aim and fired. The harpoon struck the whale in the back, just ahead of the dorsal fin. Stunned, the animal hardly reacted at all. Two other members of the pod swam over and seemed to lift the wounded whale to the surface so it could breathe, and it occurred to Bauer that they might be able to make a live capture.

Alerted at his office in Vancouver, Newman jumped into a seaplane for the trip to Saturna. By the time he arrived, the two "whale hunters" were out beside the stricken animal in a boat that a fishing company had loaned them. Pat McGeer had also arrived. A professor of neurochemistry at UBC, McGeer was a Liberal member of the provincial legislature and a future cabinet minister in Bill Bennett's government. He had joined the whale project because he was eager to get a chance to examine the brain of such a large mammal. Everyone was very nervous, fearing what the animal or the other pod members might do. Jack Scott, a writer for the *Vancouver Sun*, had summed up the attitude toward killer whales earlier in the summer. "No one can say for sure how a killer whale will react if the harpoon does not strike a vital spot and, moreover, there's every likelihood that the other bulls in the pack will attack the ship itself, as they have been known to do in the past. Since the bull killer whale runs to twenty-five feet (7.6 m) in length and has a mouthful of teeth and disposition that can only be described as perfectly dreadful, the possibilities are downright chilling."[15] But right from the beginning, the whale contradicted everything that had been believed about it and made no aggressive moves against its captors.

Newman had no idea what to do. The plan had been to kill a whale, measure it, dissect it and take whatever they needed for study. Instead, they had a live animal and nowhere to put it. The four men decided on the spot to attempt moving the wounded whale across the Strait of Georgia to Vancouver, where Newman made arrangements to house it temporarily at Burrard Drydock on the North Shore. Running all night, Burich and Bauer managed to tow the whale "like a dog on a leash" to North Vancouver, and the next afternoon it took up residence in a netted area of the drydock. Moby Doll — the name was chosen from entries to a radio contest — caused an immediate sensation. It was not every day that a fearsome killer of the deep was available for public viewing. Stories appeared in media around the world. Scientists from across North America flew in to observe what was going on. When Burrard Drydock opened its doors to visitors, twenty thousand people showed up, about the same

■ Vancouver Aquarium director Murray Newman feeds a fish to Moby Doll. *Courtesy Murray Newman*

number as flocked to see the Beatles that summer when they arrived in town to play Empire Stadium in their first stop on a North American tour.

So little was known about killer whales that no one even knew what sex Moby was or what it ate. The first question was answered by a four-year-old girl who visited the pen. "What's that?" she innocently asked her father, pointing at Moby's suddenly visible penis. Until then everyone had assumed that he was a she. The second question was more pressing, since the whale did not eat for almost two months despite being offered a wide variety of food, including seal carcasses, poultry, whale tongues and blubber, even an octopus. As yet it was not understood that unlike their transient cousins, resident killer whales such as Moby ate only fish. This discovery was made finally when a visitor to the pen held out a lingcod and Moby took it. Offered another, he ate that one, too. Before the feeding was over, Moby had devoured fifty kilograms of cod and taught his keepers another lesson about killer whales.

After several days in the dry dock, the Aquarium moved Moby across Burrard Inlet to a purpose-built enclosure at the Jericho military base on the Point Grey waterfront. Pat McGeer ministered to the animal's medical needs, using a huge hypodermic needle at the end of a three-metre pole to inject Moby with antibiotics and vitamins. Once started he ate hungrily. But something was wrong, and on October 9, less than three months after he was captured, Moby Doll died. The cause of death was aspergillosis, a fungal disease that invaded his lungs.

Sam Burich, who had been one of Moby's caretakers throughout his captivity, completed his sculpture for the Aquarium. (It hung for years in the foyer until it was removed to make way for a new pavilion.) But his widow Helen recalled that his experience with Moby altered his attitude toward killer whales. The artist seemed to bond with the animal. He recognized its intelligence and gentleness and regretted the role he had played in removing it from the wild. Burich's change of heart was symptomatic of the

■ Moving Moby Doll. *Courtesy Murray Newman*

change that took place in the wider community during and after
the Moby Doll episode. For the first time people had had a chance
to get close to a killer whale. Instead of a fearsome man-eating
predator, they discovered an amiable creature that was endearing
and apparently smart. Scientists and members of the public alike
began to suspect that they had been wrong about "public enemy
number one."

However, Moby Doll's capture also had a downside for the
animal. As Murray Newman noted in his memoirs, "the age of
innocence was over" for killer whales.[16] Once it became known
that Marineland of the Pacific had been willing to pay $25,000
to obtain Moby, killer whales everywhere had price tags on their
heads. Notice was served that major aquariums wanted live specimens and would pay handsomely for them. The result was the
equivalent of a maritime gold rush, and sea-going "prospectors"
set out to find the mother lode.

■ Moby Doll in his pen in Vancouver. Dr. Pat McGeer is seen administering medication by means of a long pole. *Courtesy Murray Newman*

■

THE TINY COASTAL HAMLET OF NAMU lies on the mainland shore of the Inside Passage about 120 kilometres north of Port Hardy, where coastal boat traffic takes a sharp right turn and heads up Burke Channel toward Bella Coola. Archaeologists have discovered that people have lived there for ten thousand years, making it the oldest known inhabited place on the BC coast. Little evidence remains today, but not long ago Namu was the site of a thriving cannery village with a population of several hundred people during the summer fishing season. It had a café and store, bunkhouses and bungalows for the plant workers and managers, net lofts, an ice plant, even a two-room schoolhouse, all connected by a lacework of sturdy boardwalks.

And in the summer of 1965 the circus came to town.

It began innocently enough.[17] Late on the evening of June 22, a local salmon fisherman named Bill Lechkobit was caught in a sudden gale south of Namu at the mouth of Warrior Cove. To avoid being swept onto the rocks, Lechkobit cut loose his net and headed for a safe harbour. Early the next morning, his friend and fellow seiner Bob McGarvey emerged from the cove to find two killer whales trapped inside the abandoned net. One was an adult bull, about 6.5 metres long; the other was a young calf. As McGarvey watched, the current suddenly opened the end of the net and he saw the bull swim free, only to return inside the circle of mesh when the calf would not follow. McGarvey and Lechkobit, who had returned to the scene, realized they had a prize on their hands. Moby Doll had received so much publicity that fishermen all along the coast knew the value of a live killer whale. They secured the captives with more netting, and within a few hours they had sent word to the outside world that they had a couple of whales for sale. Prospective buyers, including the Vancouver Aquarium's Murray Newman, immediately flew to the tiny cannery village, but they were all dismayed by the asking price, $25,000 per whale. Which, of course, did not include the expense of transporting the animals south. The deal seemed even less attractive a few days later when the calf escaped. Since it was really the younger, smaller whale that the rival aquariums wanted, the captors found themselves with one remaining overpriced animal that might escape at any time and had a healthy appetite for salmon. Meanwhile, they weren't getting any fishing done. McGarvey and his friend decided to make a final offer: "The first person here with $8,000 in cash, gets the whale."

This spurred Ted Griffin into action. Griffin was the twenty-nine-year-old owner of the Seattle Marine Aquarium, a facility he had opened on the city's waterfront in 1962. Unlike most of the other aquarium representatives, he was an entrepreneur and a showman, not a scientist. Griffin had long sought a killer whale for his facility. He had spent many hours patrolling Puget Sound by helicopter and boat looking for a specimen and he wasn't about to let this one get away. He had already been up to Namu but his initial offer had been refused. When news of the final price reached him in Seattle, it was a Saturday night and the banks had closed. Griffin grabbed a couple of shopping bags and set out along the waterfront, calling on hotels and restaurants and writing them cheques for whatever cash they had in their tills. Before the weekend was over his bags were stuffed with small bills and he was on a flight north, accompanied by a gun-toting former Mountie he picked up in Vancouver as a security detail.

Griffin got his whale, which he christened Namu. (Subsequent research has found that it was C11, a member of one of the northern resident pods. C11 was a twenty-year-old male whose mother, C5, known as Kwattna, lived until 1995, when she died at the ripe old age of seventy-one.) He then faced the challenge of moving his four-tonne acquisition seven hundred kilometres along some of the most treacherous waters on the Pacific coast. Although no one knew it at the time, Griffin was pioneering the technique that Springer's rescuers would use thirty-seven years later. With the help of local fishermen, he welded several tonnes of steel bars into a three-sided pen about twelve by eighteen metres and six metres deep, kept afloat by empty oil drums scavenged from a local salvage company. A net hung across the open side of the pen.

Meanwhile, other whales regularly visited Namu at Warrior Cove. Some of them were large males with dorsal fins towering two metres in the air. Others were cows and calves. Their high-pitched whistles and squeaks echoed against the rocky shore in a plaintive symphony. On one occasion as many as three dozen whales showed up to support Namu, splashing around the net, tail lobbing and vocalizing. While most of these whales came and went, one cow and her two calves, presumably members of Namu's family group, remained near the net almost continuously.

Once Griffin got his makeshift cage into the water, it was towed to Warrior Cove, where Namu was coaxed into it. Griffin hired a local purse seiner, the *Chamiss Bay*, to tow the pen as far as Port Hardy and on July 9 it set off, accompanied by the *Robert E. Lee*, a ten-metre pleasure tug owned by Seattle disc jockey Bob Hardwick. For the entire trip a small group of journalists aboard the *Lee* filed daily stories about Namu's progress, building public interest in the operation. Also aboard the *Lee* was Gil Hewlett, a twenty-four-year-old biologist "donated" by the Vancouver Aquarium to assist in the transfer. Hewlett was the lone Canadian involved in the expedition. Journalist Sylvia Fraser described him as "a handsome towhead who was never seen to wear shoes and who looked like a beach boy left over from the latest surf-side movie."

At Port Hardy the *Chamiss Bay* left to go seining and the tow was taken up by the *Ivor Foss*, a Seattle tug. Two hours out of Port Hardy a group of about ten whales were spotted in the distance converging on the pen. Hewlett described what happened in his journal. "When they are within three hundred yards of the pen, Namu lets out a terrifying squeal, almost like a throttled cat. He leaps out of the water and crashes against the left corner of the pen. There was terrific thrashing and he is making all kinds of sounds. Then they are there again, the same family of the cow and two calves. They came straight up behind the pen to about ten feet away, tremendous squealing going on. Namu seemed to lose all coordination in the pen. He kept getting swept against the cargo net and swimming vigorously forward. The family unit circles around towards the end of the pen. Those of us on the pen are yelling and screaming at the top of our lungs. This is an incredible experience. The excitement is almost overwhelming."

Once the tow passed through Seymour Narrows, however, the other whales disappeared. (Years later researchers would learn that the narrows form a boundary between the typical ranges of the northern and southern residents.) On the southern coast the little flotilla was joined by a growing fleet of pleasure boaters who were curious to see the captive killer. Members of the crew kept busy warning the sightseers to keep their distance. A team of researchers from the Boeing Company's acoustic division had arrived. They were taping Namu's vocalizations for possible application in anti-submarine warfare, and the constant roar of boat engines was interfering with their recording. At one point the whale developed blisters on his dorsal fin. Sunburn, it was decided. The convoy was stopped at Deep Bay, opposite the southern end of Denman Island, and Hewlett went off to track down some zinc oxide lotion. He telephoned Jane Van Roggen, a member of the Vancouver Aquarium board who was holidaying in the area and together they drove around to all the local pharmacies. "When we told the pharmacist we needed enough zinc oxide for a killer whale," Hewlett recalled, "he/she either laughed uncontrollably or looked at us incredulously, saying 'zinc oxide only comes in two-ounce tubes!' We bought every tube in the area and took them back to Deep Bay." Attaching a brush to the end of a bamboo pole, Don Goldsberry, a collector from the aquarium in Tacoma who was part of the transfer team, painted the fin with the zinc oxide mixed with mineral oil. Namu didn't much like it—indeed, after one coating he wouldn't let Goldsberry get close again with the brush—but it seemed to work. At Deep Bay, where the convoy was held up by storm warnings, two young boys with a boat charged seventy-five cents to take spectators out to view the whale. Meanwhile, at the village's only phone booth, journalists lined up to call in their stories.

On July 25 the saltwater caravan reached Deception Pass at the north end of Whidbey Island, where it paused to wait for a tide change. When Hewlett looked up at the bridge that spanned the pass, what he saw astonished him. "The bridge is crowded with people as are the banks on both sides," Hewlett wrote in his journal. "There must be five thousand people, with cars lined back for miles on each side. Namu rolls twice and then gave a smack with flukes. The crowd, upon seeing this, gave a cheer—then the Lee and the *Ivor* blew their foghorns. I think for the first time all of us realize how big this whole thing is." Three days later, welcomed by a flotilla of boats, swooping helicopters, water skiers, go-go dancers and a brass band, Namu reached his future home at Pier 56 on the Seattle waterfront.

Namu was a public relations bonanza that Griffin, whose aquarium needed a financial shot in the arm, exploited to the limit. The whale's image appeared on everything from sweatshirts to colouring books. Namu was front-page news not just in Seattle but around the world. His voice was used at station breaks on Bob Hardwick's radio station. The pilots of passenger jets arriving at the airport reported on his health as routinely as they gave the local weather report. A nightclub

■ Gil Hewlett, then a newly minted biologist working for the Vancouver Aquarium, watches over Namu in the pen that was used to transport the whale down the coast to Seattle in the summer of 1965.
Courtesy Gil Hewlett

launched a new dance craze, the "Namu," including moves like the dorsal, the spray and the dive. Griffin was filmed in his wetsuit riding on Namu's back gripping the tall dorsal fin. Within a year, the whale was starring in his own Hollywood movie, *Namu the Killer Whale*. In the film, a biologist played by the ruggedly handsome Robert Lansing convinces the people in a hostile coastal fishing community that killer whales are not the deadly predators they loathe and fear. Lansing actually did some of his own stunt work, going into the water to ride on Namu's back. These images of a benign, playful, endearing animal, no more dangerous than a large dolphin, reinforced the change that was taking place in the mind of the public about the nature of killer whales.

■

NAMU LIVED FOR A YEAR AT THE SEATTLE AQUARIUM before he drowned by tangling himself in the cables of his pen trying to escape. But he turned out to be just a dress rehearsal for Ted Griffin, who continued to capture killer whales and sell them to other aquariums. One of these animals belonged to a pod of fifteen whales that Griffin netted in Puget Sound early in 1967. Two of the captives drowned and Griffin released another five because they were too big for life in captivity, but one of the survivors remained available for purchase. Up in Vancouver, Murray Newman was still eager to obtain a whale for his aquarium, and after a spirited debate he managed to persuade his board of directors to approve the purchase. Griffin was trucking the whale to Vancouver anyway to exhibit in a tank at that year's boat show and he accepted Newman's offer of $22,000. Walter the Whale, as he was then known, was transferred to the new dolphin pool in Stanley Park, and the Vancouver Aquarium had its first resident killer whale. Soon after, it was noticed that "Walter" was in fact a female so another contest took place, resulting in a new name, Skana, roughly analogous to *S'quana*, the Haida word for killer whale.[18]

The presence of Skana at the Aquarium created new possibilities for scientific research. While her trainers taught her an assortment of manoeuvres to showcase her dexterity and intelligence, and impress the thousands of spectators who flocked to see her, a battery of researchers from the aquarium and from the University of British Columbia began studying her behaviour and recording her vocalizing. Among these scientists was a psychologist named Paul Spong. Spong was a twenty-eight-year-old New Zealander with a freshly minted PhD from UCLA who had just taken a position in the psychiatry department at UBC. At the aquarium he began by devising a series of tests to evaluate Skana's visual abilities and the ways in which she used visual information to solve problems. He was able to determine that the visual acuity of killer whales was in the same range as that of a cat. Spong began using music instead of food as a reward in his experiments, and he became aware of the whale's response to different sounds. He would play classical music for Skana and invite musicians down to the pool to play their instruments. At the same time, Spong found himself drawn to the whale emotionally. "Everything I was learning about them showed that this was an extraordinary animal in its sensory makeup and in its ability to modify its behaviour and learn things," he recalled. "I was still doing science because I was trying to do things in systematic experiments, but at the same time I was becoming more personally involved in the whales." Spong would sit at the edge of the pool with his feet in the water and Skana would swim over to have her back rubbed. On one occasion Skana dragged her teeth across Spong's feet, not biting but serving notice that she could. Startled, Spong jerked his feet out of the water but he put them back in and Skana once again showed her teeth. After several repetitions, Spong no longer felt afraid and Skana stopped her mock attacks on his feet.[19] As a result of this and other experiences, the scientist became convinced that he was the

■ Skana and Hyak, the Vancouver Aquarium's two killer whales in residence together between 1968 and 1980, entertain visitors to the whale pool. *Vancouver Aquarium*

object of Skana's experiments every bit as much as she was the object of his. "All of this stuff was really starting to open my eyes," Spong later recalled.

> What on earth was this animal that we've got here? Other things were happening too. I was still interested in acoustics and I was interested in using acoustics to find out things like how high a sound can a whale hear? I was also interested because I was personally intrigued by the whale in a more personal interaction. That's when I started coming down and sitting on the edge of the little training platform at the edge of Skana's pool

with my feet in the water. She would come over and I would rub my feet on her head and got to know her a bit more personally. It was also at the point where I was making sounds underwater to her and looking at the way she oriented to them. I had this little brass bell and I would ring it on the rung of the ladder in the pool and she loved it. She would come over and hang upside down motionless while I was ringing the bell. With the front of her head fairly close to the bell. This is so consistent with the way in which it was understood that hearing occurs in dolphins where you have a sound that is transmitted through the lower jaw up into middle ear. So it was also confirming in orcas about what was happening with dolphins.

Spong's research aside, his lifestyle was increasingly at odds with the culture of the Vancouver Aquarium. It was the sixties and the baby boom generation had embarked on its flirtation with sex, drugs and rock 'n' roll. In Vancouver this youth movement sometimes seemed to be at war with the older generation. Its mouthpiece was the *Georgia Straight* newspaper, launched in May 1967, and its enemy was Mayor Tom Campbell, whose intolerance of the so-called counterculture manifested itself in several draconian efforts to get the hippies off the streets, including the attempted use of the War Measures Act to "clean up" the city. Spong embraced the *zeitgeist* with enthusiasm. His beads, beard and long hair didn't rate a second look in the hippie hangouts of Vancouver's Kitsilano neighbourhood but he stood out around the whale pool, where, by Newman's own admission, "my staff were mostly a pretty clean-cut bunch of people."[20] Eventually Spong's personal views would lead to a rupture with the Aquarium. But whatever antagonisms existed were put aside in the third week of February 1968, when news reached the Aquarium that a pod of killer whales had appeared suddenly in a bay in Pender Harbour.

Pender Harbour is a complex jumble of islands, coves and lagoons on the Sunshine Coast about seventy-five kilometres northwest of Vancouver. The whales first appeared in Gunboat Bay at the head of the harbour, where they were discovered by local fisherman Sonny Reid. The pod exited the bay despite Reid's attempts to contain them but they returned the next day to Garden Bay, another arm of the harbour. Reid and some other fishermen managed to drop a net across the entrance to the bay and trap one of the whales, an adult male almost five metres long. By the time Murray Newman flew in late that afternoon, the captive had been secured inside a large herring pond consisting of a bag-like net suspended from a frame of logs chained together in a square. The Aquarium purchased the animal on the spot and officials decided to leave it for the time being in Garden Bay. Two months later Reid and his friends captured seven more whales in the bay, and within a few days they had sold five of the animals to various aquariums in California. A crane scooped the animals from the water into waiting trucks, which transported them to the cargo planes that flew them south. No longer vilified and shot on sight, the killer whale had become British Columbia's newest export.

The Vancouver Aquarium purchased the two remaining captives—a large bull and a calf—so it now had three whales in Pender Harbour. Newman decided to establish a satellite facility in Garden Bay where the whales could be trained and studied and the public was welcome to watch.[21] The facility, which was ready for its official opening by August, consisted of three large netpens circled by logs, with floating platforms where the captive whales could be observed. Everyone in Pender Harbour was excited at the prospect of the whales becoming a major tourist attraction. The idea was to study killer whales in their near-natural environment and Spong took charge of the research effort. He continued to use music to stimulate and reward the whales and at times the whale exhibit took on the atmosphere of a countercultural "be-in" with long-haired musicians playing to and swimming with the animals. It was all a bit too "eccentric" for Murray Newman. More importantly, Spong had concluded that the whales—Skana and the animals in Pender Harbour—were suffering from sensory deprivation in captivity and should be set free. The smallest whale, Hyak, had been transferred to the main aquarium in Vancouver, and when the other two escaped from their Garden Bay pen, Newman decided to shut down the facility.

In retrospect, the capture and sale of the Pender Harbour whales seems inhumane, but at the time everyone involved assumed that there were thousands of the animals on the coast, and there was still a great deal of fear and animosity directed at them. Graeme Ellis, who, as an eighteen-year-old, was hired by the Aquarium that summer to work around the pens, recalled the attitude that prevailed. "It's like a skeleton in my closet, when people ask me, 'You were involved in killer whale capture? How could you?' But at the time, that was what we did. It was just a natural chain of events. It was just happening..."

The following June, 1969, Spong's contract with the Vancouver Aquarium expired and Newman, irritated at his views on captivity and alienated by his lifestyle, did not renew it. Spong, who was more or less barred from the facility, camped outside the Aquarium to protest Skana's continued confinement, and the episode ended with bad feelings on both sides. Subsequently, Spong was involved with Project Jonah and Greenpeace in their initial protests against commercial whaling, then later moved up the coast to Hanson Island in Johnstone Strait, where he established a research facility, OrcaLab, to monitor killer whales in the wild. His relations with the Vancouver Aquarium remained strained but he would still play a key role in efforts to relocate both Springer and Luna.

■

LUCRATIVE AS IT SOMETIMES WAS, killer whale collecting in the 1960s was a seat-of-the-pants enterprise that relied as much on chutzpah and ingenuity as it did on science and experience.

Nothing illustrates this as well as the improbable story of how a whale from coastal British Columbia ended up halfway around the world entertaining visitors to an aquarium on the French Riviera.

In December 1969 the whales returned to Pender Harbour, and Sonny Reid and his friends were ready for them. This time they netted a dozen specimens at Madeira Park, another harbour community. Six of the captives escaped or were released, and five were sold to aquariums in California. That left one for two teenage collectors from Vancouver who were acting for a French aristocrat, Roland de la Poype, a decorated fighter pilot who was building his own marineland at Antibes on the Côte d'Azur. Despite their youth, Robin Best and Chris Angus had been collecting animals for several years. Before they could legally vote they already were advertising themselves as "dealers in dolphins, whales and other marine mammals." "We were very young," recalled Chris Angus, "but we were experts because there weren't very many."

Robin was the son of Alan Best, an animal collector himself and the supervisor of the Stanley Park Zoo. His friend Chris had spent his boyhood working around horses. When Moby Doll arrived in Vancouver, the two of them caught whale fever, spending all their spare time hanging out at the Jericho pen. Before long they were collecting river otters and seals for sale to marine parks and zoos, but their ambition was to catch a killer whale. When they heard about the whales in Pender Harbour they rushed up the coast to see if they could acquire one of the captives for de la Poype. Negotiations took place in a local beer parlour. By this time Chris and Robin were eighteen and nineteen respectively, not old enough even to be in the establishment, but they talked their way in and for $ 16,000 they purchased the remaining whale, a female about 5.5 metres long, which they named Su-san.

Then the hard part began. Angus went back to Vancouver to find an airplane. Most airlines took one look at the long-haired eighteen-year-old looking to charter an aircraft to move a whale and laughed him out of the office, thinking he was probably high on drugs. His search eventually took him to the Georgia Street offices of Lufthansa, the German airline. Lufthansa didn't even fly out of Vancouver at this time but the district manager fell in love with the project and agreed to make a Boeing 707 cargo jet available in Los Angeles. He also made arrangements for another plane to airlift the whale from Vancouver to California. Next Angus managed to find some fabricators who could throw together an aluminum cradle on a moment's notice. The plan was to transport the whale down from Pender Harbour on the back of a flatbed truck, suspended in a sling inside a vinyl bag in the cradle. Ice water would be sprayed over the animal during the trip to keep its skin wet. Three days after Christmas the two teenagers managed to get Su-san loaded onto the truck, which set off on the fifty-kilometre drive down the Sunshine Coast to the ferry terminal. As the truck approached the steep hill that carries the highway into the town of Gibsons, the compressor gave out and with it the vehicle's air brakes. The driver had no choice but to start down the incline with only a hand brake to slow them down. By the time the truck rolled through Gibsons, its clutch was burning up, its brakes were smoking and the three passengers on board were leaning out the doors ready to jump for their lives. Miraculously, they made it onto the ferry, where repairs to the compressor were carried out.

When they drove off the ferry at Horseshoe Bay, a police motorcycle escort ushered them through Vancouver to the airport, where the next surprise awaited them. When a forklift went to load the whale, it was discovered that the cradle did not fit through the doors of the cargo bay. Ever resourceful, the two teens lopped off a section of the cradle and by bending the whale's tail managed to stuff the animal into the back of the plane. At this point David Taylor took over. Taylor was the veterinarian at the Flamingo Land Zoo, owners of the whale pool in Yorkshire, where Su-san was going to be kept until de la Poype got his facility in Antibes built. He had arrived from England with his animal trainer, Martin Paddly, and the two of them took possession of the whale at the airport. The flight to Los Angeles went off without a hitch and by the next day the whale was on her way to Europe. At that point she was the largest animal ever shipped by air. But Murphy's Law seemed to be plaguing the expedition. At Manchester, where the big jet was scheduled to land, weather conditions made it impossible to put down. The airline had no landing privileges at London's Heathrow Airport, and the plane was supposed to proceed to Germany, but Taylor was adamant: the whale had to arrive in England. So the pilot radioed Heathrow and announced that he had an emergency on board and had to land. When officials learned that the emergency was a two-tonne whale they were furious, but the plane was already down. Taylor transferred Su-san to the back of a truck and drove to Yorkshire, pausing at every rest stop to buy boxes of popsicles, which he used to cool down the water inside the vinyl container. At Flamingo Park, where she stayed for several months, the whale was renamed Calypso. Later in 1970 she was transported to Marineland Antibes, but she died that December from an abscess on the lung, a year after being hoisted out of Pender Harbour. (As a postscript to this adventure, Angus recalled that when he and Best eventually met de la Poype the Frenchman gasped, "You are but a lad!", astonished that he had given so much money to a pair of teenagers.)

■

ANOTHER TEENAGER WHOSE LIFE was transformed by his encounter with killer whales in Pender Harbour was Graeme Ellis. Most of what Ellis knew about the whales he had learned growing up in Campbell River, where the fishing community hated them and Ellis himself passed the time as a boy shooting stones at them with his slingshot. He had just completed high school when Murray Newman hired him to work at the Vancouver Aquarium's out station in Pender Harbour. "I remember the first day," Ellis recalled. "[Trainer Terry McCloud] gave me a bucket and told me to walk along a log to the other end of this pool. I was terrified. First of all, walking along a log anywhere and secondly with a killer whale following me along, so it was an eye opener." Ellis quickly overcame his fear and grew attached to the animals. When his work with the Aquarium finished early in 1969, he took a job at Sealand of the Pacific, British Columbia's second aquarium. Sealand, located in Oak Bay, was owned by Bob Wright, a Victoria-area marina owner who recognized the commercial potential of captive killer whales. He had purchased his first whale, Haida, from Ted Griffin's Seattle Aquarium, and hired Ellis to train the animal for Sealand's opening that summer. "I was very excited to be working with killer whales again," Ellis said, "because you can't help but get incredibly attached to these animals. They're so bright and it's so rewarding to interact with them." The exhibits at Sealand also included a bottlenose dolphin named Chloe, a trio of Steller sea lions and a group of seabirds, but Haida was the star of the show and Wright was determined to find him a companion. When he was outbid for one of the Pender Harbour captives that December, Wright decided to go into the capture business himself, little realizing what an unusual animal he would come up with.

Most killer whales are the colour of formal dinner party attire: black back and fins with white front and lapels, and a grey patch at the base of the dorsal fin. On occasion, though, all-white albino whales occur. The first reported sighting of one of these rare animals on the BC coast dates back to 1924. Clifford Carl, director of the Royal BC Museum from 1942 to 1969, collected many references to a local albino, which he christened Alice. One afternoon in January 1970, Bob Wright, Graeme Ellis and a couple of other researchers were out in a boat looking for whales off the southern end of Vancouver Island.[22] They'd had a report of a group of five animals—transients as it turned out—in the vicinity of Race Rocks. When they spotted the whales, they discovered that one was white, probably the granddaughter of Alice. The whales swam into Pedder Bay, a narrow notch in the coast west of Victoria, where

Wright and his team managed to pen them in with the only net available, a flimsy gillnet filled with holes and too short to reach the sea floor. Concerned that the captives would escape, Wright stationed boats at intervals along the net, and all night members of his team pounded paddles on the sides of the boats and dropped seal bombs—underwater explosives used by fishermen to frighten away seals—to keep the whales from approaching the mesh. When dawn arrived, so did a pair of seiners with more nets to secure the entrance to the bay.

For twenty-four days, while Wright held the captives at Pedder Bay, they would not eat the herring and salmon offered to them. At the time the distinction between transients and resident whales was not understood, nor was the fact that transients eat other marine mammals such as seals, sea lions and porpoises, not fish. But when the white whale, now named Chimo, and another young female, Nootka, were moved to the Sealand facility at Oak Bay, Haida, the resident whale, was able to persuade the newcomers to begin eating. Ellis described what happened. "It was the most amazing thing. We had a safety net across between them and we had someone distracting [Haida] and feeding him, at the other end of the pool. We put in both of these animals and Haida kept coming, going by the net and looking at them through the web. I was in the water watching the net in case an animal got tangled. Haida came along with herring and they both came face to face in the net. He actually pushed herring through the mesh and into their mouths and that's how they started feeding. That happened within minutes of them going in the pool. In retrospect, that totally blows me away. It was really astounding." Meanwhile, back in Pedder Bay, the other three captives continued their fast, getting slimmer and slimmer. After seventy-five days one of them attempted to burst free through the net, and drowned. A few days later the remaining two finally started eating fish and began regaining their health. Wright had sold them to a Texas aquarium but before they could be moved, someone opened the net during the night and let them go. Over the next few years they were seen often on the coast.

Chimo, who was estimated to be five years old and 3.5 metres in length, attracted all the attention that Bob Wright had expected. She was the only white killer whale in captivity in the world, and following her arrival at Sealand, attendance doubled. Jacques Cousteau paid a visit to see her and Wright reportedly turned down an offer of a million dollars for her. Unhappily, she began exhibiting a series of health problems. A yellow substance appeared on her skin, lesions formed, she lost weight and her echolocation system appeared to be impaired. Chimo was eventually diagnosed with Chediak Higashi syndrome, an inherited disorder of the immune system, also known in humans, that left her highly susceptible to infections. In late October 1972 Chimo became ill and after five days she died of a streptococcal infection that developed into pneumonia. Nootka was later moved to several different aquariums until she ended up in San Diego, where she lived until 1990.

■

BY 1973, WELL OVER A DOZEN AQUARIUMS had purchased killer whales taken from the coast of British Columbia and northern Washington State, and a total of 263 animals had been captured, at least temporarily.[23] The "gold rush" atmosphere had begun to arouse concern among researchers and members of the public. It was one thing to keep a small number of animals for purposes of scientific research. It was quite another to have so many on public display, performing tricks in aquariums and oceanariums. As a first step toward protecting the killer whale population, the governments of Canada (1970) and Washington State (1971) passed legislation banning the harassment of the animals and requiring a permit to capture one. But it was impossible to establish how many whales could be captured safely without knowing the size of the population. It was widely assumed that there were thousands of the animals but nobody knew for sure.

To determine how many killer whales were on the coast, the Fisheries Research Board of Canada in 1971 launched a study in collaboration with the relevant departments of the four Pacific American states. In BC, the researcher chosen to head the study was Dr. Mike Bigg, a marine mammalogist attached to the Pacific Biological Station in Nanaimo. The project he began in 1971 would last the rest of his life and completely transform thinking about the animals, particularly about how abundant they were and how they organized themselves socially.

Bigg was eight years old when his parents emigrated from England to Canada in 1947. His father Andy found work in the cement plant at Bamberton, north of Victoria, and moved his family into a tiny house on the Malahat Highway. Andy, who had worked on newspapers back in England, began supplementing his income by writing articles for tourist publications and eventually became a well-known journalist on Vancouver Island. By that time Mike had left home to attend university. After completing graduate work in zoology at the University of British Columbia, he joined the federal department of fisheries as the head of marine mammal research on the West Coast. Initially his work involved seals and sea lions, and he was also involved in the successful relocation of sea otters from Alaska back to the BC coast, where they had once been abundant. But the killer whale project became a passion, not a job.

The challenge facing Bigg and his associates was how to count animals that spend ninety-five percent of their lives below the surface of the water and are constantly on the move. An individual that is counted today in one location can easily be the same individual that is counted tomorrow many kilometres away. At the suggestion of Murray Newman, Bigg organized a one-day census, the first animal census of its kind anywhere in the world.[24] He enlisted the help of volunteer informants up and down the coast: lighthouse keepers, commercial fishermen, tugboat operators, ferry crews, pleasure-boat owners, mariners of all types, anyone who was likely to see a killer whale in the course of their daily lives. He distributed thousands of question-naires for these volunteer spotters to record how many whales they saw, where and when. Monday, July 26, 1971, was census day. Spotting whales with the naked eye is not easy, especially in rough water, and records indicated that that date gave the best chance of good weather. Close to five hundred forms came back, a large enough response that the census was repeated in 1972 and 1973. The results led Bigg to a shocking conclusion. He estimated that the population of killer whales along the coast of BC and Washington State was only between 200 and 350 animals, far fewer than had been supposed.[25]

One thing Bigg and his researchers learned from the initial census was that whales seemed to be particularly numerous in Johnstone Strait, the long, windblown passage that runs along the northeast side of Vancouver Island. In August 1972 Bigg and Ian McAskie, an associate from the biological station, visited Johnstone Strait on a fisheries department boat to observe and photograph killer whales in the wild. The two researchers noticed that they could recognize some individual animals by marks on their dorsal fins and backs. An animal called Nicola, for example, had a large nick in her fin, while the fin of another, known as Stubbs, had been nearly amputated, leaving only a mangled stub. Wavy had a rippling fin, Top Notch had a notched fin and so on. As they observed the animals, an idea dawned. As McAskie recalled it:

> Mike and I were up there [in 1972] just to check the numbers and we thought, just go up and count them. We didn't know what to do about that. I noticed that one had had its dorsal fin sheared off about two-thirds of the way up. A great chunk. And we called it Stubbs. I didn't think too much about it until further up the strait in a different place and a different time we saw it again. We wondered then, discussing it on the bridge, if we should look for other indications of injuries. Seemed like a good idea. This meant chasing individu-

als to take photographs. Stubbs was obvious, but once you started looking you could see smaller injuries.

The use of physical markings to identify individual animals was not new. Bristol Foster, then the director of the Royal BC Museum, had done work identifying giraffes in Africa by noting the pattern of their skin patches. Roger Payne was beginning to use photographs to identify right whales off Argentina, and Steven Katona was doing the same with humpback whales in the North Atlantic. The technique of photo identification was in the air; Bigg and his team utilized it to make a breakthrough in the study of killer whales. As they made more field trips and gathered more photographs, they were able to show that not just some but *all* of the whales could be identified using this technique. And once they identified individual animals, everything changed. The whales no longer resembled a cloud of bees buzzing around a hive or a row of blackbirds on a wire, indistinguishable one from another. Instead they were individuals, each with its own physical appearance, its own family, its own life history and habits. And each individual could be followed and documented.

The study expanded over the next few years. Censuses continued to be carried out, but Bigg also took a more proactive approach. John Ford, one of Bigg's associates, described how the system evolved.

He established a network of hundreds of volunteer observers, who would telephone or call by radio whenever whales were seen in the area. When a call was received, Mike or one of his field teams would race to the location to intercept, observe and photograph the whales. Occasionally, Mike would locate a pod from a float plane, land near the whales and, with his charm and infectious enthusiasm, convince a nearby boater to take him closer to the animals for photographs. In only three years, the team collected data from more than three hundred encounters with killer whale pods. By 1976 they had identified virtually every individual on the coast and had shed the first scientific light on the natural history of these remarkable cetaceans.[26]

A key member of the research team was Graeme Ellis. Ellis had left his job at Sealand, tired of the circus atmosphere there, gone blue water sailing for a year, then taken a year of university. He was at loose ends when a group of filmmakers asked him to be part of an expedition to Johnstone Strait in the summer of 1973 to film killer whales. Camping in the strait, Ellis and a photographer, James Hunter, used a rubber Zodiac to track the whales, and it was during that summer that Ellis met Bigg. They spent time chatting on one of the research boats and Bigg invited Ellis to drop in to the biological station during the winter. One thing led to another and Ellis began working with Bigg whenever a few dollars could be found to pay him, and often when it couldn't. He was ready with his camera on a moment's notice, whenever a call came in on the "killer whale hotline," to jump in a boat and tear off in to the strait to locate and follow the animals. Meanwhile, in Puget Sound, the US government hired marine biologist Kenneth Balcomb in 1976 to carry out a census of whales in Washington State similar to the one Bigg and his team had conducted in BC. Balcomb's project produced a detailed snapshot of the southern whale population. When his government support ended, Balcomb went on to establish the Center for Whale Research on San Juan Island to continue the research.

The official killer whale study carried on by Bigg and his team also ended in 1976 because the main question that had prompted it—how to set a limit on live capture of the animals— had been answered. In early March of that year, Sea World's Don Goldsberry, who had become the most active supplier of whales to aquariums, cornered a group of six animals at the head of Puget Sound within sight of the state capital, Olympia.[27] His timing and tactics could not have been worse. Goldsberry was using aircraft and seal bombs to herd the whales at the same time as legislators were debating the creation of a whale sanctuary. Public opinion was already turning against killer whale capture. The sight of the whales being harassed and "bombed" sparked an instant protest at the capture site where a crowd of more than a thousand people demanded that the captives be set free. "It was the last capture to take place in Washington State," recalled Graeme Ellis, who was at the protest, "before they put the lid on any more captures due to public protest and so on. It really was a gong show. Those guys did a real 'ride 'em cowboy' roundup right in front of Olympia, the state legislature. Everyone was horrified. They had float planes and speed boats and all the usual cowboy stuff going on." The governor of Washington sued Goldsberry for allegedly violating his collecting agreement and ultimately a judge ordered the whales released and revoked Sea World's permit. As Ellis said, it was effectively the end of live capture on the Pacific coast. From this point, killer whales could be captured there only to replace a captive that had died or escaped. Since Bigg's censuses had already shown that the population of killer whales was too small to sustain live captures at the rate at which they had been going on, there seemed to the Canadian department of fisheries no more need to continue the research project.

But to Bigg and his associates, the work had just begun. Year after year they continued to monitor the whales, often in their spare time and with little or no financial support. Bigg himself was told by his bosses in the department of fisheries to shift his attention to harbour seals. He began leading a sort of double life, officially studying seals and later sea lions, while clandestinely spending much of his time compiling data on killer whales. Every scientist in the world who was interested in the whales knew about Bigg's research, but his boss on the other side of the building had little more than an inkling.

Once Bigg's team was able to identify individual whales, they could draw conclusions about the animals' social organization and behaviour patterns. The more they found out, the more it became clear just what a remarkable and unique creature the killer whale is. Thanks to Bigg's team, scientists recognized that there are actually two types of whales, residents and transients, who may share the same territory but are otherwise so different as to be almost distinct species; and that the mother is the focal individual of the pod and offspring associate with her for as long as she is alive. These phenomena do not occur in any other vertebrate animal. Much of what is now known about killer whales was discovered after Bigg died of cancer, tragically young at the age of fifty-one, in October 1990. But all that is known derives from his pioneering work, without which it would have been impossible to identify Springer, the lost whale in Puget Sound, or develop a plan to bring her home.

■

IF THE LIVE CAPTURE OF KILLER WHALES for display in zoos and aquariums effectively ended on the Pacific coast in 1976, the occasional rescue of a sick or injured animal still took place. One of these rescues occurred in 1977, and it foreshadowed the rescue of Springer that took place twenty-five years later.[28]

Mike Bigg and Graeme Ellis first heard about the whale that would become known as Miracle on July 4. The crew of a freighter in Nanaimo Harbour reported an animal swimming close to the ship and vocalizing actively. Since it is so unusual for a killer whale to be alone, Bigg and Ellis expected it was a false alarm, but when Ellis went out in his boat he confirmed that it was a young calf, probably just over a year old. Reports came in during the following days and weeks as the whale was tracked northward until it entered Menzies Bay, a few kilometres north of the community of Campbell River, where it was discovered by a couple of sport fishermen. By this time the calf appeared to be dying. It was cut where it had been struck by a propeller, a brown slime coated its back, white fungal patches were growing on its fins, and it was moving very sluggishly. There was also a bullet wound from a .22 rifle. Local people fed the whale herring and tried to protect it from the boaters who began gathering to gawk at it. Eventually Bigg was informed and he flew up from Nanaimo with Bob Wright of Sealand and Jay Hyman, who was visiting from the New York Aquarium, where he was the consulting veterinarian. When they inspected the whale the trio of experts had no doubt the animal was dying. After burning up the phone lines to Ottawa, Wright and Bigg persuaded Fisheries Minister Romeo LeBlanc to issue a capture permit so the whale could be confined and treated for its wounds and infections.

Wright brought a crew up to Menzies Bay and with the help of a log crane they loaded the calf onto a flatbed truck and drove it through the night down island to Victoria. Not knowing for sure what infections the whale harboured, Wright did not want it sharing a pen with the other animals at Sealand, so he arranged with the Oak Bay Beach Hotel to put Miracle in the hotel's saltwater swimming pool. The shock of the whole experience almost killed the calf. Four times she stopped breathing and sank to the bottom of the pool, and four times the rescue team was able to revive her. After a couple of days she began eating and the infection began to abate. As she recovered, Miracle received blanket coverage from the media. The *Vancouver Sun* kept daily track of her progress. Radio stations gave hourly updates. Thousands of curious spectators came to the hotel every day to get a look into the swimming pool. Just as Springer would, Miracle seemed to captivate the public. Medical treatment continued, and it was not until the end of February 1978, almost seven months after Miracle checked into the hotel, that she was airlifted by helicopter to Sealand.

But the animal's ordeal was far from over. No sooner had she arrived at her new home than she began convulsing, then seemed to withdraw into herself, refusing food and attention. During her time in Menzies Bay, the person who had discovered her, local millworker Bill Davis, had grown close to Miracle, hand-feeding her and eventually stroking her skin. The people at Sealand decided that exposing Miracle to a trusted friend might help her adjust to her new surroundings. Davis came down to Victoria and almost immediately got Miracle to respond and begin eating. The worst was over. Miracle lived at Sealand for almost four years until mid-January 1982, when she became tangled in a net that formed one side of her pool and drowned.[29] It has never been determined who her family might have been or how she came to be wounded and alone in Menzies Bay. Miracle remains a mystery.

■

AS THE 1970S DREW TO A CLOSE, it was evident that the era of live capture had done serious damage to the killer whale population of the Pacific coast. About fifty animals had been taken, mainly from the southern resident population, which by 1976 had been reduced to sixty-eight whales. Most of these were adults because collectors had favoured removing the younger animals. If live capture had not ceased when it did, this population of whales probably would have been wiped out. After 1976, the number of animals began to increase until by 1990 there were about ninety southern residents. Was this enough to ensure the long-term survival of the population? No one knew for sure.

Ironically, it was also during the live capture era, and perhaps because of it, that the killer whale underwent an image makeover. As the aquarium-going public grew familiar with them, the whales lost much of their fearsome reputation and became instead the poster animal for the marine mammal world: handsome, intelligent, graceful, sociable, even cuddly, if a five-tonne predator with a mouth full of sharp teeth could ever be considered cuddly. The attitude toward the animals changed so completely that for some members of the public and the scientific community, it became anathema to keep them in captivity. In 1964, when the Vancouver Aquarium set out to obtain a killer whale, no one gave a second thought to harpooning one. Sixteen years later, in 1980, when Skana died at the Aquarium and Murray Newman wanted to obtain two new whales, he had

to travel all the way to Iceland because it was no longer acceptable to capture them locally. And even then the relocation of the
animals was fought in the courts by environmentalists. Despite
the public popularity of the new residents, Finna and Bjossa,
captivity continued to be a hot-button issue. Finally, in 1996 the
Vancouver Aquarium adopted a policy that precluded the collection of killer whales from the wild. Finna, who died in 1997,
and Bjossa, who was moved to Sea World in San Diego in 2001,
were the last killer whales to live at the facility.

But that was far from the end of the Aquarium's involvement with killer whales. Scientists based there continued to carry
out groundbreaking field studies on the animals. It was not surprising, therefore, that when Springer showed up in Puget Sound
alone and ailing, it was the Vancouver Aquarium that developed
the plan to save her.

3 ▪ RESCUING SPRINGER

OUT IN THE WATERS OF PUGET SOUND around the north end of Vashon Island, Springer's health seemed to be deteriorating and her behaviour was becoming more and more obsessive as she played endlessly with her favourite stick. On May 24, the National Marine Fisheries Service announced that after a long delay and much discussion it intended to submit Springer to the three Rs: Rescue, Rehabilitation, Relocation. Preparations for the "intervention" took another three weeks as the NMFS scrambled to assemble a capture team and prepare a facility to hold the whale while the veterinarians assessed and treated her. At this stage it was still not certain that Springer would return to Canada. If her health was precarious or if she was discovered to be harbouring some disease that might infect other whales in her home territory, the relocation could still be cancelled.

The leader of the capture team was Jeff Foster. Foster was the son of the head veterinarian at Seattle's Woodland Park Zoo. In 1970, when he was just fifteen years old, he had gone to work for Ted Griffin at the Seattle Marine Aquarium and was involved in some of the notorious killer whale captures in Puget Sound. Later Foster took part in whale collections in Iceland and sea otter captures in Alaska. Most recently he had been a key member of the team that transported Keiko to Iceland, where he helped to prepare the famous captive for release. Keiko had as yet refused his chance at freedom but Foster saw an important difference between the two whales. "Keiko was probably the least likely candidate for release because of his history in a captive environment," he explained. "He's been in a captive situation for most of his life and was taken away from his family at a very young age."[30] Springer, on the other hand, had never been in captivity, had not been absent from her family for very long and had not had an opportunity to develop much of a relationship with the human world.

Early in June, Foster and other members of his team, who had acquired a lot of experience during the Keiko project working with wild whales in all kinds of weather conditions, began going out in a boat to visit Springer to prepare her for the capture. They wanted to get her used to having people around, so they tethered her favourite knobby stick to the boat with a rope to entice her close. In the absence of other whales, Springer loved to rub on objects, but the team did not want her actually to touch the hull for fear this would lead her to become dangerously attached to boats. Gradually they began rubbing Springer with their hands. All of this was intended to get the whale used to their presence so they could obtain a blood sample, not an easy thing to do with a free-swimming animal. Eventually they were able to get a small amount of blood using a butterfly needle and a length of tubing. Butterfly needles have short plastic wings that make for easier handling, and the flexible line allowed the whale to move slightly without dislodging the needle. Meanwhile, a holding pen was prepared at an NMFS research station at Manchester, on the western shore of the sound opposite Seattle.

Finally, everything was in place. On Wednesday, June 12, the capture team carried out a dry run. Opinions differed about the best method for capturing the whale. One option was to use a floating pen into which Springer would be lured. This method was tested successfully on the Wednesday, when Springer showed no hesitation about swimming into the enclosure. However, the experts still worried that tides and currents might disrupt the netting and so, when Thursday dawned bright and calm, they decided to go with their second, simpler option, which involved placing a soft rope around the animal's tail. (A third option,

enclosure in a purse seine, was never tried.) For all its simplicity, this was a delicate procedure that required members of the
team to spend several hours accustoming Springer to their presence and to the touch of the rope. This was a wild whale, after
all, which was allowing people to interfere with it while it swam
free. In a sense Springer was allowing herself to be caught, a far
cry from the early days of capture when animals were yanked out
of the water with head snares, tail grabs and hoop nets. During
the "bad old days," it was not uncommon for whales to die as a
result of these techniques.

On the day of the capture, several swimmers in wetsuits went
into the water with Springer to calm her. After about an hour the
rope was deployed. All this time the team was working under the
pressure imposed by intense media coverage. At least four news
helicopters were hovering overhead. The tiniest slip-up would
be witnessed by about five million people who were watching
the event live. "Boy, it was nerve-wracking," reported Dave Huff,
who was in a boat nearby, "because I can't count the number of
times he leaned over the side of the boat to put the noose on and
couldn't. There was incredible patience and then all of a sudden
the noose was on." Springer made no objection as the swimmers
manipulated her into a sling that had been borrowed from the
Point Defiance Zoo. A crane barge, donated by Cypress Island Inc.,
a local fish farming company, was in position to hoist the sling
out of the water. Once the precious cargo was on board, resting on
a foam pad and being sprayed with ice water, the barge motored
across to Manchester, where Springer was lifted into the pen. The
whole operation went off without a hitch. "Everything went as if
the animal knew what to do," reported the *Seattle Times*.

■

FLOYD FULMER, THE TLINGIT ENGINEER who worked the night
shift on the *Evergreen State*, the Vashon Island ferry, had an idea.
He had been watching Springer for several months, listening to

her calls and feeling his spiritual connection to the whale deepen. Knowing that the capture was scheduled for mid-June, he telephoned his brother Fred with a request. As a young man Fred had returned to live in the Tlingit ancestral territory in Alaska, where he learned to speak the language and studied carving, following in the footsteps of his great-grandfather, who had been a carver at the family's village in Glacier Bay at the north end of the Alaskan panhandle. Fred had come back down to Seattle in 1987 to be close to his mother, who was ailing, but he continued his involvement in Tlingit arts, including the Kuteeya Tlingit dance troupe, a group of Native Americans of all ages who performed at Native ceremonies and public gatherings.

Floyd's idea was that the dance troupe should perform a traditional killer whale dance on the ferry as a farewell gesture for Springer, the killer whale being one of the clan crests that the Tlingit displayed on their carvings and ceremonial objects. The Tlingit tell a traditional story about Natsilane, an accomplished carver and sea lion hunter. One day during a hunt Natsilane was abandoned alone on an island by his brothers-in-law, who were jealous of him. Natsilane was rescued by the sea lions and returned to his village, where he carved a large killer whale out of yellow cedar. The carving came to life and drowned the jealous brothers-in-law. After that the whale became a benefactor of the village and so the people took it as their crest.

Fred Fulmer jumped at his brother's offer and, after initially being cool to the idea, the ferry company agreed. On the afternoon of June 12, while the test capture was underway offshore, seventeen members of the Kuteeya Tlingit group boarded the ninety-five-metre ferry as it lay at the Vashon terminal between runs. They were dressed in their dance regalia: red and black cloaks adorned with abalone shell buttons, headpieces of cedar and wood decorated with ermine and rabbit fur, and deer-hoof ankle bracelets that jangled as they spun through the steps of the dances. One man wore a Chilkat blanket, one of the stunning

■ Members of the Kuteeya Tlingit dance troupe perform a farewell ceremony for Springer on the ferry *Evergreen State*, June 12, 2002. The women are wearing dorsal fin headdresses indicating that they are members of the killer whale clan. *Kellie Anderson*

robes woven from mountain goat wool and cedar bark for which the Tlingit are famous, and brandished a carved paddle. Four of the women, members of the killer whale clan, wore painted wooden fins jutting up from the tops of their heads. As the drums beat out a hypnotic rhythm, the group danced and performed a song traditionally sung by the Tlingit when paddling among the whales.

The Tlingit, many of whom had migrated south to Seattle from their northern territory, identified with Springer as a creature who was displaced in the south and longed to be back with her family pod. This feeling was expressed in a poem that was read at the ceremony:

Our heart goes out to you, little Springer. We too have lost family and friends, and sought out the company of strangers to ease the pains of solitude. As you travel through the waterways that we too call home, marveling at the beauty around you, curious about things too large to understand, we wish you well. May gentle waves trace your path, may they heal the wounds that we could not. We hope that Nature will provide you with the answers you seek as you continue on your journey. And should you think back to your time here on Vashon, we hope you will remember a gentle, caring people, working for a world that honors its past, cherishes the present, seeks to create a future that leaves no wake.

THANKS FOR THE MEMORIES.

It wasn't just the Fulmer brothers and their Tlingit friends who were saddened by Springer's impending departure. Many ferry employees had grown used to seeing the young whale. "It almost made me cry," said Kellie Anderson, one of the traffic managers on the Vashon dock, who witnessed the farewell ceremony. "It's going to be so sad to see her go." Kim Shride, one of the first people to spot Springer back before Christmas, felt bereft. She had no faith in the capture experiment and was convinced that Springer was going to her death. Ted Griffin, the former whale capturer, wrote a front-page article in the *Seattle Post-Intelligencer* predicting the operation would not go well. The fact that many people shared this pessimistic outlook, wrongly as it turned out, cast a melancholy pall over the day's events.

■

AS THE LANDING BARGE CARRYING SPRINGER to her temporary home plowed across Puget Sound, the experts had an opportunity to measure the two-year-old whale accurately for the first time. She turned out to weigh 563 kilograms and measured 3.3

■ Springer being lifted into the netpen at Manchester WA on June 13, 2002. *Robert Wood*

metres (eleven feet) in length. Killer whales cannot survive on salt water alone and must obtain some water from their food. Springer was quite dehydrated, an indication that she had not been getting enough fish. She received a large quantity of water on the barge and this seemed to stimulate her appetite, because not long after she was released into the pen she began feeding on the salmon that were waiting for her. Over the next few weeks Springer would devour around twenty-five kilograms of fresh Atlantic salmon daily, donated free of charge by the Cypress Island farm and laced with whatever medication the veterinarians wanted her to have. Caretakers fed the live fish into the pen through a long pipe. Feedings took place at random times and in random quantities, and a screen was set up so that Springer could not see her handlers putting fish into the pipe. The idea was that she should not be able to associate the food she was receiving with humans. She was expected to catch her own dinner, though she learned pretty quickly to hang around the end of the pipe. It was a crucial part of the process that she not lose any of the skills that would allow her to survive in the wild and that she not fixate on people.

The netpen was a twelve-metre-square enclosure, monitored twenty-four hours a day by five cameras, one suspended above the pen and four others viewing underwater. Human contact was kept to a minimum, though out of sight of Springer at least two minders were always on duty. As well, the veterinarian who was in charge

■ A second netpen was used to hold live Atlantic salmon for Springer.
Sandra Stone

of her health while she was at Manchester, Peter Schroeder, was staying in his camper van on shore, and security guards patrolled the perimeter of the facility in response to fears that animal activists might try to liberate the whale. Maintaining their distance was not always easy for Springer's minders, as Christine Sakhrani, a trainer from the Vancouver Aquarium, explained. "I think for many of us who have worked with whales before, the natural human instinct is that this little animal needs help and care, it's lonely with no companionship, and it's very hard to walk by without looking and giving some kind of recognition."

As she had shown before capture, Springer was fixated on rubbing against objects, dangerously so in the case of boats. To satisfy this craving, her minders provided her with small logs, pieces of kelp, and bits and pieces of other natural objects with which to interact. One of these toys was the knobby stick that had been used by the capture team to lure Springer close to the boat. Another odd piece was a wood-beaded car seat cover, the kind favoured by taxi drivers, which someone bought in a thrift shop. The seat cover was tied to a stump and Springer loved to rub on it. Perhaps it reminded her of the stones on one of the rubbing beaches in her home territory. Sakhrani described two other stimulants deployed in the pen. "We had the hose and a sprinkler so you could set the different sprays. Sometimes it would be a dribble and sometimes it would be a big spray like a fan. Stephen Classen [one of the other minders] came up with the idea of a bag of rocks. Basically it was a pillow case with a bunch of rocks in it and we tied it to the rope so that when she rubbed on it, it would feel good like a rubbing beach and it would make noise. But it hung in there and she completely ignored it. Poor Stephen, we made so much fun of his bag of rocks." The handlers were aware from their experience in aquariums how important an enriched environment was to the well-being of cetaceans in captivity. At the same time, they did not want to make the pen such a comfortable place that Springer would be reluctant to leave when the time came. For the entire time she was in captivity, her minders walked a fine line between keeping her healthy, physically and mentally, and making sure she did not become a pet whale.

Sakhrani, who was the senior trainer of the Aquarium's beluga whales, described the routine at the pen.

My shift would start at midnight and through the night we would do observations. We were sitting behind a blind, we had a cover over us and around us, but we could see Springer. We were back far enough so that she probably didn't have a very good view of us. So, every fifteen minutes we would scan the pen for Springer and we would record what she was doing, whether she was resting, foraging, vocalizing, whatever. We also counted her respirations over a five-minute period of time. This way we had a general idea of her health. If she was stressed, her respirations would go up, and if she was resting and relaxed, her respirations would go down.

One of the jobs was to send live salmon down the feeding tube into the pen. Sakhrani recalled a moonlit night when there was a lot of bioluminescence in the water. Bioluminescence is created by chemical reactions taking place in tiny marine plankton, known as dinoflagellates, which are stimulated to produce light by the movement of an object through the water.

I would see Springer start to go after the salmon and I could see a little trail of light coming off the back of the salmon. I could see the salmon moving and see a little bit of light coming from the tail. All of a sudden I saw a big flash of green from the bioluminescence as Springer kicked her tail up as she was going after the salmon. I could actually see it, even though it was dark, after midnight, she would chase the salmon. Often she would use the net to help her, she would pin the salmon against the net, shake it and then shred it. Before she would eat it, she would drape it over her rostrum and swim around carrying it on her head, and then she would eat it. For

■ Jeff Foster inserts a live salmon into the feeding tube at Springer's pen in Manchester. *Christine Sakhrani*

a while, the water was calm again and everything was quiet, then all of a sudden I would see this green flash of bioluminescence and then her going after it again. There were five or six salmon in her pen, all going in different directions. She would chase them and make them tired, and then shepherd them into a corner. From there she would pick one out, chase it around and eat it.

There was twenty-four-hour security around the perimeter of the facility. Anyone wishing to access the pen had to present their identification. The minders were in contact with the guards via two-way radio. One night while Sakhrani was on duty she heard a noise. "I looked over to the security boat that was tied up to the dock and all of a sudden it started rocking back and forth. I thought someone was on the boat so I called the security guys. They came running down. The boat was rocking from side to side and it looked like someone was jumping up and down in the boat. We got closer and closer and I was a little bit frightened, it's two o'clock in the morning. We peered inside the boat and guess what's running around in there? A little river otter." The otter became a regular visitor to the pen. "There was another night when it had been swimming around in the bay and peeking in at Springer. I could see she was really interested because her rostrum was pressed right up against the net pushing on it. You could see the otter's little nose and whiskers sticking out of the water and they were looking at each other from each side of the pen. The river otter went all the way around the net and Springer followed."

Sakhrani was typical of many of the trainers and scientists involved with Springer in that she had come to the world of marine mammals at a young age. She remembers her first visit to the Vancouver Aquarium when she was about five years old and for years afterward asking her parents for a killer whale as a birthday present. At sixteen she got a weekend job at the Aquarium supervising the children's birthday parties and essentially never left. By 2002 she had been a trainer for five years. Stephen Raverty, the animal pathologist, appeared at the Aquarium as a shy thirteen-year-old offering to volunteer. Jeff Foster, the head of the capture team and the son of a vet, had been working with aquariums since he was fifteen years old. John Ford, Fisheries and Oceans Canada's chief whale scientist, began his career as a summer cleaner at the Aquarium in his university days. As a university undergraduate, Brad Hanson, one of the American biologists, had come all the way up to Vancouver from Seattle on weekends to volunteer at the Aquarium. The other members of the team all had similar stories. These were people who had spent years in the company of whales. To them, rescuing Springer was far more than a job.

The veterinarians performed a variety of tests on Springer. When they needed to examine her or acquire more blood, they slowly lifted the bottom of the net until eventually the water was about waist deep. Five or six people would slip into the pen and hold the whale or walk her into the sling so she could be cradled during whatever procedure was taking place. Springer never objected to these interventions; indeed, she may have looked forward to them given how boring life inside a watery cage could become. On other occasions, minders had to enter the pen to make repairs to the netting, readjust the underwater cameras or check Springer's stool for worms. They were all veterans and knew they had no reason to fear the whale. Sakhrani recalled being in the water in her scuba gear when Springer began to vocalize. "Not only did I hear the clicking from Springer but I also felt it in my chest. It felt amazing. It's like the feeling you get when you are in a car with the bass pumping and you can feel the beat in your chest. Hearing the clicking, I looked over my shoulder and Springer was right behind me, only a couple of feet away. As she swam by, she cocked her head sideways and took a good look at me."

Initially it was expected that Springer would remain at Manchester for about two weeks, but it took almost a month for the medical staff to be sure that she was not a risk to herself or to the other whales she would encounter in the wild. She was checked for brucellosis, a bacterium related to birth problems in animals, and her blood was tested for leptospirosis, morbillivirus and erysipelas. As requested by the NMFS, samples were sent for testing to laboratories in Europe and the United States as well as to the Animal Health Centre in Abbotsford. In fact, the testing turned into a bone of contention between the Canadian vets and NMFS personnel. One issue was the quantity of blood that the doctors were allowed to take. The NMFS had prearranged the number and kind of tests and tolerated no deviation from the list. As a result, samples could not be used for toxicology screening or banked for further study. The Americans began to feel that Canadian authorities, particularly the DFO, were being too cautious by prolonging the testing process and unnecessarily delaying Springer's departure. They pointed out that the longer the whale stayed in captivity, the more conditioned she became to being in captivity. With the Americans saying they had cleared Springer for release, it now looked to the outside world as if the Canadians were dragging their bureaucratic feet.

In their defence, Canadian scientists pointed out that they needed to screen for all possible diseases, those that Springer could have been exposed to in her short life and those that she might introduce into wild stocks north of the border. The Canadian veterinarians felt they were not receiving the kind of material they needed to carry out these tests. As a veterinarian pathologist at the BC Animal Health Centre in Abbotsford, Stephen Raverty works to detect animal diseases and prevent their spread. Ultimately it fell on his shoulders to decide if Springer could return. He was concerned that if she was carrying a virus there was a huge potential for introducing a contagious, virulent disease to the whale population north of the border, with catastrophic consequences. The Canadians were galled at being accused of delay when in their opinion the NMFS had been unnecessarily slow to authorize Springer's capture in the first place and rigidly bureaucratic in its refusal to authorize the taking of more than a minuscule amount of blood. The Aquarium's Lance Barrett-Lennard expressed some of this frustration:

> This extra holding had a lot to do with the fact that the National Marine Fisheries Services was very reluctant after the whale was captured to give David Huff and Steve Raverty in Canada access to the biological materials — most importantly, twenty-five cc of blood — which they could use to provide the DFO with assurances that the whale was not carrying any nasty diseases. This assurance was necessary for the DFO to clear the whale for transport. This is something any government would have to do ... Any sovereign nation would insist on the

right to assess an animal's health before importing it. The Americans were well-meaning but somehow forgot that the Canadian government was accountable at the end of the day and had the right and the responsibility to make the final call.

Some even suspected the Americans of being eager to be rid of the whale before something went wrong on their watch. "Canada was really adamant that they didn't want a sick animal coming north," said Clint Wright. "And the US wanted to get the animal out of there." In the end, thanks largely to Raverty and in typical Canadian fashion, a compromise was worked out. The Canadians received a bit more material for their own tests while at the same time accepting some of the American results.

Springer may have been the darling of the media and the public, but she was not doing much for Canadian-American relations.

■

WHILE SPRINGER WAITED IN HER PEN at Manchester, fattening up on salmon and taking her medicines, preparations for her homecoming were being made on the Canadian side of the border. The lead government agency responsible for the relocation was the federal Department of Fisheries and Oceans (DFO), assisted by the Vancouver Aquarium, whose personnel would look after the details of the operation. The first item on their agenda was to find a location in the Johnstone Strait area that would be suitable to hold Springer prior to her release back into the wild. The ideal spot was a small bay, close enough to population centres that the release team would have easy access but remote enough to be off the beaten track for recreational boaters and curious members of the public. It had to be the right size: compact but large enough to handle the netpens and barge that would be used during the release. Most importantly, it had to be close to the route that members of Springer's A4 pod would likely follow when they returned to the area that summer so she could hear the vocalizations of her family as they passed. Finding such a spot was not an easy job. The team responsible for handling Keiko's release had spent months scouring the coastlines of Ireland and Scotland before they settled on the Westman Islands of Iceland. Springer's team did not have months—it had just a few weeks.

Luckily, the job had already been done. For several years, OrcaLab's Paul Spong had been lobbying San Diego's Sea World to return one of their captive whales, Corky, to her home environment in Johnstone Strait. Corky is one of several whales that performs under the stage name "Shamu." As a three-year-old, she was one of the whales captured in Pender Harbour in 1969. She is the only survivor of all the northern resident whales taken during the "gold rush" era of the 1960s and 1970s. In 2002, though she had cataracts in one eye, Corky still performed regularly and was the oldest killer whale in captivity. While preparing for what he hoped would be her release, Spong had been scouting suitable places around his base at Hanson Island to locate a killer whale "halfway house." He had already identified Dong Chong Bay, a narrow inlet on the north side of the island about twenty minutes by foot from OrcaLab. Given that Corky wouldn't be needing it anytime soon, Spong thought it would suit Springer perfectly. "It is in direct acoustic contact with Queen Charlotte Strait and Blackfish Sound, the likely route for returning northern resident orcas," he pointed out. "Setting up a crew camp with adequate logistical supports would be no problem."

Dong Chong Bay was named for a long-time storekeeper in Alert Bay. During the 1940s, Dong and two partners were involved in logging on Hanson Island, where they used the bay as a booming ground. The mouth of the bay measures about fifty metres across. Through that opening, Springer would be able to hear the members of her family as they passed and go to join them. The surrounding shore is steep, aside from a flat area at the bottom of the bay where a camp could be installed. It is open to

Blackfish Sound yet protected, and has a smooth bottom with no obstructions that might snag the pen netting. Spong already had asked permission from the 'Namgis First Nation, whose territory included the bay. Graeme Ellis and John Ford from the DFO, along with Lance Barrett-Lennard, paid the site a visit and thought it was ideal. In mid-June, Clint Wright and Jeremy Fitz-Gibbon, the coordinator of marine mammal projects at the Aquarium, came up from Vancouver to have a look.

Jim Borrowman, the operator of a whale-watching business in Telegraph Cove, ferried the visitors over to Hanson Island. Borrowman is one of the key figures in the evolution of killer whale science and tourism on the BC coast. During the 1970s, when he was still working at the sawmill in the cove, he met Mike Bigg and became part of the team of people who were studying the killer whales and taking photographs of them. As a diver and underwater photographer, he assisted Erich Hoyt when Hoyt was doing research in Johnstone Strait for his classic book on killer whales, *The Whale Called Killer* (1981). After Borrowman, his wife and their partners Bill and Donna Mackay launched the first whale-watching operation on the coast in 1981, he also began recording the whales, working closely with John Ford and OrcaLab. He was intensely involved in the lobbying effort that led the provincial government to create the Robson Bight (Michael Bigg) Ecological Reserve and more recently has taken a lead role in establishing guidelines to regulate the interaction of whale watchers and whales. Over the years, Borrowman's observations had contributed significantly to the understanding of the killer whales of Johnstone Strait.

Once Spong had shown Dong Chong Bay to the visitors from the Vancouver Aquarium, they agreed the location was perfect. Spong had also approached Stolt Sea Farm, a major player in the coastal salmon-farming industry, to see if the company wanted to get involved. A subsidiary of a Norwegian multinational, Stolt operated more than a dozen farms in the channels and inlets between northeastern Vancouver Island and the mainland, as well as a processing plant at Englewood, south of Port McNeill, the closest Vancouver Island community of any size to Hanson Island. (Stolt has since merged, in 2005, with Marine Harvest, a Dutch company.) Spong anticipated that Springer would be released directly into Dong Chong Bay, which would have to be closed off with a net across its mouth, and when he contacted Stolt, the company offered to provide this net. Later, when it was decided to use two pens inside the bay instead, one for Springer and one to hold salmon for feeding, Stolt converted their net into a barrier that wrapped around both pens and offered additional protection from seals and other possible intruders. As planning progressed, the release team came back to Stolt and the company offered to provide the pens as well. These were galvanized steel cages, used by Stolt in its farming operations, about fifteen metres square with decked walkways around the perimeter. From this frame a net bag hung down in the water about ten metres. The company's work boat, the *Sea Roamer*, a fifteen-metre landing barge equipped with a crane, towed the cages to Dong Chong Bay, and divers anchored them and the net walls into position. In the end it was decided that the barrier net presented a hazard—if Springer broke through the inner net, better she swim free than be trapped between the two barriers—and it was removed. By June 26, the pens were ready to welcome Springer.

At this point, Stolt expected to be providing farmed Atlantic salmon to feed Springer, who some people thought might remain in the bay for as long as a year. Clare Backman, the Stolt manager in charge of the project, decided he had to contact the usual regulatory officials because it was going to look like he was installing an unauthorized fish farm in Dong Chong. Backman later joked about it: "At the end of the day, I said to others that this was the fastest fish farm that I ever got approved! I got it done by phone in an hour and a half, so maybe attaching a killer whale to every application helps." At this point the politics of salmon farming on the coast came into play. Given how unpopular his industry was with environmentalists, Backman himself suggested that Springer should be fed with wild salmon and Spong thought so as well. But the whale had been eating farmed salmon in Manchester, and when problems developed obtaining licences for local First Nations seiners who had agreed to provide fresh wild fish, Backman was asked if he could deliver some of his farmed supply. The result was an embarrassing last-minute mix-up, described by Backman.

> We decided we needed the harvest boat, as it is set up to receive fish with no escapes. It is the *Orca Warrior* which is a purpose-built salmon harvesting boat, a sixty-metre vessel, a live-haul packing vessel with a large vacuum hose which is placed into the pen of fish. The internal holds are sealed and then air is pumped out which pulls water and fish into the boat. There are no moving parts so the fish are OK. It's a very slick way of moving fish. It's owned by the Orca Shipping Company and we contract with them for all our moves of fish from the cages into the processing plant. There was only a Thursday spot before Springer was due to arrive where they could free up four hours to transport fish for us. We set up fish at one of our farm sites, Midsummer Island, about ten kilometres north of Hanson Island, and graded them into a separate pen for early harvest as they were larger, faster matured, and sized eight to ten pounds. I told Jeremy [Fitz-Gibbon] to let me know if they weren't wanted and we would cancel the boat. Orca charged us about three thousand dollars for this delivery. The day before this Paul Spong did phone me to voice some concerns over the use of Atlantic salmon. I began to worry a little bit but he said he might be able to get a permit for the 'Namgis to go fishing. They wouldn't know until the morning but please don't send the fish! I told him that if I didn't give the go-ahead by ten a.m. we would miss this window to have the fish delivered. The next morning the permit has arrived and so they're

out fishing with no guarantee they're going to catch anything. I called Jeremy to ask what we should do here.
He replied that we should go with the Atlantics, so they
went. About eleven a.m. I got a call from [Clint Wright]
to say they had been successful catching fish and they
were moving them down to the bay so don't deliver the
Atlantics. By the time I got in touch with the boat they
had already picked up the Atlantics and were steaming
to the bay! I caught them at the mouth of the bay where
they stopped and I told them to turn around.

Until almost the last minute the release team was still looking for a crane capable of lifting Springer from the back of the
transport vessel into the netpen. It turned out that the crane on
the *Sea Roamer* was not large enough. Two days before Springer
was scheduled to arrive, the team, with the help of Stolt, found
a larger apparatus at Discovery Crane in Campbell River. By
Friday the new equipment was in place on the *Sea Roamer* and
that morning the crew practised manipulating the crane with
a two-tonne weight attached. Everything seemed to be ready,
although on the morning of Springer's arrival there was one
more embarrassing glitch involving Stolt. The company had
displayed a corporate banner across the front of one of the
pens, but when Spong saw it he wanted it taken down. Spong
didn't like the idea of a fish-farming company getting free
publicity from all the television coverage of the event and he
thought that the First Nations would object when they found
out. As he pointed out, the 'Namgis opposed salmon farming,
and not only was the bay located in their territory but a delegation from Alert Bay was going to be arriving at any moment
to welcome Springer. As the Vancouver Aquarium's man on
the spot, Lance Barrett-Lennard was in an awkward position.
The Aquarium felt indebted to Stolt for all its help but didn't
want the fish farm issue to boil up and spoil the homecoming.
Luckily, Backman was perfectly willing to take down the sign,
averting a potential confrontation. "Each time things changed

we just took a deep breath and carried on," Backman recalled ruefully.

The final piece of the puzzle in Dong Chong Bay was the arrival of an ice barge donated by Canfisco, the Canadian Fishing Company. The red and white barge was intended to accommodate members of the release team and act as a staging platform next to the pens in the bay. Jeremy Fitz-Gibbon was the only person from the Aquarium to have seen the barge—in fact, he rode north on it—but he did not appreciate how small Dong Chong Bay was and how noisy the barge was. It turned out to be a monster, as large as a good-sized apartment building and over forty metres long with several huge, unmuffled diesel engines turning water into ice twenty-four hours a day. In the fishery it was used to make ice for the boats, which needed it to keep their catch

■ The giant ice barge, donated by Canfisco, that was used to accommodate some of the crew on Hanson Island. *Sandra Stone*

fresh. The accommodations consisted of a trailer perched on top of the three-storey superstructure with four small bedrooms and enough bunk beds to sleep eight people. The barge was towed up from Vancouver by a tug, and it wasn't until it arrived that everyone realized how completely it dwarfed the bay. The noise would have drowned out any conversation around the pens and made it impossible for Springer to hear any passing whales. When Spong saw the barge approaching he gave Barrett-Lennard, who was on his way to the site by car, a panicked call on his cellphone. Barrett-Lennard arranged with Fitz-Gibbon to have the barge towed instead to Double Bay, about three kilometres to the west, where it was still used to house and feed most of the crew for the duration.

All this meant that the day before Springer was due to arrive, there was no staging vessel in Dong Chong Bay. Fitz-Gibbon, who was responsible for these logistical matters, went into Telegraph Cove to see if he could borrow a suitable boat for the purpose. Telegraph Cove nestles in a tiny harbour on the coast of Vancouver Island at the western end of Johnstone Strait, about twenty minutes by boat from Dong Chong. As the name suggests, it was once the northern terminus of the Vancouver Island telegraph line. During the 1920s, local logger A.W. Wastell purchased the site and opened a fish saltery and sawmill. The mill remained in operation until 1985, by which time the village had become the jumping-off point for whale watching and other ecotourism excursions.

Jim Borrowman had opened his Johnstone Strait Whale Interpretive Centre in an old warehouse at the end of the village boardwalk. Also known as the "Bones Project," the centre displays the skeletons of several whales, including an eighteen-metre fin whale that was killed in a collision with a cruise ship. Borrowman's then-fiancée Mary had had the carcass towed to the cove from Boundary Bay as a wedding present for her new husband. The centre houses the remains of a variety of other marine mammals, as well as some land animals. In the "summer of Springer," the west side of Telegraph Cove remained a picturesque spot with several old homes and buildings dating back to the sawmill days linked by the wooden boardwalk. The east side was less appealing. Developers had blasted and bulldozed a large area in preparation for a residential complex, and much of the shoreline was taken up by a drab new building that resembled a dentist's office on pilings.

Fitz-Gibbon met Barrett-Lennard, who had just arrived from Vancouver. Walking along the boardwalk the next day discussing their need for a boat, they ran into Nic Dedeluk, a coordinator with Straitwatch, a marine mammal monitoring and education program. Dedeluk pointed out a steel-hulled yacht tied up at the marina and told Fitz-Gibbon that she had just been chatting with its owner. "Why not go and talk to him?" she suggested. They went over to the boat, which was called *Shadow*, and fell into conversation with the owner, Joseph Bettis, a retired professor of religion from San Juan Island, and his friend, Sandra Stone, from Cincinnati. *Shadow* was a beautiful vessel, 16.5 metres long with a canoe stern and watertight bulkheads, fully equipped for ocean cruising. Throwing caution to the wind, Barrett-Lennard asked Bettis if he would be willing to volunteer the *Shadow*. They explained that he was likely to have lots of strange people coming and going at all hours, that the operation could easily last two weeks or more, and that the whale crew would supply its own food, but they had no money to offer. "We thought you'd never ask!" replied Bettis, and within a few hours the *Shadow* was anchored in Dong Chong Bay, where it served as an observation platform for the entire release period.

■

DOWN IN PUGET SOUND, SPRINGER'S HEALTH WAS IMPROVING. Her "bad breath" had disappeared, her skin was clearing up and she was gaining weight. As test after test came back negative for any disease, the DFO officials finally gave her the thumbs up. Springer was ready to come home and Friday, July 12 was set as moving day.

Early on in the planning Clint Wright and his colleagues had considered several options for moving Springer north. One plan was to fly her from Seattle to Port Hardy at the north end of Vancouver Island, but this proved to be the most expensive option by far. Then a twenty-seven-metre hovercraft was offered by the Canadian Coast Guard. Wright described the vessel. "The bow end of the hovercraft was an open deck. It was a fabulous looking thing with a maximum speed of forty-five knots. It had tie-down cleats in the area we were offered, the crane reached forty-one feet. It would be a fairly smooth ride as long as weather conditions were good. We could take on board a fairly large crew of people." The only problem was the noise. The vessel made such a roar that Wright worried it might spook or even injure the whale. But the experts made some tests and reported that the noise was not an insuperable problem as long as the box that held Springer was insulated from the deck's vibrations. A third option was to ship Springer on the back of a flatbed truck to Beaver Cove, next door to Telegraph Cove, where Stolt offered to load the truck on its barge and move it to Dong Chong. The hovercraft emerged as the preferred option, but it turned out that there was no reliable reserve vessel to fill in during its absence so the coast guard was reluctant to let it be used for an extended period.

At this point the "Two Bobs" made another of their timely interventions. Even though they had been discouraged by Brent Norberg and the NMFS, and had even been chased away from the Manchester pen when they came to offer help, Bob McLaughlin and Bob Wood were still playing a key role in the project behind the scenes. The Canadians involved bore no animosity to "the Bobs" and were quite willing to work with them. Bob McLaughlin talked to Matt Nichols of Nichols Brothers Boats, whom he had known for several years. Based on Whidbey Island, Nichols Brothers had been building steel and aluminum boats, including high-speed catamarans, since 1964 and they offered a Catalina Jet to transport Springer by water. On July 8 Wright visited Seattle, where the Bobs took him out to see the catamaran. Apart from being covered in seagull droppings because it hadn't been used in a while, it looked ideal. Constructed as a ferry to operate between Los Angeles and Catalina Island, it was a blue and white vessel, forty-four metres long and twelve metres wide, with big twin jet drives, large enough to handle 499 passengers. At its top speed of thirty-five knots, the trip from Manchester to Dong Chong would take less than twelve hours. Matt Nichols was keen on the whole idea. He explained that they could make modifications to remove seats from the middle deck to open up room for the special passenger. He offered to provide fuel, a crew and food for the trip, all at his own expense. The vessel was for sale and Nichols believed the publicity would improve his chances of closing a deal. The catamaran featured a wake-piercing hull design, meaning that it cut through the water rather than riding up and down on the surface, and a stabilization system that countered the effect of waves even further. The result was an exceptionally smooth, quiet ride. "It was an absolutely fabulous boat," remarked veterinarian Dave Huff. "I think all of us would agree that it was a fabulous choice and was the best, better than any of the other options we could have had. It had millions of dollars of stabilizing equipment on it as I guess it was built for the Catalina tourist trade and you can't have tourists puking all over themselves. It could go through any kind of a wake and the boat was rock-solid." Nichols's offer seemed to have no negatives. The Catalina Jet became Springer's transport vessel.

On Thursday, the day before the move was scheduled to take place, Wright and Huff drove down to Manchester together. Wright spent the trip fielding calls on his cellphone from Johnstone Strait, where the release team was trying to decide where to put the ice barge and whether to use farmed or fresh salmon. When Wright and Huff reached Fauntleroy they learned that there was no food on the catamaran so they had to load up the car with groceries from a local supermarket before boarding the ferry to Manchester. They finally arrived in the evening. Early the next morning when Wright arrived at the netpen, he found the parking lot crowded with satellite trucks and media. After running a gauntlet of microphones, he entered the pen area and checked that everything was all right with Springer, which it was. All they had to do was wait for the catamaran to arrive.

On the Catalina Jet, which was tied up on Whidbey Island, an unexpectedly large number of people had crowded on board, many of them friends and employees of the Nichols brothers. Angela Neilson, the Aquarium's media representative, described the scene. "When we went to leave there were 150 or 200 people on the boat, like it was a party cruise. My first impression walking on the boat was I couldn't believe the sheer number of people, it looked like one of those booze cruises. People were coming on with those coolers of beer and everything." Along with these guests, there were members of the transport team, Aquarium staff, officials from the DFO and the NMFS, and members of the media pool. When she saw all the people, Marilyn Joyce, the senior DFO official, was horrified. "Well, we just won't go!" she declared, hands on hips and temper flaring. Matt Nichols was adamant that all the people he invited on board be allowed to stay, including six of his grandchildren, for whom he brought along the movie *Free Willy*, the story that made Keiko into a household name. There wasn't much anyone could do given that Nichols was providing the boat for nothing.

Once the catamaran got under way it became obvious there was a problem. The vessel couldn't seem to get up to speed. At first no one knew what the trouble was. The whole exercise hung in the balance. If the catamaran couldn't go, the transfer was a wash. According to mariners' lore, voyages should never begin on a Friday, the unluckiest day of the week. Was this old superstition actually coming true? "There really wasn't anything we could do at that point and we just had to wait," recalled

Wright. In the end, the problem turned out to be a simple one. The vessel had been laid up for six months, and during that time it had accumulated a heavy growth of barnacles on the hull. It had been cleaned but there were still barnacles in the engine nozzles that prevented the boat from accelerating properly. It took until noon to clean off the growth. There would still be enough time to reach Dong Chong Bay in daylight, but not enough to ensure that Springer could be offloaded. It was an embarrassing snafu in the glare of so much media attention, but the decision was taken to wait until the next day. The boat was cleaned, taken on a test run, then moved down to Manchester, where the transport box was put on board. This was a blue fibreglass container donated by Six Flags, the world's largest chain of amusement parks, which had just used it to transport a whale from Europe to one of its facilities in Ohio. The box, 5.5 metres long and 1.67 metres deep, would serve as Springer's "bed" during the trip. It was lined with vinyl and filled with water to keep her cool.

The next day, Saturday, July 13, not nearly so many people were on board the Catalina Jet. Matt Nichols had accepted the Aquarium staff's argument that with so much media attention, the boat should not look like it was going on a party cruise, and he had cut the passenger list by about two-thirds. The team started loading at dawn. Jeff Foster and his people were in charge of getting Springer on board, and the transfer from the pen, again using the sling and a huge crane, went off without a hitch. One of the onlookers was Sue Murray, an Aquarium employee who had driven down from Vancouver with John Nightingale and several other people and was waiting to drive the van back again. She described what she saw. "Then just as they started getting things in motion to start loading Springer, I noticed circling over her was a bald eagle! I'd already been told by a Native that bald eagles signal spirit strength. When you are in a troubled time, they will come. I looked at that and said, 'Well, little one, you have your strength today!' It was so majestic, a huge, fully mature eagle and the sky was red because the sun was just coming up." As the crane lifted the sling, Springer swung around so that her head faced the dock and she wiggled her pectoral fins, almost as if she were waving goodbye.

At 7:30 a.m., right on schedule, with cameras flashing and media helicopters whirring overhead, the boat pulled away from the dock. Murray was caught up in the mood. "I had a moment to myself, all the press people left, the dock was empty, there was no one there. And it was over. I just sat there for a moment and caught my breath and watched the boat head out of Manchester into the inlet and reflected on my privilege."

After all the arguments, all the delays and all the anxiety, Springer was on her way home.

4 ▪ THE HOMECOMING

THE PLACE TO WHICH SPRINGER WAS RETURNING, the place her family knew as home, was also home to the Kwakwa̲-ka̲'wakw people. Since before recorded history began, the Kwakwa̲ka̲'wakw (meaning "those who speak the Kwak'wala language") have inhabited the northeastern shores of Vancouver Island, the deep coastal fjords of the mainland opposite and the islands in between. The early Europeans mistakenly called them the Kwakiutl, a variation of Kwagiulth. It later became clear that the Kwakiutl were simply one of several contiguous groups or tribes that comprise the Kwakwa̲ka̲'wakw people. Prior to contact there may have been two dozen or more of these groups; today there are fourteen. Their neighbours to the north were the Oweekeno of Rivers Inlet, while to the southeast lived the Coast Salish tribes — the Comox, the Klahoose on Cortes Island, the Pentlatch, who were destroyed by smallpox, and the Homalco of Bute Inlet. To the west, on the west coast of Vancouver Island, lived the Nuu-chah-nulth. All these neighbouring peoples respected and feared the Kwakwa̲ka̲'wakw, for they were known as great fighters. This was especially true of the Lekwiltok, the most southerly group, who raided the Salish First Nations in the Strait of Georgia and up the Fraser River with fierce regularity for many years. Contact with Europeans resulted in a dramatic decline in the number of Kwakwa̲ka̲'wakw, as it did for most First Nations in the province. From a contact population estimated at nineteen thousand, their number fell to as few as one thousand people during the 1920s. But then a recovery began and today the Kwakw<u>aka</u>'wakw number about six thousand.

They followed a seasonal round similar to the other indigenous peoples of the Northwest Coast. In the winter they gathered in plank houses at their main village sites to spend the rainy months in feasting, potlatching and other social activities. By the end of March the eulachon were returning to the rivers to spawn and the people dispersed to their fishing sites. Eulachon, a member of the smelt family, are long, thin fish, so oily that when dried they burn like candles. They spawn in huge numbers in the lower reaches of several mainland coastal rivers, including the Kingcome and the Klinaklini in Kwakw<u>aka</u>'wakw territory. The people dried the fish or rendered it down into oil or grease, which they used as a condiment, medicine, body oil and a valuable trade item. Boxes of the pungent oil were carried inland over ancient trading routes known as "grease" trails to trade with the interior tribes. Once the eulachon fishery ended, the people dispersed to other resource sites where they fished for salmon, gathered berries and shellfish, hunted game and otherwise made their living. With the onset of winter, the main village was re-occupied.

As the Kwakw<u>aka</u>'wakw went about their daily lives they had ample opportunity to interact with killer whales, members of what we now call the northern resident community, which visited their territory. To the Northwest Coast people generally, killer whales were special animals. The Haida of the Queen Charlotte Islands revered them as the most powerful inhabitants of the undersea world, where they lived in houses and ruled over the other creatures. John Swanton, an American linguist who spent time gathering information from the Haida in 1900–01, wrote that killer whales "were the only creatures they had a supernatural dread of hunting, and in their case the dread may not have been entirely supernatural." The Haida described the whales in their underwater houses. "Just as the towns of human beings were scattered along the shores above water," Swanton reported, "so the killer whale towns were scattered along the shores beneath it. These were located at, or rather under, every prominent cape, hill or reef: and even hills some distance back from the coast had subterranean avenues of approach from the ocean." According to Swanton, the Haida thought that in their underwater realm, killer whales took on human shape but when they appeared above water they cloaked themselves in animal form.[31] When people drowned, they went to live with the killer whales in their undersea houses.

Among the Kwakw<u>a</u>ka'wakw, the killer whale (*ma<u>x</u>'inu<u>x</u>w*) was one of the First Ancestors, the mythical beings to which each family group, or *numaym*, traced its origins. Stories describe how the First Ancestor emerged from the sea, assumed human shape and created the members of the group. These beings had special powers and their images were replicated on totem poles, masks, house fronts and other ceremonial items. According to the anthropologist Franz Boas, who collected stories among the Kwakw<u>a</u>ka'wakw, the killer whale was the supreme ruler of the world beneath the ocean. The dolphins were his warriors and the sea lions his slaves.[32]

The Kwakw<u>a</u>ka'wakw divided the cosmos into four worlds: the sky, the undersea, the mortal and the world of the spirits. The worlds were not separate and the spirit powers that inhabited them, such as the killer whale, could move freely between them, transforming into other beings as they did so. Whales, for instance, could take on the shape of a human or a wolf. Chief Bill Cranmer of Alert Bay explained how his people have many stories about the appearance of killer whales among them.

> The killer whale would come up to talk to a person and they would take the human form, and some of them decided to stay as humans and some decided to remain killer whales. There are many, many different stories. There's one story of a man walking down the beach at night and coming across a party of killer whales in human form having a gathering on the beach, and when

they found out they'd been discovered, they persuaded the Chief not to tell anyone else, in exchange he would have the right to use their killer whale mask and they gave him the song that went along with it. So there are many stories like that in our ceremonies.

Their ability to live in two worlds—breathing air yet living under the water—was one of the reasons why killer whales were so respected by the First Nations. They were also thought to have healing powers. A sick person who saw a whale would take a mouthful of sea water and blow it toward the whale, asking it to take away the sickness. The return of the killer whales to the area around Johnstone Strait each summer signified the return of the salmon and the renewal of the life cycle. In mythic terms, they were returning to the people who they had created. Given that the First Nations were such close observers of the natural world, it is not surprising that Kwakwaka'wakw elders have said that they knew about the rubbing beaches at Robson Bight long before they were "discovered" by white scientists in the 1970s, and that the people have always known that individual whales could be identified by distinctive dorsal fins and body markings.

Among the Nuu-chah-nulth and the Kwakwaka'wakw, killer whales are thought sometimes to embody the souls of deceased chiefs and it is considered unwise to kill or otherwise mistreat them for fear that they will seek revenge. Long time whale watcher Bill Mackay tells the story of the late Chief Peter Smith, who told him about two men from his village who went out in a boat many years ago and tried to put a knife in the back of a killer whale. Chief Smith warned them not to, but they did it anyway and one was able to stick his knife into a whale. A year later to the day, a killer whale appeared next to the dock on which the men were sitting plucking ducks and splashed them, lifting the dock and dumping the men into the water. Chief Smith knew that there would be serious trouble for the two men and sure enough, they died not long after. Mackay asked the chief if he could occa-

■ Kwakwaka'wakw killer whale mask. *Sandra Stone*

sionally tell this story to the passengers on his whale-watching cruises. The chief replied, "You must! If a killer whale sprays you when it blows, if you have ever brought harm to any of the chief's ancestors, you will die." From then on, if ever there was spray from a killer whale coming toward his boat, Mackay would close the windows quickly. Ethnologist Peter Macnair relates a similar story told to him by Tommy Hunt, a Kwakwaka'wakw seine fisherman from Fort Rupert. When he was out fishing, Hunt usually kept a rifle in the wheelhouse of his boat. When he saw killer whales approaching, he would throw four bullets overboard to show that he meant the whales no harm. Others might cast tobacco into the water to honour the whales.

The 'Namgis First Nation, one of the Kwakwaka'wakw groups, are particularly closely associated with killer whales because their territory at the head of Johnstone Strait encompasses a good portion of the whales' summer range. When

Captain George Vancouver passed through Johnstone Strait in July 1792 during his monumental survey of the Northwest Coast, he stopped at the mouth of the Nimpkish River, at a village he referred to by the name of its chief, Cheslakees. According to *Kwakwaka'wakw Settlements*, a definitive study of the ethno-geography of the Kwakwaka'wakw territory, the people never named a village after an individual.[33] The 'Namgis knew this spot as *Xwalk* or Whulk. When Vancouver visited, it consisted of thirty-four houses and had a population of several hundred.[34] The 'Namgis were already trading furs and European goods with the Nuu-chah-nulth from Nootka Sound via a trail that crossed Vancouver Island to Tahsis Inlet. The Kwakwaka'wakw were not as deeply involved in the sea otter trade as other coastal First Nations, but with the decline of that trade during the 1820s and the subsequent rise of the land-based fur trade, they were drawn deeper into the Euro-American economy. When the Hudson's Bay Company placed its steam vessel *Beaver* into service visiting the various villages along the coast to collect furs, Whulk was one of its ports of call. In 1849 the HBC established Fort Rupert, near present-day Port Hardy, the first permanent white settlement in Kwakwaka'wakw territory. Logging and commercial fishing followed the fur trade, transforming the Kwakwaka'wakw economy.

In 1870, a coastal entrepreneur, Wes Huson, and his partner, Stephen Spencer, opened a store and later a small saltery for curing salmon on Cormorant Island in 'Namgis territory. Wishing to attract a permanent workforce to the island, they persuaded the Anglican missionary James Hall to move his mission from Fort Rupert to the island in 1881, and the small community of Alert Bay was born. Gradually the 'Namgis moved from Whulk across the strait to Alert Bay. Hall built a school, a church and a sawmill and, with the relocation of the Indian Agency from Fort Rupert in 1889, the community became the business and administrative centre of the north island. Today, Alert Bay continues to be the main community of the 'Namgis people.

When the 'Namgis learned that Springer was returning, they decided to pay an unannounced visit to Dong Chong Bay. Joseph Bettis was standing on the deck of his boat *Shadow*, waiting for the whale's arrival on the afternoon of July 13, when a cedar canoe carrying three tribal elders materialized in the water next to him. Chief Bill Cranmer had come from Alert Bay, along with Harry Mountain of the Mamalilikala and Bill Peters of the Da'naxda'xw, both Knight Inlet tribes. As well there were representatives from the Tlawitsis and the Musgamkw, the latter associated with Gilford Island. The coast guard had placed buoys to create a "zone of exclusion" to keep the number of boats in the bay to a minimum and were patrolling back and forth in their twenty-metre cutter, the *Sooke Post*, but they were not about to

■ Native canoes at Dong Chong Bay on the day of Springer's arrival, July 13, 2002. The boat beyond the canoes is the *Shelmar*, belonging to Bob Wood, one of the "Two Bobs" who played a key role in monitoring Springer in Puget Sound. *Sandra Stone*

stop a group of chiefs paddling through their own territory. No one had expected them and no one was quite sure what their intentions were. "We didn't know whether they were protesting or supporting," said Marilyn Joyce. A second traditional canoe appeared, filled with paddlers who were drumming and singing. A number of seine boats began dropping off spectators, some of them wearing button blankets and cedar headgear, who gathered on the surrounding cliffs. "Every direction that you looked the woods were full of people with their button blankets and all regalia, cheering and clapping," Lance Barrett-Lennard recalled. "It was wonderful."

The bay had been transformed into a huge amphitheatre filled with First Nations people of all ages. At his boat, Joseph Bettis had no idea what to do. He'd been told to keep people away but he wasn't about to deny hospitality to people in whose territory he was a guest. Bettis had a snow-white beard,

■ Joseph Bettis (l.) waits on board his boat, the *Shadow*, with a group of local elders who have arrived for the welcoming ceremony. *Sandra Stone*

wore bib overalls and looked, as someone said, like a character out of *The Waltons* television show. He had a gracious, open manner and as Barrett-Lennard said, "if anyone could deal with the delicate politics involved, surely a retired professor of world religions could!" He welcomed the elders on board and together they settled in to await the arrival of the whale.

■

THE TRIP NORTH PROCEEDED WITH NO SERIOUS MISHAPS. Springer rested peacefully in her sling inside the tank on board the Catalina Jet, showing no signs of stress or fear. Her back was covered with wet towels. Several handlers comforted her by rubbing her skin and rinsing her with cool sea water, which was changed continuously so as to acclimate her to the changing water temperature of the outside world. As the boat sped up the coast it was accompanied by three helicopters carrying members of the press corps and several escort vessels, first from the NMFS, then from the DFO. "It gave a feeling of being rather special," said Dave Huff, the veterinarian on board. At the border, American and Canadian officials staged a small "hand-off" ceremony for the media, with an unexpected twist. As the group grinned for the cameras, Brent Norberg reached under his jacket and presented his DFO counterpart, Marilyn Joyce, with a video copy of the movie *Free Willy*. "You should have seen Marilyn's face," laughed media coordinator Angela Neilson. "I was horrified. This is not the film we want to be associated with. I had said we don't want the *Free Willy* connection because it idealizes a lot and is totally not accurate. So when he passes this live in front of the camera her face just looked horrified for a brief second, then she had this forced smile to say thanks."

The water in Springer's tank was cooled with ice, and when the vessel paused at Campbell River to refuel, the team seized the opportunity to take on a hundred more bags of it. "We had a chain gang going on," described Huff. "It was unbelievable how fast that ice got on. Then, to our surprise, pizzas started coming on-board."

Matt Nichols had radioed ahead to Boston Pizza to order forty large pies. Before the boat continued on, a First Nations delegation from Cape Mudge appeared at the stern in a Zodiac asking to come aboard. They had brought a carved mask representing the spirit of the forest, and they presented it to John Nightingale as a way of welcoming Springer back to their territory.

While the passengers enjoyed an apparently flawless ride, there was a fair amount of tinkering going on down in the engine rooms. Three engineers had volunteered to make the trip and they were kept busy dealing with a series of small emergencies. "There were a lot of little things that happened," admitted Mike Downey, the head engineer. "An engine alarm might go off for overheating, oil pressure losses. A fuse might blow and an alarm would go off. It kept the three guys hopping just troubleshooting the whole way along. Most of this was because the boat had sat idle for so long and now was going on a long run." The most serious problem was that the ride control pumps began to fail, threatening to make the trip very bumpy. "The portside ride control pump was the first to go out and they got that one fixed when not twenty minutes later the starboard pump went out. So they were going from one hull to the other to fix these problems... Down there it is hot and noisy and you certainly don't want to let anyone know there is any problem. You just have to keep the boat running and keep a smile on your face at all times. You just hope that no one sees you running when you have a crisis on your hands."

No one was happier than the crew to round the final point and arrive at the rendezvous at the entrance to Dong Chong Bay. An informal welcoming committee of dozens of pleasure boats had been waiting all afternoon. Among the crowd of boats was the *Sea Roamer*, the Stolt barge, equipped with a crane to hoist Springer on board. The catamaran came alongside and, working in a light chop, the crane operator managed to lift the sling onto the barge, where Springer was deposited onto a bed of wet mattresses. From there it was a short run into the bay, where the

■ Chief Bill Cranmer from Alert Bay awaits Springer's arrival.

Sandra Stone

crane lowered the whale into the pen. Applause and cheers from the cliffside onlookers echoed across the water.

As this was happening, the canoe of First Nations elders left the *Shadow* and approached the pen. 'Namgis Chief Bill Cranmer gave a brief speech of welcome in Kwak'wala and English. He was holding a rattle and wearing a Chilkat blanket, a cedar bark headring decorated with ermine skin and abalone shell, and a cedar bark neckring. "I just welcomed Springer and asked our Creator to look after her, and then sang a song to ask the Creator to be with us, to be with Springer at this time." In one of the canoes, a person wore a killer whale transformation mask and the ceremony was accompanied by rhythmic drumming. Lance Barrett-Lennard found tears welling in his eyes and he was not alone. "It was the first time that I, and I think many others involved in the operation, had really reflected on the symbolic significance of what had just happened," he recalled. "We'd repatriated a whale, a First Nations icon as well as an icon of a different kind to people around the globe, to its birthplace and ancestral home. And the First Nations had co-operated and blessed the event, which made it so much more fulfilling." After the speech the elders returned to their canoe, the people onshore got back in their boats and together they quietly left the bay.

Helena Symonds had walked across the island from her home at OrcaLab to witness the arrival of the young whale whose voice she had recognized six months earlier. She found a good viewpoint with some others from the lab on one of the prominent bluffs that form the entrance to Dong Chong Bay and watched as the barge brought Springer in. "But as we were sitting there," Symonds recalled, "and the sun was getting lower in the sky and everything, this eagle swept over us—one eagle— just swept right over us and went right the whole length of the bay, over the pen, and up. Totally silent. Absolutely no calls at all. And then this bird was joined by another and they just circled over top." It took a while to manoeuvre Springer into position for the transfer into the pen, during which time the eagles continued to drift and soar. "Then we could see Springer being lifted up," Symonds continued, "and she was brought over the pen and she was lowered gently down into the water and just as she hit, touched the water, the eagles started calling. And we all just looked at each other and went…"

The eagles seemed to close a parenthesis around the entire trip. That morning, as the sun came up over Puget Sound, Sue Murray had watched a lone bald eagle circle the netpen at Manchester while Springer was loaded onto the catamaran. Now, as the sun began to go down in Johnstone Strait, more eagles were there to witness the whale's return to her home territory. For members of the transport team, the unexpected appearance of the First Nations and the eagles seemed to augur well for the success of the relocation.

■

ONCE SHE WAS IN HER PEN, Springer showed no signs of stress from her voyage north. She swam briskly around the enclosure, slapped her tail, chased the salmon that had been placed in her pen, breached and even spyhopped to get a look at her surroundings. With the arrival of evening the small army of minders and experts who had brought her this far began to disperse. Vancouver Aquarium and DFO officials went over to Telegraph Cove to talk to the press. Jeff Foster and his team, who had been up since before dawn, hitched a ride over to the *Sea Roamer*, where they went to bed. Sharon Jeffery and Donnie Reid, divers from the Aquarium who had been in the area for a couple of days helping to set up the pen, remained watching until after midnight, then went off to get some sleep on the *Shadow*. That left Lance Barrett-Lennard, Clint Wright and Jeremy Fitz-Gibbon on the pen, along with Joseph Bettis and Sharon Stone from the *Shadow*, and Pete Schroeder, the vet from Manchester who had come up on the Catalina Jet. Alexandra Morton was recording sounds from her small boat nearby and David Howitt, a researcher with OrcaLab, was also recording.

The plan was to wait for members of Springer's family to swim by; with luck this might happen within the next few days. Her closest relatives were in the A24 matriline, led by Springer's grandmother, Kelsey. Scientists sometimes referred to this matriarch, born in 1967, as "dysfunctional" because so many of her offspring had died very young. Kelsey had seven known calves and four of them died within four years of their birth. Springer's mother, Sutlej (A45), lived long enough to begin giving birth. Her first calf died, then she gave birth to Springer shortly before her own death. In 1983, members of this group were the victims of a tragic shooting at Robson Bight. A pair of boaters on their way from Alert Bay to Campbell River opened fire with a high-powered rifle on the whales that were at the rubbing beaches. Among the whales were A10, Springer's great-grandmother, and one of her calves, A47, which had just been born. They were never seen again and were presumed killed. Kelsey (A24), Springer's grandmother, was probably there as well, but she survived. This horrific incident recalled the days when killer whales were routinely shot as vermin. It is impossible to say whether it had some lingering impact on A24 but the matriline seemed cursed in some way. A better home for Springer might be with the A11 matriline, led by her great-aunt, Yakat, the sister of A24. Both groups associated with each other regularly and their dialects were so similar that only the most experienced "eaves dropper" could tell them apart. Both groups had been seen in the area already that summer.

At the pen, Springer was vocalizing loudly, but no one expected anything to happen very soon and the minders decided to get some sleep in shifts. The stars glittered in the night sky and the trees formed black silhouettes along the top of the cliffs. Springer's soft breathing and gentle splashing and the distant sloshing of surf outside the bay's entrance were the only sounds to break the silence. It was another night of bioluminescence and the minders could see the ghostly shapes of the salmon as they darted around the pen. As she exploded after them, Springer left a swirling trail of light. For Wright and the others it was a moment they had been working toward for the past six months. The interminable scientific meetings, the frustrations of dealing with reluctant bureaucracies, the anxieties of having the whale's life in their hands, the pressure of working under the relentless gaze of the world's media, the knowledge that any number of things might go wrong with fatal consequences, all these responsibilities were behind them. The whale was back where she belonged in her home territory with her family somewhere in the vicinity.

The calm was shattered at about 1:30 in the morning, just as Lance Barrett-Lennard climbed into his sleeping bag. Helena Symonds radioed across to say that David Howitt was picking up sounds from a group of whales travelling in the direction of the bay. Based on what she was hearing, Symonds thought the group contained members of Springer's natal pod. Barrett-Lennard leapt

■ Springer swimming near the Vashon Island ferry terminal in Puget Sound the day before she was moved to the pen at Manchester. *Kellie Anderson*

▲ When Springer was
first discovered in Puget
Sound, her skin was very
blotchy and unhealthy-
looking. With proper
diet and medical care,
the condition cleared up
before her departure to
Canada. *Kellie Anderson*

▶ Springer underwater
in her Puget Sound "box."
Robert Wood

▲ The US Coast Guard monitoring Springer in Puget Sound. *Robert Wood*

▲ Passengers line the decks of the car ferry *Evergreen State* to catch a glimpse of Springer. The little whale seemed to form a strong attachment to the huge ferry. *Kellie Anderson*

▲ Floyd Fulmer (l.) and Mike Gannon look on as Springer appears beside the *Evergreen State*. *Robert Wood*

▲ Springer spyhopping alongside Brad Hanson, a scientist from the US Marine Mammal Lab in Seattle. *Robert Wood*

▲ Members of the Kuteeya Tlingit dance troupe performing on the deck of the *Evergreen State*, June 12, 2002. *Kellie Anderson*

◀ Another breath sample is taken on capture day. The Vancouver Aquarium's Clint Wright is at top left; Jeff Foster is in the water, at lower right; the veterinarian Peter Schroeder leans down over the water.

Robert Wood

▲   June 13, 2002. While she was on-board the landing barge, a crew kept Springer cool by applying wet towels to her back and dorsal fin. Here she is being prepared to be lifted off the barge into the netpen. *Robert Wood*

▶ Springer plays with her dinner in the netpen at Manchester.
Christine Sakhrani

▲ Springer's favourite stick was tethered to a line strung above the netpen. A variety of other "toys" were attached to the line and used to keep Springer stimulated. *Christine Sakhrani*

▲ The Catalina Jet shortly after its arrival at Dong Chong Bay late on the afternoon of July 13, 2002. Preparations are being made to lift Springer onto the barge using the crane, which is visible extending up to the left. *Sandra Stone*

▲ A 'Namgis drummer on the *Shadow*, dressed in a ceremonial button blanket, welcomes Springer back to her home territory. *Sandra Stone*

▲ 'Namgis chief Bill Cranmer aboard the *Shadow* waiting for Springer's arrival. *Sandra Stone*

▲ Springer splashing in the netpen at Dong Chong Bay on Hanson Island the evening of her arrival. *Sandra Stone*

◀ A group of paddlers arrive in Dong Chong Bay from Alert Bay in a cedar canoe to take part in the welcoming ceremony. *Sandra Stone*

▶ Veterinarian Peter Schroeder, who had accompanied Springer on the Catalina Jet, stands at left. The two Vancouver Aquarium divers are Donnie Reid (r.) and Sharon Jeffery. *Sandra Stone*

▶ Springer is held in the netpen just prior to her release on July 14, 2002. In the water Clint Wright (top left), Jeff Foster (top right) and other members of Foster's crew await the green light from the scientists monitoring the whales outside the bay. *Sandra Stone*

■ Springer, on the right, four days after her release. She is in the company of A51 (l.), the young adult female member of A5 pod that "adopted" her initially. The fin behind Springer belongs to A61, the younger brother of A51. *Lance Barrett-Lennard*

▲   Luna following his mother, Splash (L67), near San Juan Island in the autumn of 1999.
Candice Emmons/Center for Whale Research

▲   Luna enjoyed pushing on rudders and auxiliary outboard motors like this one. He may have
been trying to disable the boats so as to keep them nearby. *Ed Thorburn*

▲ Luna the whale finds a friend, Henry the dog, at the Gold River dock. *Deborah Brash/ Victoria Times Colonist*

▶ On at least one occasion during his interaction with boats, Luna was slashed by a propeller, leaving gashes on his dorsal area. *Ed Thorburn*

 Luna nuzzles up to a Department of Fisheries and Oceans Zodiac. *Margaret Butschler*

▼ Lisa Larsson, a researcher with OrcaLab, observing Luna from her clifftop lookout. *Orcalab*

▶ Luna wake surfing in Nootka Sound. His persistent interaction with boats raised concerns that he might accidentally harm either himself or a boater. *Ed Thorburn*

▶ The Aquarium's Clint Wright was in charge of masterminding Luna's capture, and his planning was meticulous. *Vancouver Aquarium*

Open gate
Drop curtain - check functioning
Dive - check
Bring whale in - Ed closer
jet boat attention
Curtain up 2 people - Kevin
Small boat under dock - push to close - 2 pins avail
veil flipped in before cutting
Hang net
Regroup - jet boat idle - keep attention
½ hr
Attach line to crane from boat
Lift boat out - delay until net
Pull up slow - L98 @ dock end
2 people each side for line — extra hold
Bring up fast or slow - Jeff
in suits
Jeff
Shallowing up net — 2 teams first in
drawing

◀ Two members of the Vancouver Aquarium team at Gold River, (l.) Lance Barrett-Lennard, senior marine mammal scientist, and veterinarian Dave Huff. *Lloyd Murray*

◀ The floor of the pen is being lifted by a crane to shallow up the water, as the crew planned to do when Luna was inside. *Vancouver Aquarium*

▼ The jet boat lures Luna toward the netpen on June 22, 2004. *Margaret Butschler*

▲ Chief Mike Maquinna speaks at a memorial service for Luna in Gold River on March 13, 2006, three days after the whale's death. *Deddeda Stemler*

▲ Ellen Hartlmeier's tribute to Luna's memory on the beach near Steveston. *Ellen Hartlemeier*

■ Springer in the netpen in Dong Chong Bay. *Sandra Stone*

from bed, dressed only in his underwear, and began madly setting up hydrophones, preparing the tape recorder and communicating with Symonds. "Are you telling her you're naked?" asked Clint Wright as he watched this flurry of activity.

Paul Spong described what happened from his perspective at OrcaLab:

David is in Dong Chong Bay recording Springer on one channel and listening to what is happening outside on the other. For over an hour this wonderful acoustic event happened. When Springer heard the other whales she was so excited she couldn't speak, she couldn't form the calls, just barrages of sound—"blahh!"—coming out of her. It took her ages before she was able to vocalize normally. The whales on the outside, you could hear the calls in the distance. Eventually, what sounded like a young whale came right into the bay. This lovely exchange happened. By then Springer had calmed down enough that she was able to enunciate her calls normally, and it was this lovely exchange between her and this other whale. And then the other whale left the bay and joined up with the other whales and they left, they went back up Blackfish Sound.

In the pen Springer was very excited. She leaped free of the water, slapped her tail, emitted high-pitched calls and pushed her nose against the net at the front of the pen. As Barrett-Lennard told reporters the next morning, her calls were so loud that they almost blew his headphones off. "Wherever she moved she left a trail of light. As she was screaming, the fish would dart off and she would chase them and seem to catch them. Then she'd come back and scream some more. It was a wonderful event. It went on for two and a half hours with the whales gradually getting louder and then getting fainter. We're not sure if they heard her [Springer] because they were vocalizing actively in their own group so she would've been one distant little voice for them. But for her they were a whole cacophony of different sounds."

Eventually the whales left and Springer settled down. By this time it was four o'clock in the morning. Suddenly, Barrett-Lennard, Wright and Fitz-Gibbon, the only three people awake, noticed that the pen was full of what appeared to be eels, some as much as a half-metre long. They were bright with bioluminescence and swarming by the hundreds through the pen just below the surface. (They turned out to be a kind of polychaete worm known as a ragworm.) Still giddy with excitement, the trio decided to collect some of these intruders for the Aquarium. Rounding up a pail and a net, they managed to catch a few, saved one and threw the rest back. "We were all bumping into each other and not making much sense," admitted Barrett-Lennard. "Actually, we were a bit delirious." And on that note, the eventful day ended.

■

NO ONE COULD PREDICT HOW LONG SPRINGER would be living in Dong Chong Bay but the Vancouver Aquarium's planning team did not want her getting comfortable. "We were adamant

... that her experience in the netpen should be as unfamiliar and unmemorable as possible," Clint Wright explained.

We didn't want her to have any familiar objects, we didn't want her to have any toys, we didn't want her to have anything that she could associate with being fun ... When we originally talked about the netpens, Stolt said they could give us a one hundred-foot-diameter circular pen. And we thought that would be great if we were going to be holding the animal and we wanted it to be comfortable. But I was happy with a fifty-by-fifty-foot pen. I didn't want her to feel that this was a great place to be, to eat fish and play with toys. No, this wasn't going to be home. Home is way out there somewhere."

As things turned out, Springer had hardly any time at all to get comfortable in her new surroundings.

When the sun came up on day one in Dong Chong Bay, members of the release team roused themselves and began working out a schedule of duties to cover the next few days. At about 7:00 a.m. the group of whales that had passed the night before slipped by the mouth of the bay again, travelling west into Blackfish Sound. There they paused at the Plumper Islands, a collection of rocky islets at the west end of Hanson Island. Springer herself was still active in the pen. Lance Barrett-Lennard took a boat and ran into Telegraph Cove on an errand, and he bumped into Mark Miller, who was filming the release for the Discovery Channel, and his camera operator, Kevin Mills. Because the film-makers had agreed to share their footage with the other media, they had clearance to be in Dong Chong so Barrett-Lennard ferried them back to the site. If it had not been for this fortuitous meeting, there would have been no cameras in the bay to film the extraordinary events that transpired over the next few hours.

Barrett-Lennard next motored over to the ice barge in Double Bay to pick up Jeremy Fitz-Gibbon. On their way back, they met John Ford and Graeme Ellis, the two DFO scientists, who were in their own boat watching the small group of whales that had left the Plumpers and was proceeding slowly along the side of Hanson Island back through Blackfish Sound toward Dong Chong. Among these whales were some of Springer's natal group. It dawned on Barrett-Lennard and the others that zero hour might be approaching a lot sooner than anyone had anticipated. They radioed the netpen to tell the rest of the crew what was happening and asked them to fit Springer with the locators that had been prepared. These were telemetry tags that attached to the animal's back with suction cups and sent out signals that allowed her location to be tracked, at least for a few days until they were expected to fall off.

By this time it was early afternoon. The crew at the pen got into the water and prepared to drop the net. This was the moment they had all been working toward. For many of them it was the high point of their entire careers, a chance to put all their expertise to work to rescue an imperilled animal in the wild and return it to its home. As the whales approached outside the bay, Springer began to get excited. The group at the pen grew more anxious by the minute. Could they release her? The veterinarian, Dave Huff, had already said the animal was healthy. There was no medical reason to delay. Out on the water, the scientists were trying to come to a decision. They were waiting for some sound from the whales, some sign of recognition. They asked the coast guard and the DFO boats to shut off their engines so they could hear better, but the pod had gone silent.

"The responsibility was overwhelming," recalled Barrett-Lennard, "and really none of us had anything to go by. We all knew the possibilities, including that she would swim out only to have the other whales, the whales on the outside, tear her to pieces because she was an unknown whale using their dialect. They might attack and leave her bleeding and crippled. They might swim away from her at top speed. She might panic and swim back to the pen. There were a lot of possibilities." Thinking about it, Clint Wright had already formed his own opinion, though he knew the final decision was up to the scientists who studied the animals in the wild. "If the animal is just quiet and logging in the water and trying to hide, then that wouldn't be a good time to do it," he thought. "When she was showing signs that she wanted to go, that will be the time to do it." And Springer was showing every sign, wiggling and vocalizing, that she, at least, thought the time was right.

Then a very strange thing happened. As the whales began to pass across the entrance to Dong Chong Bay, they turned abruptly and swam through the opening. Killer whales almost never enter small bays. Obviously they had heard something. They came to within about three hundred metres of the pen and stopped. Wright was in the pen at Springer's head. From his vantage he could look out into the bay and see the other whales approaching. "We could actually see the dorsal fins of these whales and the tension started to rise. We were wondering, will we let her go? ... They were getting closer and there was pec [pectoral fin] slapping going on. We could actually hear the blows and pec slaps. It was very, very exciting."

At this point the scientists in their boats and the crew on the pen had different impressions of what was taking place. When Barrett-Lennard radioed to ask that the suction cup telemetry tags be attached, the team had concluded that a decision had been taken to go ahead with the release. At this point, divers went into the water and cut some of the lines securing the net, meaning that going back would have been difficult. As a result, the people in the water holding Springer were extremely anxious to let her go. At one point Wright called up to Dave Huff standing on the deck of the pen and asked him to tell Ford and the others, "I need a single word from you, and it has to be yes or no." There was a pause and then Ford answered, "Dave, what's the question?" Out in the boats the scientists didn't know the lines had been cut and saw no reason to rush into a decision. They continued to watch carefully for assurances that the approaching whales were interested in Springer and not showing any signs of aggression.

Finally it appeared to the scientists that there was never going to be a better opportunity to do what they had come for.

Helena Symonds, who was listening in on the radio, agreed, and after a quick discussion and canvas of opinion, Ford, Barrett-Lennard and Ellis gave the okay. Ford radioed the pen. The net was dropped and the crew in the water gently shoved Springer under the decking. A chorus of cheers and applause rose from around the pen and she was free. "It was absolutely incredible," said Wright who scrambled from the water onto the deck to watch her go. "Absolutely unbelievable. We were just standing there in disbelief that this was really happening."

This was the moment of truth. How would the other whales receive her — as an intruder or a prodigal child? The whole bay fell silent as every set of eyes was riveted on the little whale to see what she would do. Springer made directly for the group, which seemed to be waiting for her. They had been identified as members of the A11 matriline, including Springer's cousins. Halfway there she paused to investigate a piece of kelp, seeming to buy time, the way a person might in a socially awkward situation. Then she swam to within about fifty metres of the other whales and stopped, her head pointing toward them. They lay motionless, their heads pointing toward her. For the release team, time stood still. After a couple of minutes, the other whales turned and swam slowly away from her, heading east. She turned, equally slowly, and headed off to the west. Barrett-Lennard had a hydrophone in the water the entire time and did not hear a peep from Springer or from the others. She found a stick and nestled it briefly. Then she was gone.

Barrett-Lennard, out in his boat watching Springer swim away, felt momentarily devastated. It was not the happy moment that everyone had anticipated or at least hoped for. Instead of starring in a family reunion, Springer seemed like a lonely little whale in a big ocean, rejected by her relations, with no one to take her in. Barrett-Lennard was happy she was back in her home waters but apprehensive about what might happen next. He trailed along behind her for a few

■ The team awaits word to release Springer. Note the two transmitters that were attached to her back with suction cups. One fell off a few minutes after release, but the other remained in place for several days and was useful for tracking Springer's location. *Sandra Stone*

kilometres but she made no sign of turning back toward the other whales.

Rob Scott, an officer on the *Sooke Post*, was also watching the whales turn away. It was such a poignant moment that he found himself with tears in his eyes. One of his fellow crew members asked him if he was crying. "No, why would I cry?" he replied. "I'm a 210-pound guy with tattoos. Why would I cry? I've just got something in my eyes." Back at the pen, the release team also was caught up in the emotion of the moment. Wright felt as if he just wanted to tell somebody. "It was the most amazing event ever and nobody knew!" But that was about to change.

SINCE THE ARRIVAL OF SPRINGER on Saturday, Telegraph Cove and Port McNeill had been gripped by a media storm. Killer whales had come a long way since they were hunted as pests in the early 1960s. In the public mind, they had changed from vicious predators of the deep to gentle emissaries for the marine environment, and they were big news. The story of this particular killer whale — its plight in Puget Sound, its "rescue" by scientists, its return to live again with its family — captured the attention of the world. A fleet of satellite trucks and an army of reporters descended on northern Vancouver Island. They required a steady diet of information to fill the daily newscasts and newspaper columns so the Aquarium's media representatives, as well as John Nightingale and some of the scientists, kept busy meeting with reporters and updating them on events in Dong Chong Bay. Occasionally boats carried small numbers of reporters out to Hanson Island, but they were kept at a distance from Springer's pen so as not to disturb her. Residents of the area were swept up in the story. Springer was the main topic of conversation in town that summer. As Margaret Butschler, one of the Aquarium's media representatives, observed, "when you went into Port McNeill they had the Springer coffee special and the hamburger special. All the store windows had 'Welcome Home Springer' on them. That is their whale, the people of the North Island think she belongs to them."

Once Lance Barrett-Lennard had seen Springer on her way he had to hurry into Telegraph Cove for a press conference to announce the release. While the press seemed ready to celebrate, his mood was sombre. "It was extremely intimidating going up the dock in Telegraph Cove," Barrett-Lennard recalled, "because it was covered by satellite trucks and scores of jostling reporters, all of whom wanted to talk to me. A little section at the bottom of the ramp was cordoned off so that I could talk to John Nightingale and Angela Neilson privately. I told them that it wasn't looking like a good story so far, that I was quite worried, and that I wasn't looking forward to breaking the news to the press." Nightingale and Neilson told him not to worry. In their view the press was determined to make it a good news story. Tell them the truth, they advised, but don't be surprised if they are only interested in the positive. And that is exactly what happened. The press had no interest in the fact that Springer and her pod had gone their separate ways. Caught up in the moment, they only wanted to hear about Springer's return home.

No one knew what would happen next. The experts were elated that the release had gone so well. But they were deflated by the fact that Springer had not immediately joined the other whales. "It took the fizz out of the champagne," was how Barrett-Lennard put it. Still, as he told the media, Springer needed to decide what group of whales she wanted to associate with. She was back in her home range with an opportunity to make that decision, which was, after all, the objective of the whole exercise.

Behind the scenes, while all the preparations had been going on for Springer's relocation and release, there was another campaign underway. It was an expensive proposition to intervene in nature. All told, it cost about one million dollars to move Springer. Much of this was covered by the many private individuals and companies that donated equipment and personnel to make her return a reality. For the Puget Sound portion of the project, Sea World in San Diego provided a veterinarian and the use of its laboratory for analysis of some of the medical data. Home Depot contributed supplies. Manson Construction, a Seattle company, provided the crane that lifted Springer onto the catamaran. Cypress Island offered live salmon from its fish farms and a barge for moving Springer to the pen. Nichols Brothers provided the Catalina Jet that took Springer north, the Point Defiance Zoo provided the sling and Six Flags offered the transport box. The scuba tanks, some of the medical equipment, the monitoring cameras, the foam padding on which Springer rested, all these important supplies were donated to the effort. In Canada, Stolt Sea Farm,

Canfisco, Discovery Crane and several other companies did the same. Hundreds of thousands of dollars were donated from private hands.

However, the Vancouver Aquarium still faced a shortfall approaching $100,000 to cover its own costs. On the American side of the border, the NMFS funded the effort in Puget Sound—the capture and rehabilitation at Manchester. But in Canada, the equivalent agency, the DFO, told the Aquarium it had no money for the operation. The Aquarium, a non-profit, completely self-supporting organization, was going to have to find its own funds and it would have to do so by appealing to the public. This launched the Aquarium into an unprecedented fundraising effort. As Dan Peiser, the head of external relations at the time, explained, "this was a very interesting campaign for us because it was crisis fundraising, which is very different from an ongoing development program where we cultivate donors and bring them on-board and get them involved. The normal fundraising approach is to work on broadening the inner circle of family members, if you will, of board and staff and going out into the community to identify people and engaging them and getting them involved. Fundraising flows from that as a process. But it is a very different methodology from raising money for disaster relief such as a famine or some sort of international crisis. Usually that is the kind of crisis fundraising that gets people who don't give to an organization traditionally. We really didn't have any experience with that kind of fundraising."

It was not until the end of June, when the DFO gave the green light to Springer's repatriation, that the Aquarium could even begin its campaign. Until then it was not certain the whale would be returning home. "The other challenge we had from a fundraising perspective," Peiser explained, "was that July was traditionally the worst month of the year to do fundraising. People do not raise money in July." On July 9, John Nightingale held a press conference to outline the project and appeal to the public for money. A toll-free number was announced and the phones started ringing off the hook almost immediately. It was obvious the plight of the young whale had touched the emotions of the public. Money was also collected through a special website, managed by Christie Hurrell, which was updated hourly with reports from project personnel, photographs and information about how to donate. The goal was set at $85,000. By July 19, less than a week after Springer's release, the campaign was almost halfway there. And the donations just kept rolling in, from friends of the Aquarium as well as from people who had never given the Aquarium a second thought but were captivated by the Springer story and believed the scientists were doing the right thing. "We rarely get such a volume of positive feedback from our donors," admitted Peiser. Countless donors said that they were either against whales in captivity or not particularly engaged by what the Aquarium did, but they felt that on this occasion the institution was doing the right thing. One donor's comment was typical. "Please accept this small donation toward the release of Springer. In a world so caught up in dollar bills and bottom-line profits, it is so refreshing to follow a story giving moral values such as this. I want to commend you and your staff for doing everything possible to prolong and enhance the life of this young whale."

On September 5 the Aquarium was able to announce that it had exceeded its goal, thanks to a $10,000 donation from the Six Flags Marine World Foundation in the US, and that all extra money would go to the facility's Marine Mammal Rescue and Rehabilitation program. The campaign was not just a great success financially; it turned out to be an unexpected educational and public relations triumph for the Aquarium. "What is so important about this," Peiser emphasized, "was that the Aquarium desperately needed it. After a year and a half of real difficulty starting from April 2001 when Bjossa left, to September 11, which had a great impact on tourism, the Aquarium had a tough financial year. Coming out of the whale debate of the late 1990s, this project really helped let the public know about the Aquarium and to get its conservation message out there. The

Aquarium could not have gotten any better publicity for any amount of money. It isn't because it is a feel-good story either — it was an important conservation effort."

Back in Dong Chong Bay on the day of the release, Clint Wright also contemplated the meaning of what had been accomplished.

It really was such a team event, so many people from so many different backgrounds and different ideals all working together for that common cause. If you had laid it out in some kind of film script and said, this is the way it's going to go, you would have said, "Are you completely insane? That would never happen in real life!" But it did. Springer is a good demonstration that this kind of thing really can work. There were rifts and real turning points throughout the whole thing. Some of Dave Huff's pushing and urging made a big difference. All along the way he really believed something had to be done. The planning and thought processes that Lance and John brought to it were great. It really was a true team effort. It was a bureaucratic nightmare and could have become even worse and gone nowhere. A lot of people ignored a lot of things that could have been insults or injury to get this done. At the end of the day they kept the clear knowledge in their head that they needed to do something for this whale.

"I think that was really the very special thing," Wright continued. "We were involved in something that was really, from my standpoint, a once-in-a-lifetime opportunity. In terms of adventure I have had a chance to do a lot of pretty exciting things and had the opportunity to go to some great places. This ranks up there with some of my dreams. Really, this is part of why some people go into working with marine mammals, because you love working with animals and you want to help them out. You want to have some kind of impact. And boy, did we have an impact on this little animal's life."

5 ▪ AT HOME IN THE WILD

IN THE AFTERMATH OF THE RELEASE, the scientists who were monitoring Springer by boat lost visual contact, but the signal from the telemetry tags gave them a good idea where she was going. About nine o'clock that evening they located her swimming along the shoreline of Johnstone Strait. She exhibited no signs of distress. She was not following boats — all the whale watchers had been asked to keep their distance — and she seemed eager to explore her environment. Lance Barrett-Lennard had worried that she might create a small box, as she had in Puget Sound, and simply park herself in it. He was relieved to see that this was not happening. But it was worrisome that she continued to be alone. As darkness fell on Springer's first day back in her home range, her minders were still concerned.

The next day, Monday, Alexandra Morton picked up the trail not far from where Springer had been seen the previous evening. All that day the little animal cruised around Blackfish Sound, apparently shadowing the same group of whales that had been at Dong Chong for her release. By now the scientists were convinced that this group, the A11 subpod, presented the best opportunity for Springer to reattach to an adoptive family. The two sides seemed to be feeling each other out. "The glue in killer whales takes a long time to harden," explained Barrett-Lennard, who was watching through his binoculars from a distance. "They are very cautious animals." When the whales sped up, so did Springer. When they rested, she did likewise.

■ Alexandra Morton, an anti-fish farm activist and killer whale researcher based in Echo Bay, was on hand with her daughter (r.) and a friend to watch the release. *Sandra Stone*

At the end of the afternoon, the whales went through Blackney Pass and across Johnstone Strait to the rubbing beaches in Robson Bight. As they approached the bight, Barrett-Lennard, who had a hydrophone in the water, could see them speed up and hear them vocalizing excitedly, typical behaviour when the whales visit the beaches. At this point Springer caught up with them. For the first time she intermingled with the other whales, jostling with them and rubbing on the stones herself. Barrett-Lennard was elated that Springer seemed to have connected with the group. After about twenty minutes the whales left the Bight and set off in the direction from which they had come. Barrett-Lennard lost sight of Springer during the commotion at the beach. He took his boat in among the group to find her, without success. Then he spotted her, trailing some distance behind the others. As they left the beach they had re-formed into their matrilines and she did not have one to join. Once again, Barrett-Lennard's initial optimism was followed by disappointment. Not only that, but over the next few days he would notice that Springer's body was covered with superficial wounds most likely made by the other whales raking her with their teeth. The cuts were not bleeding or very deep but they were extensive. Obviously the reunion at the beach was not as friendly as Barrett-Lennard had thought. Springer seemed to have endured some pretty rough treatment from the other whales as they showed her that she was not yet welcome among them.

On Tuesday the event watchers had been dreading occurred. Springer found herself a boat to play with. Wayne Chambers was a sport fisherman from Pitt Meadows in the Fraser Valley east of Vancouver. He holidayed each summer fishing in the waters around Johnstone Strait in a small runabout equipped with a seventy-horsepower outboard. Chambers was fishing for halibut off the southwest corner of Malcolm Island when Springer appeared in the water right beside him. He was familiar with killer whales from his previous visits to the area and he had heard about the famous orphaned orca, so he was pretty sure who it was. When Chambers tried to move away, Springer wouldn't let him. She wanted to play. She was rubbing up against the bottom of the boat's aluminum hull just ahead of the engine. Chambers couldn't go forward without hitting her and when he tried to reverse away she followed, continuing to rub. Terrified that he might be overturned or that his propeller might strike the frisky whale, Chambers radioed for help.

To the rescue came Barrett-Lennard and Graeme Ellis in the DFO research boat *Squamish*. "Don't worry, I'll help," announced Barrett-Lennard as he clambered on-board. "I told him that if he let me run his boat, it would be my fault if I injured the whale — I'd take the blame. But of course, I really thought I'd be clever enough to manoeuvre away from the whale relatively easily." Barrett-Lennard took the controls of the runabout and discovered to his embarrassment that he couldn't shake the persistent whale either. Springer stayed so close to the propeller that he was afraid to accelerate away. "I desperately wanted her to develop some negative feelings about boats and slapped her back with my hand several times. This was, of course, entirely ineffective. In fact, she seemed to enjoy the sensation." At one point, Springer rubbed so hard against the boat that she dislodged one of the suction cup transmitters from her back. Chambers retrieved it from the water, saying that at least he'd have a souvenir for all his trouble. "Sorry, Wayne," replied Barrett-Lennard, "I'm afraid I'm going to need that," and he pressed it back onto the whale. At this point he gave up trying to drive Wayne's boat away from Springer and passed a line to Ellis, who towed the smaller fishing boat away at speed. Springer was unable to keep pace and a relieved Chambers was able to escape under his own power.

This incident, comical in retrospect, was discouraging for Barrett-Lennard. Prior to the release, he and his colleagues had been optimistic that even if Springer did not reattach to a group, she would do fine living by herself in her home range. Now he began to suspect that this middle ground probably did not exist. If Springer was not accepted into a pod she was likely going to be a problem. In her playfulness and need for company she might overturn a small boat or a kayaker or end up getting injured by a propeller. Faced with these possibilities, would they have to recapture her? Ellis had the same misgivings. "That's when I actually thought we were going to have to catch her again," he said, looking back. "She's going to either scare someone to death and turn the boat over or get injured by a propeller." The feel-good story of Springer's release had the potential to turn tragic in a hurry.

■

ON THE WEDNESDAY FOLLOWING SPRINGER'S RELEASE, several of the Americans who had taken part went to Village Island to attend a welcoming ceremony for the whale. Joseph Bettis and Sandra Stone of the *Shadow*, along with the veterinarian Peter Schroeder, who had come north aboard the Catalina Jet and stayed on with Bettis and Stone, had met Tom Sewid, a local tour operator, and he had invited them to be present. They brought along Jeff Foster and his team from Dong Chong. Bob McLaughlin, who had been one of the drivers of the catamaran, and Bob Wood, who came up on his boat *Shelmar*, were also there.

Village Island is located north of Hanson Island at the mouth of Knight Inlet. It is a very historic spot, the site of Memkoomlish ('Mimkwa̱mlis), a former village site of the Mamalilikala people, one of the Kwakwa̱ka̱'wakw tribes. In December 1921 Dan Cranmer hosted his infamous "Christmas potlatch" at Village Island. The term *potlatch*, which derived from a Chinook jargon term meaning "to give," referred to a constellation of traditional ceremonies held to mark many different occasions, from marriages to funerals, from births to house raisings. Guests who were invited to witness these important events received gifts for doing so and the celebrations lasted for several days. Potlatching had been illegal on the coast for many years as part of the government's attempt to stamp out non-Christian practices, but First Nations, particularly the Kwakwa̱ka̱'wakw, continued to hold potlatches in defiance of the law and for the most part government agents turned a blind eye. Early in 1922, however, Indian agent William

Halliday, determined to teach the Kwakw<u>aka</u>'wakw a lesson, ordered the RCMP to arrest some of the people who attended the Cranmer ceremony. The police collected many pieces of ceremonial regalia and charged more than fifty participants. In the end, twenty-two people were sent to the Oakalla Prison Farm outside Vancouver to serve their terms. Many of the ceremonial pieces, including masks, coppers, headdresses and whistles, ended up in museums in eastern Canada and

■ The whole of northern Vancouver Island was transfixed by Springer's return. This sign at Village Island was typical of the community involvement. *Sandra Stone*

the United States. Later the people moved away from Mem-koomlish, though they continued to visit seasonally. In 1951 the federal government ended its ban on the potlatch. After prolonged negotiations, many of the items seized as a result of the Village Island ceremony were returned to the Kwakwa̱-ka̱'wakw to be held in museums at Cape Mudge and Alert Bay.

The people gathered at Village Island to honour Springer's return welcomed the Americans as special guests. Schroeder described the setting.

There's only one way to approach the village [by boat], from due west, and you approach and see just a small brown weather-worn building, with a dock, and that's where you anchor. There's a little gift shop where you can get refreshments and gas I believe. From there the people who are going to see the ceremonies gather there and are taken by trail which goes up a hill and then down to the left. You are sort of walking up into the unknown and then see a big old ancient totem pole just lying there. Then there are a couple of old broken-down houses which were probably part of the old village. In between are a couple of those big, old lodge poles that they have in front of the lodge house where they stretch a banner, tell the stories and do the dancing. The banner frames the event in among the big old cedar posts, obviously old-growth. It was very moving to see, and the weather was perfect, just little spits of rain that you hardly noticed.

Schroeder had carried Springer's favourite stick with him on the trip from Puget Sound. It was the same knobbly branch that he had given the whale to play with while she was in the netpen at Manchester. He had thought that perhaps he would give it to her again at the pen in Dong Chong Bay, but events had developed too quickly. After the drumming and dancing, he approached the participants and offered the stick to them. They accepted it and agreed to encourage all the local people to keep well away from Springer until she had settled in to her surroundings.

■

JOHN FORD, THE DFO MARINE MAMMALOGIST, was one of the monitors out on the water that day. Ford, who was forty-seven years old the year of Springer's release, had spent his entire career studying the killer whales of the Pacific Northwest. As a young university student he had worked in the marine mammal department of the Vancouver Aquarium and eventually became interested in recording and analyzing the sounds of the beluga whales there. By 1978 he was in graduate school, where his research focus shifted to killer whales. With a small grant from the federal government he purchased a Nagra tape recorder, state-of-the-art for the time, and with the help of Mike Bigg, who had been carrying out his groundbreaking photo identification studies, Ford started recording the killer whales in Johnstone Strait. This research went on for several years, producing exciting new understandings about how the whales communicate and socialize. Ford and Bigg together, along with Graeme Ellis, came to recognize the existence of the two separate populations, residents and transients, a discovery they revealed at a research conference in Vancouver in 1985. At this time, Ford was working at the Pacific Biological Station in Nanaimo with Bigg. Not long after, he moved back to Vancouver, and in 1988 he became curator of marine mammals at the Vancouver Aquarium. (By the time of Springer's release, Ford was back working for the DFO in Nanaimo.)

Meanwhile, Ford's acoustic research continued. Using photo identification, it was possible to sort out the social organization of the resident pods with some clarity. Knowing which

families individual animals belonged to, Ford was able to iso-
late particular sounds or dialects that belonged to one pod or
another. Based on acoustics, he and his colleagues identified
a grouping that they called a clan. A clan comprises pods of
whales that share a vocal dialect. Among the northern resident
whales there are three clans; the southern residents all belong
to the same clan. It is theorized that all the pods within a single
clan probably trace their ancestry back to a common pod that
grew and fragmented down through the generations. Yet member whales have retained recognizable similarities in the sounds
they make. In other words, members of a resident pod vocalize
using a common dialect, and this dialect shares some characteristics with the dialects belonging to other pods that make up
the clan. Scientists use these vocal similarities to identify different groups of whales. Sometimes, as in the distinctive calls that
Springer made when she was first seen in Puget Sound, they are
able even to identify an individual whale.

Not surprisingly for an animal that vocalizes so much,
killer whales have exceptional hearing. Their eyesight is good
but it is sound that helps them navigate in the murky underwater world and enables them to communicate. Externally,
a killer whale's ears are not obvious. Their streamlined shape
precludes the floppy outer ear of humans or other land-based
mammals. Instead, the whales have tiny pinholes located on
either side of the head just below the white eye patches. But
this is not where they detect sounds. That is done by the hol-
low lower jawbone, which has an area referred to as the acoustic window. From there sound is transmitted by fatty tissue to
the middle and inner ears, where the eardrum is located, protected by hard bone and gas-filled tissue that corrects for the
air-pressure changes the animal experiences as it dives and
surfaces. Whales can detect a much broader range of sounds
than humans. While humans hear sounds as high as 20 kilohertz,
killer whales are known to detect high-pitched sounds of up to
one 110 kilohertz. In this regard they resemble dogs, rodents, bats

and other animals that are able to hear sounds to which humans are deaf.

Killer whales vocalize but they do not "speak" in the human sense. Humans make sounds by passing air across our vocal cords and shaping the sounds with our mouths. Whales produce sounds by using muscles to squeeze air through the convoluted nasal passages located below the blowhole. Some of these sounds are rapid bursts of echolocation signals or pulses, known as click trains. They radiate out from the melon, the animal's forehead. The melon acts like an acoustic lens, focusing the sounds into a cone-shaped beam that is projected in front of the animal. When the sounds strike an object in the water, they bounce back and the whale is able to form an acoustic picture of what it is "seeing." This enables the whale to "size up" its prey, calculating from the echo not only the location of a fish, for instance, but also its size and species. Other sounds are high-pitched whines, squeaks and squeals. They have been compared to the sounds of rusty hinges on a quickly closing door. In fact they are a set of calls and they can be heard for many kilometres through the water. To the practised ear, they are the equivalent of a name tag, identifying the whale as a member of a particular group.

Through his research, Ford discovered that resident pods have as many as seventeen different calls, and every member of the pod shares the entire repertoire. This is the pod's dialect. Much as human youngsters learn to speak, every calf in the pod learns the dialect from infancy by mimicking the sounds made by its mother. Another Vancouver Aquarium researcher, Valeria Vergara, has reported on her work with Aurora and her son Tuvaq, two beluga whales at the aquarium. Vergara noted that immediately after Tuvaq was born, in July 2002, Aurora started producing a unique call over and over again, much like a human mother might repeat the same word to her newborn baby. Whenever Aurora wanted to communicate with Tuvaq, she would make this call. When he was four months old, Tuvaq began trying to reproduce the call, clumsily at first and then with improved facility until by the age of twenty-one months he could produce a call that was indistinguishable from that of his mother. What Tuvaq was doing was engaging in a form of babble talk, making sounds or perhaps fragments of sounds that in themselves did not mean anything until they meshed into a fully formed call. This is very similar to infant humans babbling away to themselves as they practise sounds they have heard and learn to speak.

Transient whales are different. They are much more stealthy creatures who do not advertise their presence by chattering away like the residents. If they did, the seals and other sea mammals that make up their prey would hear them. Transients emit echolocation clicks much less frequently than residents and produce them in series that are shorter and less intense. During his graduate research, Lance Barrett-Lennard had discovered that transients also use isolated and odd-sounding echolocation sounds, what he termed "cryptic clicks," that hide within the background noise of the underwater world.[35] This allows them to navigate and avoid obstacles without giving themselves away. To find prey, however, they usually remain completely silent and find their way to dinner by keying on the noises made by the animals they are stalking. When they do vocalize, the repertoire of calls used by transient whales is limited to perhaps a half dozen, none of which are used by their resident cousins. At least some of the calls seem to be recognized by every transient. Because these whales are socially promiscuous, changing their group affiliation frequently, they require a dialect that is familiar to all members of their community.

The fact that dialects are learned, not inherited, makes killer whales and other cetaceans unusual in the animal world. "It...seems most reasonable to assume," wrote John Ford in a 1990 paper, "that a killer whale's repertoire of discrete calls is acquired through imitation and learning, and thus is passed from generation to generation by cultural, rather than genetic, transmission."[36] The calls allow the whales to remain in touch even when widely dispersed, such as when they are foraging for food. Because calls are unique to specific pods they may also play a role in keeping groups socially cohesive. What Ford was able to describe was something entirely unprecedented. Apparently the killer whale is the only mammal, except for humans, that exhibits vocal variations among social groups that occupy the same geographic area and routinely mix with one another.

Vocal dialects appear to play a role in killer whale mating habits as well. As Barrett-Lennard showed in his groundbreaking research analyzing killer whale DNA, resident female whales invariably choose their mates from outside their own pod and usually outside their clan. By recognizing dialects that are too similar to their own, the whales avoid possibly harmful inbreeding. At the same time, they only mate within their own community (i.e., northern resident, southern resident or transient), likely by recognizing the appropriate dialects. In human terms, females are attracted to partners that sound a bit exotic but can still be understood. "Residents have figured out a way to stay in small communities and very effectively avoid mating with their kin," explains Barrett-Lennard. This becomes a problem when a community of whales becomes too small, as may be the case with the southern residents of Puget Sound. In such a case, females have fewer and fewer potential mates to choose from.

Because the acoustical environment is so crucial to killer whales, human-generated sound, particularly the noise from boat traffic, can pose an important threat to their well-being. The Broughton Archipelago is part of the seasonal range of some of the northern resident whales, as well as the hunting ground for groups of transients and even, very rarely, groups of offshores. In 1993, fish farms in the archipelago began using underwater noisemakers to deter seals from preying on the farmed salmon. A study conducted by Alexandra Morton and Helena Symonds concluded that these acoustic harassment devices (AHDs), known as seal scarers, had a significant impact on local killer whales, masking their vocalizing with each other, perhaps causing pain and injury and driving the whales from this portion of their habitat. Morton and Symonds warned that noise pollution of the marine environment was only going to get worse.[37] This is why scientists asked boaters to remain well away from Springer following her release, allowing her an underwater environment free of background noise so she could identify and connect with her family.

Similarly, whale watchers have worked out protocols for approaching whales that require boats to reduce their engine noise and keep their distance from the animals. In 2004 a study of the southern residents, published in *Nature*, suggested that killer whales had learned to alter their calls to compensate for the prevalence of boat noise in their environment. This study found that when boats were around, the whales actually were lengthening their calls to be better heard, another example of the amazing ability of the animals to learn from experience and shape their behaviour.[38]

Because they use sound for both communication and finding prey, residents are susceptible to noise pollution. But as Barrett-Lennard determined in his research, transients are at even greater risk. While residents may use their extremely loud vocalizations to make themselves heard above the din, transients find food by eavesdropping on their prey. If they can't hear properly, they can't get dinner. For both transients and residents, a quiet underwater environment is crucial to their ability to forage successfully for food.

■

IN THE FIRST DAYS FOLLOWING HER RELEASE, Springer was observed interacting with other whales once or twice but she did not appear to be joining any particular group. Then everything changed. On the Thursday (July 18) Barrett-Lennard and Ellis were out in the *Squamish* looking for her when they received word of a large number of killer whales near Robson Bight. When they arrived, they found that a superpod was just leaving the area. Superpods are aggregations of several resident killer whale pods. They occur two or three times a year in Johnstone Strait, the whales typically remaining together for one to three days. In this case the superpod contained more than seventy-five whales in small groups spread out across two kilometres or more. The two researchers identified pods from all three northern resident clans, including members of Springer's family. They set about searching the different groups for any sign of Springer. The weather, which had dawned sunny and bright, began to deteriorate and by mid-afternoon there was a steady drizzle. At four o'clock Ellis and Barrett-Lennard were sizing up the last group (A5 pod) when Ellis realized there was one more calf present than the group had had the previous fall. Ellis and Barrett-Lennard were observing through binoculars from a distance and could see the calf tucked close against the side of Nodales (A51), a sixteen-year-old female just old enough to have her own calf. They wondered if she had given birth during the winter, but peering through the mist they thought the calf appeared to be too big. Then the calf began to swim toward the *Squamish* and as the two men backed away they could see without any doubt that it was Springer. Not only was she associating closely with her relatives but another whale was exhibiting maternal behaviour toward her. At that moment and for the first time since the release, Barrett-Lennard felt as if the operation was going to succeed. Moments later Nodales interceded and forcefully directed Springer away from the boat. This was another special moment for the scientists. They had not been sure how to cure Springer of her dangerous predilection for approaching and rubbing on boats but now it seemed that other whales would do it for them.

Keeping track of Springer in the weeks following her release required long, arduous days on the water. Other business called

Ellis away but Barrett-Lennard maintained his watch using the Vancouver Aquarium's research boat, the *Tsitika*. Following the sighting on July 18, the superpod drifted eastward toward Campbell River and the groups were not seen for another five days. This was a worrisome period. Barrett-Lennard had no idea whether Springer was alive or dead, alone or with the other whales. Late in the afternoon of July 23 he finally spotted her, still with Nodales. Apparently the "glue" had held. Barrett-Lennard had to return to Vancouver, but other watchers spotted the little whale during the next ten days, after which she disappeared again until August 27, another long, worrisome period. When she did reappear, it was in the company of Nahwitti (A56), a twelve-year-old female who belonged to her natal pod (A4). This was disquieting for the scientists, who had hoped that Springer was firmly associated with Nodales. But it fit with their initial expectations that she would end up with her own pod. As fall approached Springer seemed to be equally comfortable with both groups.

The last Springer sighting of the season occurred on October 6, when she was observed leaving the Johnstone Strait area with members of both A4 and A5 pods. This is the time that the northern residents usually migrate northward along the coast. It was encouraging for everyone involved in her relocation to see Springer apparently settled in with her extended family. But the months ahead were a dangerous time. Killer whale mortality increases during the winter, especially among calves, as the food supply dwindles. She was now leaving the range of human assistance. Would she be able to keep up with the others? Would they continue to accept her? Would she return in the spring? "This is the real test, whether she makes it through this winter," John Ford told a reporter. "We'll just have to wait and see."[39]

It was a nerve-wracking few months for the Springer team, though in a sense, no news was good news. If the whale separated from her pod, she might well go looking for company and find it with a boat or a ferry, as she did in Puget Sound. "What I've dreaded all winter," said Barrett-Lennard, "is hearing the phone ring and picking it up and some guy from Bella Bella or fishing off the west coast, says 'Gee, I have this friendly little whale alongside the boat'."[40] But the phone remained silent and Springer's whereabouts unknown.

Bill Mackay is a long-time whale watcher on the coast. He and his wife Donna co-founded Stubbs Island Charters with Jim and Mary Borrowman, then he started his own operation using the purpose-built thirteen-metre *Naiad Explorer*. Mackay had helped out at Springer's release and was the last person to report seeing her in early October as she departed for the north. During the winter he kept an expectant eye out for the whale as he went about his business on the water. In February he was returning from delivering a charter up Kingcome Inlet when he ran into a group of about thirty whales near the entrance to Fife Sound. Among them, Mackay identified Nodales and her brother. Springer had been swimming with them when she departed the area five months earlier but there was no sign of her now. Mackay's heart sank, but it was far too early to draw any dire conclusions.

The entire whale-watching community was holding its collective breath. In mid-March there was an excited report from Johnstone Strait that the A5s were back and Springer was with them, but this sighting was never confirmed with photographs and was probably a mistake. On May 30 Barrett-Lennard did receive the dreaded phone call from an excited fellow in Prince Rupert named Gareth Scaife reporting that his friend on a tugboat in Tuck Inlet had a small killer whale nuzzling up to him. Barrett-Lennard called the tug and verified the story but the description of the animal was ambiguous. Scaife agreed to speed out in a boat and snap a digital photograph to email to Vancouver. Meanwhile, Barrett-Lennard made plans to fly north early the next morning, anticipating the media circus that would ensue if the whale turned out to be Springer. It would also present the Aquarium with the challenge of deciding what to do about her. He breathed a huge sigh of relief when the photograph arrived on his computer screen showing that the animal was not Springer but a false killer whale, possibly Willy/Foster, the wandering pseudorca who had recently left its usual stomping ground at Roberts Bank. Barrett-Lennard cancelled his plane ticket to Prince Rupert and left for a weekend in the interior, as far from the coast as possible.

The watching and waiting continued. Early in June several members of the A4 and A5 pods were seen around Prince Rupert but not Springer. Her great-aunt's group was also absent so there was reason to think she might be swimming with them. Finally, on June 9, Rachel and Lewis Penney, two participants in the Cetacean Sightings Network, sent a photograph of a young whale they had spotted in Fisher Channel at the top end of Fitz Hugh Sound in the heart of the Inside Passage. Graeme Ellis was able to say it was Springer. Whether or not she had ever left BC waters, she was definitely back.

Confirmation came on July 9 when a sport fisherman contacted Bill Mackay to tell him that he was watching six killer whales passing Doyle Island off Port Hardy in Queen Charlotte Strait. Mackay hurried out in the *Naiad Explorer* to have a look, taking along his friend Rolf Hicker, a seasoned whale photographer, and a full load of whale watchers. Soon they were surrounded by about thirty dorsal fins. Suddenly a female came straight up out of the water near the boat, and alongside her came Springer. Mackay had been the last one to see her go out in the fall. Now he was the first to see her return. It was an exhilarating moment. Hicker snapped some digital photographs, which were immediately sent to Ellis, as well as to Alexandra Morton and to OrcaLab, for confirmation. Springer was swimming with Nahwitti, the young female she'd been with the previous summer, along with her great-aunt Yakat (A11) and another, older male (A13). She was fat and appeared completely healthy. What's more, she showed no interest in the boat. Everything seemed normal.

As the summer progressed, it appeared that Springer had found a middle ground after all. She had reappeared with Nahwitti, but it turned out that she was not as bonded with this surrogate as an actual offspring would be. As more sightings were reported, it became apparent that Springer was a bit of a roamer, occasionally joining Nodales's group (the A5 pod) or swimming alone for short periods. Nonetheless, the most important things were that she remained healthy and steered clear of human/boat contact. Scientists continued to monitor her and there appeared to be no cause for concern. She was small for her age, probably because she was undernourished when she became separated from her mother, from whom she was still nursing. Otherwise, she has been seen every summer since her release, usually near or with Yakat or Nawitti. There is every reason to believe that the relocation was a success.

Springer's story was unprecedented. Never before had a killer whale become separated from its family and then returned to live among them. It was also against the odds. One of the things that had been running through Barrett-Lennard's mind as he watched Springer swim away from the netpen toward her family that fateful day was that he and his colleagues were relying on killer whales to be totally unlike any other animal. Any other animal would reject the outsider. "When you think about other mammals, the other highly social, large-brained set of species, the primates, can be absolutely brutal to each other. A wolf outside its pack would perish if it met another pack. When you are a member of a species with a highly social structure, being outside, being at odds with a group, not having a strong identity with a group is usually fatal." Yet here was Springer, wandering naïvely up to the door, giving it a loud knock and apparently being welcomed inside. And it wasn't just about Springer,

■ Springer (l.), in the summer of 2007, swimming in Johnstone Strait in the company of Yakat (A11), her great-aunt (c.), and Yakat's son, A13 (r.).
Lance Barrett-Lennard

it was about the other whales as well. What advantage did the group gain by allowing Springer inside? "You can imagine them asking, 'What's in it for me?'" continued Barrett-Lennard. "What's the benefit for the pod even to let her hang out with them? It's another mouth to feed." The answer, he concluded, is that resident killer whales must have strong inhibitions against being physically aggressive with other members of their clan, and they would have recognized Springer by her calls as one of their own. "In a lot of ways this vindicates Mike Bigg's use of the word *community*. A killer whale population is an interacting group with a social agreement." If Springer had met up with some of the southern residents, Barrett-Lennard speculated that they would probably have chased her away. But in her own community, she was welcome.

■

SPRINGER'S RELOCATION may have been unprecedented but by an amazing coincidence, at almost precisely the same time that she was discovered swimming alone in Puget Sound, another lone whale was spotted in Nootka Sound on the west coast of Vancouver Island. This was Luna (L98), a young male member of the southern resident community. Once Springer was back with her family, attention naturally shifted to this other lost animal. Could humans once again intervene to "rescue" a whale? Should they intervene or should they leave the animal alone to let nature take its course? As it turned out, the story of Luna offers little of the good feeling that Springer inspired. Fraught with misunderstanding, clashing interests and political intrigue, it ended not in success but in tragedy.

6 ▪ LUNA

FRED AND DARLENE LAZUK were heading into Muchalat Inlet in their seven-metre charter boat one afternoon in early July 2001, bound for Gold River and home, when a small killer whale vaulted out of the water ahead of them. The Lazuks, who had been running a sport-fishing charter on Vancouver Island's west coast for years, knew enough about whales to wonder what such a young one was doing in the Inlet all by itself. Over the next few days they saw the whale several times, always near Mooyah Bay at the mouth of the inlet where it widens around Bligh Island and merges into Nootka Sound. Realizing that something wasn't quite right, Fred Lazuk left a message about their sightings with the BC Cetacean Sightings Network at the Vancouver Aquarium. "I see orca quite often," he reported, "but in thirty years of boating in Nootka Sound this is the first time I have seen a young orca unaccompanied by a pod." It wasn't long before word reached John Ford and Graeme Ellis.

Researchers who spend their careers following whales on the West Coast rely on information coming in from a wide range of volunteer spotters. It is in the nature of their jobs to follow up on every report but they also know that false reports are part of the business. It is not easy to pick out a dorsal fin or a gust of spray against a backdrop of black water and breaking waves. Mistakes are common. Mike Bigg once received a report of a killer whale in a kelp bed that upon investigation turned out to be a dead black and white cow, but many more mundane objects have been mistaken for whales by inexperienced spotters. In the case of the Mooyah Bay animal, Ford and Ellis figured it was probably a Dall's porpoise. As far as they knew, killer whales seldom ventured into Nootka Sound, certainly not alone. A Dall's porpoise has similar colouring to a killer whale, though it is smaller with a far less prominent dorsal fin. From a distance a hurried glance might easily confuse the two animals.

Since there was no pressing need to investigate, it was October before Ellis, who was flying over the area on a sea otter survey, detoured to Mooyah Bay and spotted the little animal down in the water. To his surprise, he confirmed it was a killer whale. Believing it might be a southern resident, Ellis and Ford used photographs borrowed from Ken Balcomb at the Center for Whale Research on San Juan Island to identify the calf as L98, Luna, a two-year-old male who had been reported missing and presumed dead earlier that year.

Ellis began making periodic trips out to have a look at their discovery. The presence of a solitary whale in Nootka Sound was odd but for the time being there didn't seem to be anything that needed doing. Luna appeared to be healthy. He was not in any apparent distress and was not growing over-fond of people. Much like Springer, Luna had created his own small comfort zone outside of which he rarely ventured. In both cases, this imaginary "box" measured about 1.5 kilometres square. Possibly both whales were following an instinct to remain in one place when separated from their group, much like human children are taught by their parents to stay put if they get lost. Late in the year, Ed Thorburn, a federal fisheries officer based in the sound, went out in his Zodiac and found Luna right where he had been reported at Mooyah Bay. The calf more or less ignored the boat. He was spending most of his time pushing drift logs through the water. He would get on the butt end of a long log and push it ahead of him with his head. If the log started to curve, Luna would straighten it out. At this time, logs seemed to be his main form of recreation, just as Springer had been preoccupied with a large stick in Puget Sound.

The Department of Fisheries and Oceans decided to keep news of Luna's presence quiet so as not to attract public interest and to wait and see what happened. "We worried that it would become a sensation," recalled Marilyn Joyce, the DFO's marine mammal coordinator, "and next thing you know we'd have a circus." Although well intentioned, this decision was consistent with a bureaucratic obsession on the part of the DFO to control information whenever possible, a pattern that did not sit well with many of the people that the department later turned to for help. It was a full two months before Ford, Ellis and Joyce revealed Luna's presence to their closest colleagues, including Lance Barrett-Lennard, part of whose job was to oversee the BC Cetacean Sightings Network that had received the original report. They finally chose to do so at a closed-door meeting of a hand-picked group of whale experts who happened to be attending a large international marine mammal conference hosted by the Vancouver Aquarium in December 2001. The meeting was cloaked in secrecy and most of the attendees had no idea why they were being called together (even though conference organizers accidentally posted the "special killer whale meeting" time and location on their announcement board). Ford shared what was known about Luna to that point. Several people challenged the notion that his presence in Nootka Sound could, or even should, be kept secret and expressed disappointment that they had not been consulted earlier. But all agreed that contact with large numbers of people would not be in Luna's best interest. Then, in January, Springer appeared in Puget Sound and Luna more or less fell off the radar.

■

LUNA WAS BORN SOMETIME DURING THE EARLY HOURS of September 19, 1999. It is possible to pinpoint his birth accurately because Tom McMillen was almost in the "delivery room." McMillen operates a whale-watching business in the San Juan

Islands and Puget Sound. He is based in Roche Harbor on San Juan Island during the summer and moves south to Seattle in the winter. Then in his sixties, he had served with American forces in Vietnam in 1966–67 and the events he witnessed there had left him with a series of post-traumatic stress-related problems. Early in the 1990s, McMillen and his wife had moved to Spieden Island, a privately owned island north of San Juan, where he worked as the caretaker. By this time he had acquired a boat and a charter licence. One morning he was out fishing when a group of killer whales swam directly beneath his boat. In that moment, his interest in the animals was kindled. He started learning everything he could, mainly from the whales themselves, following them everywhere on their travels through the islands. After years of therapy and distress going back to his Vietnam experience, McMillen found that his fascination with the whales helped him to recover an equilibrium in his life that nothing else ever had.

McMillen always took his dog along with him on his trips and the dog, a cross between a golden retriever and a chow, had developed a relationship with the whales. He was able to hear them when McMillen could not without the aid of his hydrophone. The dog never barked at the whales but instead made a low whine that McMillen was convinced was mimicking the sound of the whales. The dog would be lounging under a table, apparently indifferent to what was going on, when suddenly he would jump up and run to the side of the boat. Sure enough, the whales invariably breached or made some other change in their behaviour. McMillen thought the dog was listening to the pod and knew when something interesting was about to happen.

On the morning of September 19, McMillen was out on the water by nine o'clock when he saw a female whale heading toward him with a newborn calf. It is very unusual for a new mother to be alone while giving birth. Usually she is surrounded by other members of the pod, who are there to play the role of midwife. Ken Balcomb and one of his assistants from the Whale Center, David Ellifrit, were on the water as well and they identified the mother as L67, Splash, a fourteen-year-old southern resident whale. McMillen noticed that the calf seemed to be wandering aimlessly and Splash was simply staying close by. The southern resident population of whales consists of three pods, J, K and L, numbering at the time of Luna's birth about ninety animals. Splash belonged to L pod and also to the L2 matriline, meaning that the reigning matriarch of the family was her mother L2 or Grace. The group also consisted of three of Grace's brothers. One of these brothers, Orcan (L39), would take on great significance in the newborn calf's life.

Later on the day of the birth, McMillen brought another group of whale watchers out. They were observing Splash and her calf when several members of K pod arrived on the scene. After some mingling on the surface, a strange thing happened. Three members of K pod swam rapidly away and the calf followed them, leaving Splash behind. A short time later Splash reconnected with her own pod. McMillen was perplexed. Normally, killer whale calves and their mothers are inseparable. Yet here was a newborn that seemed to switch mothers just hours after birth.

Pregnant killer whales give birth after a gestation period lasting about sixteen months. Three or four days before the birth, a cervical plug of mucus which has been helping to hold the calf in the womb dissolves and washes away. To an observer, a thread of mucus in the water is the sign that birth is imminent, much like the waters breaking in pregnant women. Labour generally lasts three to four hours, with the fetus emerging from the womb tail flukes first, followed by a gush of afterbirth that stains the water red with blood. Struggling to the surface to breathe, the calf at first seems awkward and frantic. It throws its head up gasping for air through its blowhole and flopping about, apparently in danger of drowning. Yet within a few hours, calves are usually swimming along beside their mothers, breathing and diving in synchronicity. Being air breathers living in water, cetacean babies are more precocious than many land animals. In this respect they resemble their closest land relatives, the ungulates, which are often able to walk within hours of birth. Because killer whale calves need to breathe more often than adults, mothers alter their own breathing patterns to accommodate the young. As the calf matures, its breathing rate drops and the mother's returns to normal.

During the first twenty-four hours after birth, a mother killer whale generally does not eat, instead focusing all her attention on the calf. When it is between twelve and thirty-six hours old, the youngster begins nursing. Much like a newborn cow or horse, the calf bunts its mother's mammaries with its head, apparently stimulating the release of the milk. Killer whale milk has a high fat content so as to promote the rapid development of a thick layer of blubber in the offspring. Shortly after birth, the milk is as much as forty-eight percent fat, a ratio that declines to about twenty-eight percent as the weeks pass. By comparison, the fat content of the milk produced by nursing humans is less than ten percent.

Suckling while moving under water is not a simple procedure. The calf attaches to the mother by curling its tongue like a tube around the nipple, achieving a firm seal. A bout of nursing may last just a few seconds, and several bouts may constitute a feeding, after which mother and calf resume their normal swimming. For the most part, the calf hitches a free ride in the mother's slipstream, much as bicycle racers are carried along in a flow field created by the lead cyclist. In the case of the killer whale, as the mother moves forward she displaces a quantity of water that is pushed forward and around her. The space behind her is filled with moving water, which carries along the calf as it hugs its mother's body. It is during these months of intimate contact that the bond between mother and child that will last a lifetime is sealed.

Unlike all other mammals, killer whale and dolphin mothers barely sleep for at least a month after giving birth and their calves do not sleep at all. In the case of other mammals, mothers and babies require a great deal of sleep. The human baby, for example, hardly wakes during its first days except to feed. Yet the whales remain awake and on the move twenty-four hours a day, allowing them to avoid predators and helping to maintain body temperature in the newborn until it develops its insulating layer of blubber. Neonates and mothers eventually do start resting, of course, and over a period of several months the amount of time they rest increases to normal adult levels. Killer whales have apparently learned to compensate for sleep deprivation during the post-natal period but researchers do not know precisely how.

Given the closeness of the typical killer whale mother and its offspring, McMillen concluded that Splash could not have been the mother of the calf after all. He decided the calf must belong to K pod and that Splash was merely alloparenting or babysitting when he first spotted her. For the next two or three days, as McMillen continued to observe, the calf remained with the Ks, seeming to confirm that it belonged with them. But then Splash reappeared, the calf rebonded to her and as far as anyone could tell Splash turned out to be the mother after all. It is speculated that the explanation for this unusual behaviour may be that one of the K whales with whom the calf was associating, Kishka (K18), had just given birth herself to a stillborn baby and that she was lactating when she encountered Splash's calf. If that was the case, the calf might have gone off with her temporarily. Whatever the reason, this initial dissociation of the youngster from his mother was an eerie portent of what was to come.

When the whales returned to the San Juans in the spring of 2000, the young calf, now known as Luna (L98), a name chosen for him in a Seattle newspaper contest, was swimming with Splash and the rest of L pod and everything seemed normal. For the remainder of the summer there was no indication of any dysfunction in the pod, and on September 23 Luna was seen leaving the area with the rest of the matriline swimming beside his uncle, Orcan. But that was the last anyone would see of Orcan and the last sign of Luna until he showed up all alone on the far west coast of Vancouver Island the next summer. What happened?

It is not uncommon for young male whales to associate with older males. Researchers speculate that during the winter of 2000–2001 Luna may have been swimming with Orcan when the older whale died. Given that Orcan was only twenty-five years old, it was likely a catastrophic event that took his life. In fact, L pod as a whole suffered unprecedented losses during that winter. A total of five individuals from the pod disappeared forever, as compared to a typical mortality rate of up to two animals per year. Alarm bells rang on both sides of the border. It was unlikely to have been a sudden food shortage because K pod, which also leaves Puget Sound each winter, was unaffected. Had the Ls run into an oil slick, gotten entangled in fishing nets, been affected by military sonar experiments or encountered some other deadly event? No one knew, but Luna may have been a survivor of whatever had taken place. Separated from his family, he was left behind, eventually to end up in Nootka Sound where the Lazuks found him.

■

NOOTKA SOUND IS ONE OF FIVE LARGE SOUNDS that indent the west coast of Vancouver Island. The area has the landscape common to the outer coast: archipelagos of surf-beaten rock, labyrinthine channels strewn with thick beds of kelp, shorelines overhung by low branches of hemlock and cedar, all set against a backdrop of the snow-capped Vancouver Island range of mountains. The waters of the outer sound extrude into several fingerlike inlets that penetrate into the interior, their steep sides cloaked in the timber that has brought loggers to this remote spot since the 1930s. But trees were not the first natural resource to attract the attention of outsiders. It was the sea-otter trade at the end of the eighteenth century that first focussed world attention on Nootka Sound, the so-called "birthplace of British Columbia."

In March 1778, Captain James Cook, the famed British explorer, was cruising the North Pacific in search of the Northwest Passage across the top of America when he wandered into Nootka Sound. As Cook sought shelter for his two ships, *Discovery* and *Resolution*, his expedition encountered a welcoming party of local Natives. David Samwell, surgeon aboard the *Discovery*, described the scene in his journal:

> As we were coming [in] we were surrounded by thirty or forty Canoes full of Indians who expressed much astonishment at seeing the ship; they stood up in their Canoes, made many strange Motions, sometimes pointing to the shore and at other times speaking to us in a confused Manner very loud and shouting, and presently after they all sung in concert in a wild Manner ... we made Signs of Friendship to them and invited them along side the Ship where they soon ventured and behaved in a peaceable manner, offering us their Cloaths and other things they had in their Canoes, and trading immediately commenced between us.[41]

Cook anchored at a small harbour now called Resolution Cove on Bligh Island, not far from Luna's stomping grounds at Mooyah Bay. The British remained for twenty-seven days repairing their vessels, taking on wood and water and learning what they could about the surrounding area. This was the first time that Europeans had set foot in what would become British Columbia.

Through a misunderstanding in conversation with the local people, Cook decided that they called themselves *Nootka* so that is what he named them. This name stuck for many years, but in fact Nootka Sound was home to several different tribal groupings that together formed part of the Nuu-chah-nulth Nation. Nuu-chah-nulth people occupy the outer coast of Vancouver Island from Jordan River in the south to Quatsino Sound in the north and are also related to the Makah people on the Olympic Peninsula in Washington State. The word *Nuu-chah-nulth* translates as "all along the shining mountains," a reference to the spine of snow-capped peaks that runs almost the entire length of Vancouver Island and in whose western shadow the Nuu-chah-nulth live. Each tribal group had its own name and territory. Cook had anchored in the territory of the Muchalaht people but interacted mainly with the Mowachaht, who were centred at the nearby village of Yuquot, which Cook called Friendly Cove, and led by a chief named Maquinna. During the 1930s, these two groups amalgamated and today are known as the Mowachaht/Muchalaht Nations.

Cook's visit to Nootka, brief as it was, might have had little impact on the local people had it not been for the plentiful number of sea otter pelts his men obtained in trade. In Canton, China, on their way back to England, some of the British sailors sold their prime skins at a huge profit that signalled there was a fortune to be made on the Northwest Coast. By 1784, when the official account of the expedition was published, rumours of riches had already piqued the interest of the merchant community and traders were about to launch a stampede to the coast that would last for twenty-five years and seriously disrupt the lives of the Nuu-chah-nulth.

Nootka Sound was also the centre of a spirited diplomatic rivalry between Britain and Spain that was not resolved in favour of the British until 1795. But the traders didn't let that stop them. They began to arrive on the coast in increasing numbers, first from Britain, then mainly from the eastern United States. Between 1793 and 1825, when the fur business was past its peak, just over four hundred trading voyages were made to the coast.[42] Pelts were transported across the Pacific to China, where they were exchanged for tea, silk, cotton, porcelains, sugar and teak.

Initially, Nootka Sound was the centre of the otter trade. The Mowachaht obtained pelts from their own territory and by trading for them from surrounding tribes from as far away as the other side of Vancouver Island. It was not long, however, before sea otters became scarce at Nootka and the harbour lost its preeminence. Ships continued to stop there to replenish their supplies of wood and fresh water, but the trade expanded to other harbours on the west coast of Vancouver Island and then, as the coastline became more familiar, north to the Queen Charlotte Islands and the Alaskan archipelago. Nootka Sound and its Nuu-chah-nulth inhabitants were left in the wake of imperial expansion. In the end, the sea otter disappeared everywhere on the British Columbia coast and the interest of the European outsiders shifted to land-based furs such as beaver and other animals.

The Nuu-chah-nulth groups who lived in Nootka Sound seemed to follow a seasonal round of subsistence activities. They passed the stormy winter months at villages located up the protected inlets of the inner coast. In the spring they moved to the more exposed outer coast to fish, gather shellfish, and hunt waterfowl and sea mammals. Within this seasonal pattern, the people developed an elaborate material culture that depended in particular on the red cedar tree to provide the raw materials for their log canoes, their plank houses, their myriad utensils and weapons, even the clothes on their backs. Whales played a significant role for the Mowachaht, perhaps more so than in any other First Nations culture on the coast. Archaeologists tell us that sometime around AD 800 hunters at villages on Nootka Island began to pursue the giant gray whales and humpbacks that migrated offshore. Oral tradition says that these people took up whaling, dangerous as it was, because they lacked access to salmon-rich streams. Armed with long wooden harpoons tipped with heads made of giant mussel shells, the hunters paddled out onto the ocean and waited for their prey to appear.

A whaler believed that a specific whale gave itself to him, through a mysterious power. Prayer and cleansing the mind and body made the whaler worthy of the great whale's gift of life. When the whaler went out to sea and reached the place where thousands of whales were

migrating up the coast, when he got there he didn't harpoon the first whale he saw, he identified the one that he
was intended to kill. That one was looking for him, too
They recognized each other.[43]

Once the canoe was manoeuvred almost onto the back of
the animal, the harpooner stood and made his thrust. According
to John Jewitt, an American sailor who lived as a captive among
the Mowachaht for two years (1803–5), the animal belonged to
the chief.

> The whale is considered as the king's fish, and no other
> person, when he is present, is permitted to touch him
> until the royal harpoon has first drawn his blood, how-
> ever near he may approach; and it would be considered
> almost as sacrilege for any of the common people to
> strike a whale, before he is killed, particularly if any of
> the chiefs should be present.[44]

The stricken whale thrashed and sounded, towing a line
of cedar bark that connected the harpoon to a series of inflated
sealskin floats designed to tire the wounded animal. The ensu-
ing chase might last for many hours, even days, before the whale
weakened from exhaustion and loss of blood and could be
approached and killed. Then the hunters faced the gruelling task
of towing the carcass back to the village.

Not only was a whale an important source of food, oil and
bone for the villagers, the hunt itself lent prestige to the male
members of the tribe. As a result, it was surrounded by elaborate
ritual and festivity that was a unique feature of Mowachaht society. A whaling chief engaged in ritual bathing, cleansing his body
with water and scrubbing it with different plants while mimicking the behaviour of his prey. He would sing and pray and abstain
from sexual relations, sometimes for several months. When a
hunt was successful, the whale carcass was butchered on the
beach and shared among the members of the tribe, again amidst
great ritual. The focus of much of this ceremonial activity was
a unique shrine, known as the Whalers' Shrine or the Whalers'

Washing House. Located on a small island in Jewitt Lake on Nootka Island, just a few minutes' walk from Yuquot, it was an assemblage of human skulls and wooden carvings, some of whales and some of human figures, that were used as part of the ritual magic associated with the whale hunt. In 1904 the shrine was sold under questionable circumstances to the American Museum of Natural History and shipped to New York City where it has remained ever since, for the most part out of public view.[45] The Mowachaht/Muchalaht consider the removal of the Whalers' Shrine a serious blow to the spiritual life of their community. In 1991 a delegation of Mowachaht/Muchalaht travelled to New York to view the elements of the shrine, which they found stored away in drawers in the museum's basement, and a process began by which the people hope to reclaim the shrine and place it back in their territory.

According to the anthropologist Philip Drucker, the people considered killer whales (*kaka-win*) too difficult to catch, though apprentice hunters pursued them as a form of practice.[46] The Nuu-chah-nulth respected killer whales as the guardians of the laws of the sea. In his book *Living on the Edge*, Chief Earl Maquinna George relates that his people did not hunt the *kaka-win* for food because it had spiritual powers. In particular it was able to go onto dry land and transform into a wolf.[47] Like the Kwakwaka'wakw, the Nuu-chah-nulth believed that sometimes killer whales carry the spirits of the departed, especially chiefs. As it happened, just a few days before Luna appeared in Nootka Sound, Chief Ambrose Maquinna of the Mowachaht First Nation passed away. Shortly before his death, the chief had reportedly either expressed a wish to return as a *kaka-win* or had predicted he would do so. In July 2002 Ambrose's son, Mike Maquinna, who had succeeded his father as chief, announced that it was his family's wish that Luna be named *Tsu'xiit* in honour of Ambrose. Whether or not the chief's death and Luna's appearance were related, the coincidence would prove to be vital in the developing discussions over the whale's future.

■

ONCE SPRINGER SEEMED WELL ESTABLISHED in her home territory, attention shifted to Luna. To an outsider, the situations of the two animals seemed identical. Based on the success of the Springer relocation, why would a similar effort to "rescue" Luna not be a straightforward decision to make? To the research community and to government officials, however, Luna was an entirely different case. Springer had been a sick animal which had meandered out of her normal range into a very public area with little or no chance that, in the normal course of events, she would be exposed to members of her natal population. Her mother was dead and if something had not been done, it was fairly certain that Springer would have died as well. Luna, on the other hand, was healthy and in a fairly isolated location where boat traffic and human interference initially did not appear to pose a problem. He was apparently feeding on pilchard, a sardine-like fish, extremely rich in oil, that had been the focus of an important fishery from the mid-1920s until the mid-1940s. Pilchard reduction plants, where the catch was rendered into fish meal and oil, operated at several locations in Nootka Sound during this period. The fishery collapsed in 1947 as a result of overfishing and changes in ocean temperature, but since the 1990s pilchard stocks have been rebuilding on the West Coast. Pilchards were probably sustaining Luna between salmon runs. DFO officials also believed there was a chance that the whale might leave Nootka Sound as he had arrived, under his own steam; it was unlikely, but not impossible. What's more, any plan to move Luna would involve relocating him to Juan de Fuca Strait or Puget Sound, areas of high vessel traffic where he might get into serious trouble if the relocation did not "take." This was the reverse of the Springer situation, in which the animal had to be removed from a high-traffic situation for her own safety. For all these reasons, officials felt less pressure to intervene with Luna and saw fewer grounds on which an intervention could be justified legally, scientifically or practicably.

Nonetheless, by August 2002, basking in the euphoria of Springer's successful release, some people began to suggest a similar rescue scenario for Luna. The calf was then almost three years old and had been alone in Nootka Sound for more than a year. Word had spread about the little whale. Boaters ventured into the area to have a look and some locals visited him regularly. That summer the DFO posted signs in Gold River warning recreational boaters to keep clear and arranged with a Victoria group called the Marine Mammal Monitoring Project, known more familiarly as M3, to keep an eye on Luna. M3's job was to educate the public about the whale and the need to give it space, and to intervene when sightseers got too close. M3 began sending pairs of monitors to Mooyah Bay at the beginning of August. The first pair had only been on the water in their Zodiac for a few minutes when they encountered the whale and found out for themselves how uninhibited and playful he had become with boaters. Luna nudged their boat, spun it around like a toy in a bathtub, bounced it up and down by pushing on the hull and spy-hopped directly in front to keep it from speeding away. It was not the behaviour of a wild animal shying from human contact. As the summer progressed, he became more insistent in his interactions and harder for boaters to escape. At the same time, boaters became more inventive in their excuses why they were stopped in the vicinity of the calf. It was surprising to the monitors how many people experienced "engine trouble" exactly where they knew the whale to be.

Initially, Luna kept to a well-defined area that included Mooyah Bay and the entrance to Muchalat Inlet. But by early September monitors reported him swimming well outside this zone, including visits for the first time to the docks at the mouth of the Gold River at the head of Muchalat Inlet, perhaps following the run of salmon. Luna had also taken to tagging along beside the *Uchuck III*, a former World War II minesweeper that ferries supplies

■ The *Uchuck III* is a coastal freighter working out of Gold River taking passengers and supplies to destinations around Nootka Sound and beyond. Luna became particularly attached to it. *Lance Barrett-Lennard*

and passengers from the Gold River dock to the remote communities and camps that are sprinkled throughout Nootka Sound. Disturbingly, the M3 monitors noticed marks on Luna's back that looked like injuries from a propeller, and other scrapes and blemishes appeared regularly. The level of marine traffic, even into September, was substantial, including water taxis, the *Uchuck*, tugs, float planes, boats associated with logging operations and fish boats of various types, not to mention recreational boaters, and even canoeists and kayakers. Unconfirmed rumours circulated about sightseers holding babies over Luna's open jaws to snap photographs and feeding him beer and snack foods. As one of the monitors observed, "the level of interference that continues, regardless of our presence on the water ... makes it clear that as long as Luna is here, his interaction with boats and interpreted 'friendliness' will be exploited and his future jeopardized."[48] The monitors were there to see that this didn't happen, but it was ironic that one of the best ways they found to steer Luna away from other boats was to attract him to their own. DFO officials began to worry that the presence of the monitors might actually be encouraging Luna to become habituated to people. The M3 people recognized the paradox themselves. As one of them recorded in the project journal, "I have mixed feelings this morning. It feels weird to deny him [Luna] any contact. He seems so lonely, but it doesn't feel right to interact with him either or to allow/encourage others to do so. And it was weird to discourage others by engaging him ourselves. It's confusing."[49] This ambivalence was typical of so many people who were attracted by the whale's vulnerability and sociability even as they knew that for the animal's well-being they should keep their distance.

The M3 monitoring ended in mid-September with the situation as ambiguous as ever. Three weeks later the DFO organized a scientific panel to advise it on Luna's long-term future. The government was reluctant to make a precipitous move. As Marilyn Joyce explained to the Washington State-based NGO Orca Network in a letter dated October 11, 2002, "we are very concerned that if L98 were moved and failed to connect with his pod, he might be faced with spending the winter in a less desirable location than his current one, both in terms of food availability and increased human interference. At this time, L98 is healthy and in a good, clean environment with plenty of food. The monitoring program by the M3 program that was established over the busiest summer months was successful in reducing the inappropriate human interactions with L98. Nootka Sound is a very isolated inlet on the West Coast of Vancouver Island and it is expected that human interference will be minimal over the winter."[50] But the Orca Network disagreed. In his response on behalf of the organization, Doug McCutcheon noted that Nootka Sound was not so out-of-the-way that Luna had not been involved in numerous troubling incidents with boaters during the previous summer. McCutcheon also pointed out the pollution problems related to the former pulp mill and accused DFO of ignoring the risks posed by Luna's interactions with boats, hoping that the whale would "just go away." Without specifying exactly what he wanted the DFO to do, he accused it of dereliction of its obligations and hinted at a hidden agenda to capture Luna permanently for an aquarium.[51]

As the letter from the Orca Network indicated, Luna was fast turning into the biggest challenge of Marilyn Joyce's career. Joyce had begun working for the DFO as a young biologist in 1986, and after several years in the field she had gravitated to the management side of the department, dealing with conservation issues relating to different fish species. Marine mammals had been an early interest, though, so she was excited to take up the position as the DFO's marine mammal coordinator in the summer of 2001, just a few months before Springer appeared in Puget Sound. It was a classic case of being careful what you wish for. Almost immediately she was thrust into the complex negotiations that preceded Springer's return to Johnstone Strait. As difficult as that episode was, it turned out to be far less complicated than the web of interests and intrigue that spun itself around Luna. "It was probably the most complex operation I've ever been involved in," Joyce would say about Luna's relocation, after the project fell apart. First, she faced the decision about what to do with the whale. Once that was made, there was the need to coordinate many different organizations, under intense media scrutiny and constant criticism from people who did not trust the DFO to do the right thing. Joyce had to co-operate with American government officials, somehow find enough dollars in a budget that had no money earmarked for animal rescue, appease a series of activist NGOs (not to mention her own bosses) and negotiate with the local First Nations people. In the end, it would be her failure to manage the last of these that would jeopardize the entire operation.

In the winter of 2002–2003 did not convene its panel of experts until February. The panel, chaired by Joyce, included representatives from the DFO, Vancouver Aquarium, OrcaLab, the US National Marine Fisheries Service and the Puget Sound research community. By a strange coincidence, on the same day the panel held its first discussions (February 12), the *National Post* reported that the RCMP in Gold River had charged a local woman with harassing Luna. It was the first time the charge had ever been laid in the province and it came after repeated attempts by the police to stop people from gathering on the dock at the river's mouth to touch and feed Luna. The whale, a more-than-willing participant in these games, had taken to hanging around the dock looking for company. "We have heard of people swimming with him," reported RCMP Corporal Jacquie Olsen, "dangling children in his mouth ... There was a report of people going down to the dock after the bar emptied out and trying to feed him beer and stuff something in his blow hole ... It's got to the point where people feel they have the right to do what they want with him. And of course they don't."[52] A co-owner of the local float plane company, Lorraine Howatt, reported seeing as many as seventy-five gawkers at a time on the dock wanting to see the whale. She expressed a fear that was growing among everyone who cared about Luna. "What happens if he sees a kayak and gives it a nudge? What happens if he kills someone? Remember in the sixties when people in the national parks were getting out of their cars to feed the bears? Then the bears were killing people around Banff and Jasper, and then the bears got shot. That will be Luna's fate if this goes on."[53] (In May the woman, Sandra Lynne Bohn, pleaded guilty to the charge of disturbing a killer whale and was fined one hundred dollars.)

Despite the growing climate of concern, members of the scientific panel believed they had the luxury of time. They did not want to be rushed into a decision by public pressure. Instead, they wanted to come up with a formal process for assessing risks and managing the situation. Officials were aware of the escalating interactions between Luna and curious members of the public but they also saw the downside of intervention. Would they be putting the animal at greater risk by moving it than by leaving it alone? Wouldn't it be better to manage the human side of the equation by policing the interactions and leave the animal alone? John Ford expressed some of the concerns that the panel had. "People are making a lot of assumptions," he said. "But I'm not completely convinced his [Luna's] separation was an accident. Maybe there's something wrong with him and he was rejected by his pod. Or perhaps he didn't want to be with them anymore. We just don't know. We'd all like to see him back in his pod but we don't want to inadvertently put him in a worse predicament than he's in now. And there's a real possibility of that happening if we don't think this through properly."[54] It was still not beyond the realm of possibility that during the next summer Luna's pod might arrive in Nootka Sound and save everyone a lot of trouble.

It may seem strange for Ford to suggest that animals as social as killer whales would reject one of their own, but in fact the social dynamics of the killer whale pod are not entirely understood. Harald Yurk, one of Ford's graduate students and a research associate at the Vancouver Aquarium, observes that resident killer whales in a location where food is easily obtained are quite capable of living on their own; they simply don't want to. So what might account for Luna's solitary situation? Yurk wonders if some traumatic event separated him from his family. Did his mother think he was dead and leave him behind? Or did Luna have trouble fitting in with the group for some reason? While an individual derives benefits from belonging to a group, Yurk speculates, so the group must derive some benefit from having an individual as a member. "In human society we have laws that are enforced by a police force," he points out, "and there are social rules that are enforced by everybody. These rules most likely exist in killer whale society as well." Researchers are not aware of any instances of a young whale being rejected by its group for violating social norms but that does not mean it could not happen. One possibility is that Luna may not have learned a sufficient number of calls to allow him to function as a member of the group. The scientists asked themselves whether the group would even accept Luna back, given that the other members would have to teach him how to adapt. Among such intensely social animals, it would not necessarily be the mother who would decide Luna's fate. Instead, the group as a whole might conclude from an instinctual cost-benefit analysis that the young whale was a drain on resources. If Luna was transported to the south and, like Springer, released to members of his family, scientists had to consider the possibility, even the likelihood, that he would be rejected—and rejected in the glare of world publicity. This time there might be no Hollywood ending. And even if the other whales accepted Luna back, would it be possible for him to make up the deficit of learning that he had suffered because he was absent from the group for so long? Springer had only been on her own for perhaps six months, but by the summer of 2003, Luna would have been alone in Nootka Sound for at least two years. Questions like these brought the experts up against the limits of their knowledge and made it difficult for them to recommend what to do.

Another concern shared by some of the experts was that Luna, who had become used to interacting with boats and people, might transfer his "bad habits" to the other members of his family group should he be reunited with them. In the case of Springer, monitors had seen the other whales take her in hand following her release and stop her from approaching boats. But there have been other instances when one or two whales have "taught" others to engage in learned behaviour. A notable case involved killer whales in Alaska and the longline fishery for Alaska black cod. The whales learned to distinguish the sound of the lines being hauled into the boat. Like a dinner bell, the sound attracted the whales, which stripped the fish from the hooks as they came to the surface. In the beginning, just a few whales were observed feeding this way but soon these few had taught the others. In Marineland in Ontario a young killer whale was

seen setting a seagull trap. He would spit a fish onto the surface of the pool, then submerge and wait for an unsuspecting
gull to appear. When it did, he lunged. Within a few months he
had taught his brother and his mother to play the same game.
"It was once believed that most animal behavior, from the food
they ate to the places they slept, was based on instinct," said
Michael Noonan, a professor of animal behavior at Canisius Col-
lege. "This new discovery supports the growing view that animals like killer whales are very prone to learning by imitation,
and that they are 'cultural' in nature."[55] All of these observations
raised concerns that when he returned to live among the southern
residents, Luna might teach the other whales to interact with
boats, with disastrous results.

Yet another concern stemmed from the fact that Luna was
a male. Before too long he would start to become amorous.
Some researchers worried that he would "come on" to objects
in his environment, having no other whale to approach. From
observations in aquariums, it was known that when young
killer whales become sexually aroused they are very rambunc-
tious: breaching, flopping about on the surface, charging other
whales and rubbing up against objects. The erect penis of a
killer whale may reach almost two metres in length and when
it appears it causes acute interest and often embarrassment
among aquarium visitors. Parents with young children are very
creative when it comes to explaining what is on show. Clint
Wright recalls on one occasion hearing a mother explaining to
her youngster that the penis was a tube by which the mother
fed her young. On another occasion, as Vancouver Aquarium
staff waited tensely for Bjossa, a female killer whale, to give
birth, a volunteer excitedly reported on her two-way radio that
she could see the baby emerging. It turned out she was watching Finna, the male killer whale, having an erection. The volunteer was so embarrassed by her mistake that she fled the
building and never returned. In the case of Luna, the experts
wondered whether, if he remained solitary as he matured, he

would channel his sexual aggressiveness toward boats, with potentially dire consequences.

There were other, deeper issues at play in terms of killer whale sexuality. Mating among killer whales is the choice of the female. So-called "coercive mating" (rape, in human terms) is fairly common among other mammal species but is difficult, if not impossible, among whales. The physical structure of the animal, notably its absence of arms and hands, and the environment in which it lives, simply do not allow it. "Mating among killer whales is like refuelling a jet plane in mid-air," is how Lance Barrett-Lennard puts it. It is all but impossible to accomplish without an elaborate choreography involving the co-operation of both partners. At the same time, studies carried out by Barrett-Lennard indicate that among the northern resident killer whales, it is mostly older males that succeed in fathering viable calves. The average life expectancy of a male killer whale is twenty-nine years and most whales that succeed in siring offspring are in their middle to late twenties. Barrett-Lennard speculates that if females are choosing who to mate with, there is logic to their choice of older males. By choosing older males, the females ensure that fathers will not be alive when their daughters reach mating age themselves. A female whale in a family group "knows" her siblings and "knows" her mother but she has no idea who her father is and, given the small size of the resident population, could easily end up mating with him if he is still around. The choice of older partners turns out to be a way that females avoid inbreeding.

Not all male killer whales enjoy the same reproductive success. Most females produce offspring but the reproductivity of males is more skewed. Some males are very successful reproductively speaking; others father few if any offspring and contribute almost nothing to the gene pool. This is true of almost all animal populations. The scientists had to wonder whether Luna, if he was returned to his group, would turn out to be reproductively successful. If he was not going to benefit the southern resident population by fathering calves or fostering the survival of the group, then from a conservation perspective, his own survival was irrelevant. But surely Luna's sexual future was impossible to predict? Perhaps, but given that Luna had grown up on his own apart from the group, it seemed to Barrett-Lennard there was little chance he would turn out to be socialized enough to master the complex behaviours males use to make themselves attractive to females. For some of the scientists on the panel, no matter how they felt about Luna as an individual whale, it was hard to make a case that returning him to his family was vital to the future of the population.

■

THE CONSENSUS THAT EMERGED from the February 2003 meeting of the advisory panel, to the extent that there was one, was that Luna would probably have to be moved but at the moment there were too many unknowns to make a definite plan. For a start, the DFO wanted to determine with certainty the state of the animal's health. The Vancouver Aquarium agreed to send a team to Nootka Sound to try to obtain a blood sample and make other observations, as they had done with Springer. Early in March, Clint Wright, Lance Barrett-Lennard, the veterinarian Dave Huff and Brian Sheehan, the Aquarium's curator of marine mammals, arrived in Gold River.

Motorists reach the village of Gold River by driving west across Vancouver Island from Campbell River. The highway passes through Strathcona Provincial Park, with its scenic views of Upper Campbell Lake and the dramatic snow-capped peak of the Golden Hinde, the highest mountain on the island. The instant community of Gold River was created in 1965 to provide homes for workers at a nearby pulp mill. It is located on the river fourteen kilometres inland from the head of Muchalat Inlet. The mill, owned initially by the East Asiatic Company, was built at the mouth of the river on land belonging to the Muchalaht band. At about the same time, the mid-1960s, the Mowachaht/Muchalaht decided to move from Yuquot to a former village site near the mill, called A'haminaquus. Relocation placed the people closer to schools, jobs and health care but the promised economic benefits did not occur and the site proved to be an environmental disaster. In 1996 the people relocated again, to the newly built community of Tsaxana, north of Gold River village. The mill operated until 1998, when its closure left the economic future of the area up in the air. At the time of Luna's arrival, Gold River was trying to reinvent itself as a retirement community and a hub for west coast tourism. Naturally some local people thought the presence of a "tame" killer whale might be the sort of tourist attraction for which they were looking.

Muchalat Inlet extends about fifteen kilometres from the mouth of the Gold River, where the docks, a seaplane float and a log-booming ground are located, out to Nootka Sound. From there a boat still has to travel another fifteen kilometres or so through the sound before reaching the open ocean. The Aquarium team jumped into a DFO Zodiac at the Gold River dock and a fisheries officer hurried them out into the inlet to look for Luna. It was a beautiful, sunny day and they found him without much trouble halfway down the inlet. Luna swam right over to the boat, wanting to be touched and played with. It looked as if they would have no trouble obtaining their blood sample.

Dave Huff deployed his apparatus, consisting of a hypodermic needle, a long tube and a syringe, the same equipment used on Springer. The killer whale has an artery running up its dorsal fin and a great deal of skill is required to locate it. Leaning out over the animal, Huff moved the needle slowly forward from the trailing edge of the fin near the base until he sensed he was at the right spot, at which point he inserted it. Huff hit the artery on his first try. But he wasn't able to adjust the depth of the needle because Luna was moving. Luna had not reacted to the needle going in but when Huff began pulling it out, the needle bent, causing the whale to flinch. From that point on, Luna understood what they were up to and refused to co-operate, shying away whenever he saw the needle. On the whole, the animal looked healthy. His skin was clear; his breath and teeth were clean; he looked a good weight; and there was no sign of any infection. It was a far cry from the state in which Springer had been found just over a year earlier. As the afternoon waned, the team decided to lure the whale back to the Gold River dock, where they hoped to have more luck. Luna followed happily enough but he was no more co-operative. Wright managed to get the needle in once more but Luna immediately jerked free and swam away into deep water, where he remained.

The team collected a few eyewitness stories about Luna's involvement with local boats; the most unsettling account was from Nootka Air's Lorraine Howatt, who told them the whale had started approaching float planes to rub on their pontoons. Howatt said that Luna sometimes approached incoming planes as they were touching down, raising the possibility that one might strike him and crash. By this time it was clear to the team that they were not going to obtain a blood sample by leaning over the side of a boat with a syringe so they returned to Vancouver to make a report. While the NGOs and scientists had all reached the conclusion that some form of intervention was going to be necessary, there was no consensus on what that form would be.

On May 29 Marilyn Joyce called together the scientific panel for another meeting at which she told the members that later that day the DFO would be announcing that it was not prepared to intervene with Luna but would continue monitoring his situation in Nootka Sound. Government officials felt Luna's health was good, he was eating and there was no obvious threat to his well-being, so there was no justification for intervention. They also believed that there were several factors that mitigated against a successful reintroduction of Luna to his natal group. As Harald Yurk explained, there was a possibility that Luna was a "loner" and would not be welcomed back or would not actually want to return to his family. In this case he might well end up in a worse situation, not a better one. Moving him also meant transferring him from an environment where he had learned to thrive to one that would be completely new and where he would have to learn all over again how to feed himself. Lastly, the officials were concerned that if they moved Luna to a site closer to the southern resident population of whales, they might be exacerbating the problem of his interactions with people, not solving it. Barrett-Lennard explained:

We are obviously concerned about public safety as well as the well-being of the whale and there's some real concern about him in Nootka Sound, but it would likely be worse elsewhere for two reasons. One is there would likely be more people in other areas than where he is now. Secondly, the public education in Nootka Sound has been very successful. People are interacting less with him now than they were a few months ago. So if he goes where people are more naïve, where boaters are not expecting him and are less savvy about what to do, then they are more at risk. It's not a good thing for him or for them.[56]

At this point, May 2003, Springer had not yet returned to Johnstone Strait with her family after the winter, so scientists were not as confident about the relocation process as they would be a few months later.

The DFO had solicited input from the advisors, but this was a decision its officials reached themselves and it did not please all members of the panel, some of whom would have preferred to see at least a limited intervention. For instance, Nootka Sound was a popular spot with sea kayakers and there was concern about Luna accidentally flipping a kayak. Perhaps steps could be taken to teach the whale to leave kayaks alone. Paul Spong, a member of the panel, worried that if an accident occurred the public pressure to do something immediately would be intense and the government might have to act when it was not the best time to do so. Better, Spong thought, to develop a plan to move the whale before disaster struck, not after. Some participants in the discussions were thinking that it might be possible to "walk"

Luna back to his home territory. This would involve teaching him to follow a boat, which would then lead him down the west coast of Vancouver Island and into Puget Sound, or at least close to his group. The trouble with this plan and one of the reasons why the DFO rejected it, at least for the time being, was that it required making Luna even more attached to boats and people than he was. But American activists in Puget Sound were growing restless. They wanted "their" whale back and they thought Canadian officials were simply afraid of failing.[57]

Everyone wanted what was best for the whale but there was little consensus about what that was. Those who favoured moving Luna thought the Canadian government was dragging its heels. Some even suspected there was a hidden agenda to ultimately take the animal into captivity. DFO officials felt it would be a mistake to move the whale out of what they saw as a manageable situation in Nootka Sound to an unknown and possibly more dangerous situation in the south. The DFO did not want to take Luna into captivity but feared that captivity might end up being the only recourse if an ill-thought-out relocation plan went sour. What the NGOs and the government scientists failed to appreciate at the time was that they had one thing in common — they were all outsiders to Nootka Sound. The Mowachaht/ Muchalaht people, who had lived in the area for centuries, had their own ideas about what should be done. For the moment they were keeping their own counsel but when they chose to enter the debate it would have a dramatic impact on Luna's future in the sound.

7 ▪ PLANNING FOR RELOCATION

LUNA COMMENCED HIS THIRD SUMMER in Nootka Sound (2003) by hijacking a party of sport fishermen and holding them captive. The incident proved to be a warning to officials at the DFO that perhaps their hands-off, wait-and-see approach was not going to work after all. The four boaters, one of whom was Darlene and Fred Lazuk's son, Chris, were on their way back to Gold River in mid-June after a day's fishing when they ran out of gas. They were paddling for shore when Luna showed up, ready to play. He good-naturedly treated the 5.6-metre vessel like a large beach ball, nudging it with his head and making it spin in circles by thrashing his flukes. He even managed to get hold of a rope and towed the boat away from shore just far enough to prolong the fun. This went on all night, until a passing prawn fisherman rescued the exhausted foursome early the next morning.[58] In retrospect the incident was a bit of a joke. At no point did the fishermen fear for their safety—they knew by now that Luna meant no harm—but it indicated how practised he had become in his interactions with people. The incident inaugurated a summer of such encounters, each one carrying the potential for a catastrophe that most observers expected to happen sooner or later.

The monitors from M3 had returned to Nootka Sound, staying mainly at the Gold River dock, where they reminded people who arrived to get a look at Luna not to touch or otherwise

■ This boat needed a tow after Luna damaged its steering. Luna can be seen continuing to play around the vessel. Obviously it took a lot to discourage him. *Ed Thorburn*

harass the animal. Renamed the Luna Stewardship Project, this group did its best to police the situation but public interest in Luna was just too strong. People could not resist the opportunity to encounter a whale in the wild, especially one that was so active and friendly. They found it difficult to believe that it was wrong to engage with an animal so obviously seeking human contact. Thirty years earlier, people would have been frightened to get close to the "killer" whale. Now everyone thought he was harmless, like a large pet. In a sense Luna was paying the price for the domestication of the image of the killer whale that had occurred over the previous three or four decades.

Luna spent a lot of his time at the dock, hemming in boats and not allowing them to depart. He was still approaching float

■ Luna's attraction to float plane rudders was a particular concern. *Hal Nelson*

planes to rub against their pontoons. Although the whale had become a magnet for tourists, the mayor of Gold River, Dave Lewis, told journalists that he wanted Luna moved. "Someone is going to get hurt," he warned.[59] On July 12 media reports revealed that a DFO contract employee was under investigation for allegedly hitting Luna with a board. It was said that the employee had lost his temper when he couldn't get the animal away from his boat. (The man was later exonerated by the court.) In August a commercial fisherman from Vancouver was fined $ 250 for touching Luna at the Gold River dock. These incidents drove home the realization that, in Clint Wright's words, "managing the people was more the problem than managing the whale."

Aside from making trouble at the dock, Luna continued to be drawn to boats out in the inlet, especially sailboats, which were slower and were easier for him to keep pace with. He discovered that he could break off their transducers, small

■ These boaters near the Gold River dock were typical of the many curious people who wanted to see and interact with Luna.
Vancouver Aquarium

mechanisms on the hull that measure speed or depth and send a signal to a display in the cockpit. These instruments emit a whirring noise, which is probably what attracted Luna's attention. Ed Thorburn, the DFO officer, reported that Luna had bitten the transducers from about thirty boats, and these were only the ones Thorburn had heard about. Luna also took to bumping rudders, perhaps realizing that if he disabled a boat it would be unable to get away from him. In contrast, he seemed to have a healthy respect for propellers and only infrequently suffered injuries from them, given how often he was rubbing up against moving boats. Still, he did make the occasional mistake. In August he was struck by a propeller that opened a small gash in his head. The boat was trolling for salmon at a low speed so the injury was not serious. A week later, another cut appeared, probably sustained when he pushed up against the rudders of a seaplane or was slashed by another boat propeller. When these incidents became public, they increased both the concern about Luna's safety and the pressure on the DFO to do something. Marilyn Joyce reported receiving more than one thousand emails about Luna and constant calls from the media. "The whole issue has reached a fevered pitch!" wrote one exasperated DFO official.[60]

The American NGOs, led by the Orca Conservancy, stepped up their campaign to force the hand of the Canadian government. The Conservancy's Michael Harris came to Nootka Sound and announced that his organization was prepared to raise the money necessary to pay the costs of taking Luna "home." In Campbell River, a woman named Gail Laurie had become interested in Luna. On a visit to Gold River to see the whale she was dismayed to witness people touching him, spraying him with water and feeding him snack foods. Laurie knew the situation was dangerous for the whale. After contacting Paul Spong for advice, she set up a website, ReuniteLuna.com, to inform people and to ask for help. Laurie devoted every waking minute that she wasn't working at her job at the Campbell River hospital to the website and to attempts to rally support for her belief that Luna needed to be reunited with his family. She was convinced that if only the experts got together they would come up with a way to help the lost animal. She searched the internet herself for organizations and individuals that had anything to do with whales, then contacted them to tell them about Luna. Laurie and her website became a main source of information about Luna, as well as a sounding board for local people who wished to vent their frustrations about the whale and his interference with boaters.

The DFO's Marilyn Joyce felt herself to be seated painfully on the horns of a dilemma. She recognized that following a policy of non-intervention no longer seemed possible. There were too many people interacting with Luna to make simple monitoring effective. An accident was waiting to happen. And activists on both sides of the border were mobilizing public opinion in favour of government action. However, Joyce believed that intervention carried a high probability of failure. For any number of reasons, Luna might not reunite with or even locate his family group. If that happened, the animal would probably have to be recaptured for his own safety, an outcome that Joyce knew would be very unpopular with the public. Through all this, the Vancouver Aquarium tried to keep aloof from the controversy while remaining ready to provide its expertise if asked. The Aquarium board's financial committee was wary of getting involved in an open-ended exercise that might turn out to be a long-term drain on its budget. The Springer experience had demonstrated that it was expensive to intervene in nature. Committee members feared that the Aquarium would be left paying the bill not just for an intervention but for an intervention that might remain unresolved for a long time. If Luna was relocated but didn't reattach to his pod, or if his health declined, what would be the Aquarium's responsibility? If he presented a danger to the public after translocation and had to be recaptured, it was clear that many of the NGOs would blame the Aquarium.

During the summer the idea of carrying out a "natural relocation" gained some traction. Michael Harris was promoting the idea and Chief Mike Maquinna of the Mowachaht/Muchalaht was reportedly in support. "Natural relocation" involved leading Luna by boat down the outside coast of Vancouver Island to an area where he might be expected to encounter his natal pod. "Natural" in this sense meant the animal would be swimming free the whole way and not confined in a pen or transported by boat or truck. The plan appealed because of its apparent simplicity. It did not require elaborate capture plans or equipment. Advocates of this approach believed it could happen quickly, possibly as soon as that fall, and many people felt it was urgent to get Luna away from Nootka Sound sooner rather than later. Natural relocation also appealed to activists who feared that any capture was a prelude to permanent captivity. Members of this group generally felt there was little to lose by trying.

But the plan made little sense to fisheries officials and

whale scientists, the people who would be held accountable if the attempt failed. First of all, it involved training Luna to follow a boat. This was exactly contrary to all the attempts that had been made to discourage his attachment to humans. Once he learned to follow boats, he wasn't simply going to forget about them. He was likely to become even more playful, only this time in an area of high traffic volume where an accident was almost assuredly going to occur. It was also a long way down the coast, about three hundred kilometres from Nootka Sound to the Victoria area. The weather was unpredictable and the waters treacherous. There was no guarantee that Luna would not stray from the boat or get lost, leaving him in a more precarious situation than he was at present. Finally, there was little expectation that the plan was even feasible. Ed Thorburn had been experimenting with Luna, trying to lure him out to the mouth of Nootka Sound so that he could be there if his family came past. Luna was very reluctant to venture that far and seemed definitely opposed to crossing the invisible line joining Escalante Point to Nootka Island. Thorburn concluded there was no way that Luna would follow a boat out of the sound into the open ocean.

No one spent more time in Luna's company than Thorburn. Born in Newfoundland in 1946, he had migrated to the West Coast following university graduation. He ended up in Campbell River working for the Bank of Montreal, then ran his own small construction company before he began training as a fisheries officer in 1986. By the time Luna showed up, Thorburn was field supervisor for the Nootka Sound area, working out of offices in Gold River and Tahsis. He began keeping an eye on the whale as part of his duties, trying to discourage boaters from interacting with the animal. Typical of the kind of thing people were doing was an incident involving kayakers in Mooyah Bay. When Thorburn arrived at the scene in his Zodiac, he found Luna, all fifteen hundred kilograms of him, looming up out of the water next to a kayak while the woman paddler inno-

■ DFO official Ed Thorburn at his desk. *Courtesy Ed Thorburn*

cently rubbed his nose. Thorburn had to explain to the woman
how dangerous this was, not to mention illegal. It took twenty
minutes to disengage Luna so the kayak could reach shore. On
another occasion Luna came up underneath the stern of a kayak
and gently lifted it clear of the water, then laid it back down again
without disturbing anything but the paddler's peace of mind.
Incidents such as these convinced Thorburn that someone was
going to get hurt. He could see Luna's behaviour changing as he
became more acclimated to boats. At first Luna had been merely
curious and would not remain around a boat for long. As time
passed he spent longer and longer with boats, actually seeking
them out to play with, nudging them and pushing them around.
Eventually he began trying to disable the vessels by butting their
rudders or biting off their transducers. As time passed Thorburn
developed a deep empathy for the whale. From the vantage point
of someone who was out on the water witnessing Luna's antics,
he was convinced the animal had to be moved back to his family,

and the sooner the better.

On September 10, amid growing public pressure and con-flicting points of view, the DFO reconvened its scientific panel. Many panel members were irritated at the way the DFO and its senior officials in Ottawa seemed to be exploiting them. Earlier, the panel had recommended intervention, albeit reluctantly, and the DFO had ignored its advice. Now Ottawa seemed to want the panel to rubber-stamp its belated decision to move the whale. The decisions Ottawa was taking seemed to many panel mem-bers to be based on politics, not the interests of the whale.

Marilyn Joyce informed the panel that because of the increased interactions between Luna and boats that summer, the department had changed its mind and now believed the public and the whale were at risk. The DFO was ready to autho-rize an intervention if a workable plan could be devised. She asked the panel to advise her not only about how an interven-tion might take place but also about contingency plans should relocation fail. In other words, the DFO wanted to know under what circumstances Luna would have to be captured and either put in captivity or, *in extremis*, euthanized. Members of the panel agreed that some sort of relocation was necessary given that the situation in Gold River had become untenable. At a second meeting, on September 17, the panel agreed to a plan that would see Luna captured in a pen, as Springer had been, and moved by truck or boat to Pedder Bay near Victoria, the same bay in which Chimo and four other transient whales had been captured thirty-three years earlier. There a reunion with L pod would be attempted. By early October, the final elements of the plan were in place and the DFO invited applications for a licence to carry it out. Initially, both the DFO and the American government said they did not have any funds in their budgets to pay for the project and that it was up to private organizations to come up with the money. In other words, both governments expected a licensee to fund the operation while they sat on the sidelines directing the show and possibly imposing conditions that would ratchet up the costs. At the end of October, the US National Marine Fisheries Service suddenly announced it would make at least a hundred thousand US dollars available, a gesture that was then exactly matched by the Canadian government. It was no surprise to anyone when the proposal submitted by the Vancouver Aquarium was accepted. With the success of the Springer relocation, the Aquarium had proven it had the expertise to carry out such a difficult project.

With money on the table and a plan in place, the relocation looked like an immediate go. But so much time had been spent ironing out the details that the window of opportunity had closed for another winter. Everyone involved agreed to wait until the spring of 2004, when members of Luna's family would be in the right spot and Luna himself would have ample time to find them and, it was hoped, readjust to a life among whales.

■

IN THE LATE FALL OF 2003, once the DFO had announced that any attempt to relocate Luna would wait until the following spring, a number of people in the NGO community were concerned about what was going to happen to Luna over the winter. The scientists among them also felt there was an opportunity to collect data about the whale's behaviour. These discussions included OrcaLab's Paul Spong, a member of the panel advising the DFO. Spong was extremely disappointed that the agency had not come up with a plan to move Luna that fall, but given that the whale was not going anywhere, he and his wife Helena Symonds offered to put together a research project to study and monitor him. Lisa Lamb, the operator of a whale-watching company out of San Juan Island, found a boat, the *Henrietta*, an old fisheries patrol vessel built to look like a Columbia River gill-netter, and Spong asked two of OrcaLab's research assistants, Lisa Larsson and David Howitt, to take part in the project. By March 2004, the Luna Research Project had obtained a scientific licence from the DFO. At this point Spong and his team sat down with Chief Mike Maquinna to explain what they intended to do and ultimately the Mowachaht/Muchalaht endorsed the project.

In keeping with OrcaLab's commitment to non-intrusive monitoring, the plan was to establish a pair of observation posts—one on a cliff overlooking the Gold River dock and the other on the north side of the entrance to Muchalat Inlet—and to use remote hydrophones to record Luna. The *Henrietta* was used as a ferry between these locations and also as accommodation for the researchers. As it turned out, David Howitt's stay in Nootka Sound was limited. Howitt, a native of Cornwall on the coast of England, was a veteran environmental activist who had worked for several years with the Sea Shepherd Society campaigning against whaling and the driftnet fishery. In 1992 he came to Hanson Island, where he became involved with OrcaLab, eventually working on the "Free Corky" campaign and then helping with the lab's live internet broadcast, Orca Live. Howitt was at Dong Chong Bay when Springer arrived and recorded her vocalizations. When ReuniteLuna and OrcaLab decided to launch the Luna Research Project in Nootka Sound, he helped to move the *Henrietta* up from Friday Harbor and install the hydrophones. But Immigration Canada had never allowed him to remain permanently in the country and on this occasion restricted his stay to no longer than a month. That meant Larsson had to carry on the research by herself.

Larsson had appeared at OrcaLab in the summer of 1992 during a visit to the west coast from her native Sweden. She had been an active volunteer there ever since, becoming a valued assistant to Symonds in her acoustic work. The Nootka Sound assignment was no picnic. The sound is not a comfortable place in March, especially not for someone working outdoors and clambering up and down steep cliffsides. It is swept by cold winter storms that bring gloomy skies, heavy rain and hurricane-force winds. The average temperature barely reaches five degrees Celsius. Larsson was alone at the observation post perched atop a cliff overlooking the Gold River dock, where cougar and black bear were frequent visitors. With the departure of Howitt, who was an experienced boat mechanic, she was also responsible for operating the *Henrietta* and keeping it in working order. Yet for all these challenges, she managed the entire project for several months, collecting data about Luna's behaviour. In March she observed that Luna was preoccupied with whatever was happening at the Gold River dock, where he remained almost all the time. In April he moved west to Mooyah Bay, presumably because the spring run of chinook salmon became available there. His interactions with boat traffic decreased and he spent more of his time foraging. Luna was a proficient hunter with a huge appetite that he appeared to have no trouble filling. He was also very vocal, his calls echoing loudly through the deep waters of the sound.

Because Luna appeared to be "behaving himself," Spong and other members of the project began to think that perhaps it was not as crucial to intervene with the whale as he and others had assumed the previous fall. Quite a few people still held out a faint hope that members of Luna's family group might find their way to the sound. Occasionally, southern residents travelled up the west coast of the Island. Michael Harris of the Orca Conservancy described for a reporter what he termed "the Pied Piper or walking-the-dog approach," by which he meant that Luna might be led into a reunion with his pod. Harris argued, rather optimistically, that if Luna could only make acoustic contact with his family, "the whales will do the rest."[61] In mid-May, K pod and a part of L pod were sighted at Tofino. "To our mind," read an entry in the Luna Research Project journal, "the possibility of a 'natural' reunion between Luna and his orca community is still there, though the chances must realistically be considered slim."[62] Spong arranged with Keith Wood, a software engineer who owned a large sailboat, the *Anon*, to take his yacht to the entrance of Nootka Sound and listen for the southern residents on a hydrophone. It was hoped that if they arrived, somehow Wood and the *Anon* could facilitate their reunion with Luna. Chief Mike Maquinna agreed that this would be a positive outcome. In late May hopes ran high for a natural reunion, which had become known as Plan A.

But the southern residents did not arrive, and early in June Luna resumed his old habits. He returned to the Gold River dock and began interacting with boats and float planes again. Air Nootka had installed an underwater noisemaker at its dock to discourage Luna from coming around but the device only worked when someone was around to operate it, and on June 9 Luna visited the dock and damaged a rudder on one of the planes. His actions were becoming dangerous once again. It looked as if it was time for Plan B.

■

ONE VESSEL THAT ROUTINELY ATTRACTED Luna's attention was a ten-metre steel tug called the *Sand Point*, used to tow logs from around Nootka Sound up Muchalat Inlet to the waterfront sort at Gold River, where the logs were prepared for loading onto a barge. Brian Konrad, a deckhand on the tug, got to know Luna well and was amazed at how smart he seemed. For one thing, the whale was able to calculate the tug's speed from a distance, to know whether it had a boom in tow or not, and thus to figure out whether it could catch up to the vessel. Using the *Sand Point*'s speed and direction, Luna seemed to be able to triangulate the route he had to take to intercept it. Luna swam along close to the bow and seemed to enjoy rubbing up against the hull. The tug's propeller was fitted with a round metal nozzle to protect it from logs and deadheads. Luna liked to play around the rear of the tug, but the nozzle kept him from injuring himself by getting his nose too close to the whirling propeller. He would bang against the nozzle. Konrad decided he was trying to disable the tug so as to keep it from moving away, just as he buffeted the rudders on so many pleasure boats.

When the log barge arrived at the Gold River sort to pick up a load, so did Luna. He loved to play among the dozer boats, the small mini-tugs used to manoeuvre the bundles of logs into place for the crane operators on the barge to pluck from the water. It took several hours to load a barge and Luna remained for the whole time. Konrad worried that the whale was at risk of being run over by one of the boats or having a bundle of logs drop on him.

As they lay in the water the bundles were surrounded by an outer ring of logs, called boomsticks, each about twenty metres long, chained together to form an enclosure. Usually a circle of ten boomsticks linked end to end held a "bag" of fifty to sixty bundles. One of Konrad's jobs was to attach and unattach the chains holding the boomsticks together. Each boom chain was about two and a half metres long with a metal ring at one end and a swinging bar, or toggle, at the other. Using a long pike pole, he hooked the toggle end of the chain hanging down in the water and lifted it up to attach to the end of the next boomstick. Luna swam along below Konrad, watching him perform this task, and one day the whale approached a chain hanging in the water, draped it over his head and rose to the surface to "hand" it to the astonished deckhand. Konrad needed no more evidence that he was dealing with an extremely intelligent animal.

Luna was displaying the type of learned behaviour that is commonly observed among killer whales in captivity. Naturally it raises the question: just how intelligent are these animals? In Luna's case, Lance Barrett-Lennard had been astonished, when he first visited Nootka Sound back in March 2003 to collect a blood sample from the whale, how quickly Luna figured out that the scientists were interested chiefly in his dorsal fin. This is when it dawned on Barrett-Lennard that "we were dealing with an animal that was capable of high-order logic." Not only that, but Luna seemed to test ideas. He very quickly understood that his visitors were attempting to trick him into presenting his fin, and he was at pains not to do so.

■ Brian Konrad
at work on the
boomsticks.
Hal Nelson

■ A dozer boat at work at the log dump. Luna was a regular visitor to
this area. Buildings belonging to the abandoned pulp mill are visible in the
background. *Hal Nelson*

"It was completely different than dealing with an animal, say, like a dog," said Barrett-Lennard. "He did things that a dog wouldn't be able to do in your wildest fantasies. It felt like I was dealing with a human."

It is known that toothed whales have very large brains compared to their body size. Humans have the largest brains of any mammal, again compared to body size, but toothed whales are not much smaller. A large brain-to-body ratio correlates to higher intelligence so it is no surprise that killer whales and other dolphins demonstrate abilities that were once ascribed only to humans and some other primates. They solve problems, as Luna did with the boom chain. And they seem to recognize themselves in mirrors and photographs. When he was with the Vancouver Aquarium, John Ford discovered that Hyak, one of the killer whales, took an immediate interest when pictures of killer whales were held up to the window of his tank for him to look at. He showed no interest in photographs of other types of whales or of any other animals. Yet another indicator of intelligence is the phenomenon of "cultural learning" discussed earlier; that is, the transmission of behaviours, such as feeding habits, hunting skills and vocalization, from one generation to the next. No one has developed an IQ test for whales, but for all these reasons it seems plausible to say the killer whale is a highly intelligent animal.

■

DURING THE WINTER AND EARLY SPRING of 2004, the Vancouver Aquarium was preparing its plan to relocate Luna. The Aquarium faced considerations familiar from the Springer move. Arrangements had to be made to move the whale south, by boat or truck, once he had been captured. As in the case of Springer, the intention was to hold Luna in a netpen in Nootka Sound while medical tests were conducted. During that time he would be fed fresh salmon so a source had to be located. Pens had to be set up in Pedder Bay, where the Aquarium planned to install Luna while waiting for his pod to appear. Luna would not be captured until L pod was in the vicinity of the bay or at least until the time of year when the pod typically appeared. Meanwhile, there was a myriad of details that Clint Wright, who once again was managing the operation for the Aquarium, had to work out.

In retrospect, Marilyn Joyce admitted that the DFO's delay in moving Luna ended up having a significant disadvantage. The longer the government waited, the more problems accumulated, the more challenging the relocation became and, according to the advice of its own expert panel, the less likely it was that Luna's pod would accept him back. For Joyce, "problems" meant the involvement of various interest groups, each with its own opinion about what was best for the whale and how the move should be accomplished. Ideally, she would have liked the "professionals," by which she meant the team from the Vancouver Aquarium and Jeff Foster's crew, to be able to do their job the way they thought best. However, Joyce was frustrated at the ability of different interests to complicate the situation by talking to the media when they didn't agree with something that was going on. "We not only had to plan a move," she complained, "we had to fit various organizations' ideals of how it should look." Among the watchdogs were animal rights activists who believed that the DFO was being inhumane in what it was proposing to do. Despite the success of Springer's relocation and the fact that there had been no attempt to divert her into permanent captivity, people were still unwilling to give the DFO the benefit of the doubt about its intentions regarding Luna. Joyce recognized that many activists believed that once the government got its hands on Luna it would not give him up, that he was destined for an aquarium. Nothing she could say would convince the skeptics of anything different.

Another issue for the DFO was the attitude of the Mowa-chaht/Muchalaht, who remained unconvinced that a move was necessary. Chief Mike Maquinna had told the press the previous autumn that his people had not been consulted adequately about the relocation and preferred that Luna be left alone.[63] From that point, his position really did not change. At the end of May 2004, Joyce, Wright and representatives of the RCMP and other agencies met with Chief Maquinna. Joyce and Wright explained that the relocation was going to go ahead. From their point of view, the window of opportunity was closing. Something had to be done soon. The whale was becoming bigger, stronger and more determined in its interactions with boats. Maquinna made it clear that he disagreed. He did not trust the DFO and suspected the Vancouver Aquarium of wanting to take Luna into captivity. There was also the respect that was due his deceased father. Chief Maquinna believed it was better to leave the animal alone and try instead to limit the public's interaction.

Relations between the government and the First Nations were complicated by the fish farm issue. Grieg Seafood, a Norwegian-owned, Campbell River-based salmon farming company, had purchased farms in Esperanza Inlet north of Nootka Island. In 2002 these farms were devastated by huge plankton blooms that killed many fish. The company asked the government for permission to move their netpens south into Nootka Sound, around Bligh Island, and despite the opposition of the Mowachaht/Muchalaht, permission was granted. Worried that wild salmon migrating past the farms would be infected with sea lice, the First Nations sued the government and Grieg. As a result, sour relations between the Mowachaht/Muchalaht and the DFO may have spilled over and contaminated the talks surrounding Luna. "I suspect there were other things going on in a bigger picture," remarked Marilyn Joyce.

The lack of common ground with the First Nations became the focus of a great deal of acrimony as events unfolded. Each side thought the other was motivated by secret objectives about which it was not being frank. Discussions between them were characterized by mistrust and a lack of candour. Officials from DFO, as well as from the Vancouver Aquarium, were impatient with what they saw as the intransigence of the Mowachaht/Muchalaht. It was obvious to them that Luna could not stay where he was. Someone was going to get hurt. The animal was not yet fully grown and already he was terrorizing kayakers and putting float planes at risk. What would happen when he reached full size? They had worked out a feasible plan to move him, one that had been successful in the case of Springer, and they couldn't understand why the First Nations objected. For their part, the Mowachaht/Muchalaht resented being pushed around. The government was offering them an ultimatum, not a choice. Once again outsiders were coming into their territory and telling them what to believe and how to behave. In retrospect, Joyce conceded that at the time she had not recognized as clearly as she should have the need to involve the Mowachaht/Muchalaht in discussions from the very start. Still, as the date for Luna's relocation loomed, there was no indication that the First Nations intended to interfere in the capture.

As the Aquarium prepared its plan, the nagging question of who was going to pay for it remained. The total cost of the capture and relocation was expected to reach between five and six hundred thousand dollars. The American government had pledged a hundred thousand US dollars and the DFO committed an equivalent amount, leaving the Aquarium to make up the difference. Naturally, the Aquarium had nothing in its budget to cover the cost of the project. Some of the money would come from NGOs in Washington State, but the Aquarium would have to rely on in-kind donations and a public fundraising campaign for the rest, as it had with Springer. A variety of organizations and companies stepped forward to donate services and equipment. BC Ferries, for example, offered to waive fares for project personnel as they made their way to and from Vancouver Island. Budget Car Rental provided vehicles and WestJet free flights. Fish farm companies offered the netpens and a supply of salmon to feed Luna while he was in captivity. The "Two Bobs" from Washington State—Bob McLaughlin and Bob Wood—were involved with a non-profit group called Global Rescue and Research (GRR), which provided the underwater cameras that were set up at the netpen for monitoring Luna. Green Island Energy Ltd., an alternative power company that had taken over the pulp mill site in Gold River, agreed to allow the Aquarium to use its dock and facilities.

Despite this generosity, the Aquarium was facing a possible shortfall. On June 6, John Nightingale wrote to Marilyn Joyce to say that in spite of the fact that the fundraising campaign had managed to collect about $65,000 in cash, the operation was still short about $60,000. And that assumed that everything went off without a hitch, an unlikely scenario. The Aquarium could not be expected to put its other programs at risk for the sake of Luna, who was not even one of its animals. Realistically, said Nightingale, the Aquarium needed a commitment that should it be short of money for the relocation, the DFO would step in. Three days later, Joyce responded that the government would cover any shortfall. From the Aquarium's point of view, the last piece of the organizational puzzle had fallen into place.

On June 1 the DFO had authorized the Aquarium to start setting up the netpens in Nootka Sound. No date had been set for a capture but an intervention seemed like a sure bet. DFO officials were only waiting to hear that members of L pod had returned to Juan de Fuca Strait before giving the green light to the operation. Meanwhile, there was a lot of preparation to be done—a pen to install, crew quarters to organize, equipment to move on-site—and this work began. On June 9, the DFO gave the Aquarium the official go-ahead. The process of capturing and relocating Luna could begin.

8 ▪ STANDOFF AT GOLD RIVER

CLINT WRIGHT ARRIVED IN GOLD RIVER during the first week of June to prepare for Luna's capture. Wright was under no illusion that because Springer's relocation had been a success, moving Luna would be a simple matter of doing the same things again. Every capture had its own challenges. Luna was an older, larger whale who had had time to grow comfortable in his new home. How would he react to leaving it? In Springer's case, there had been a consensus that the whale had to be moved. With Luna there were many interests involved and differing viewpoints about whether an intervention should even take place. The press and the public were not as uncritical as they had been about Springer. The Vancouver Aquarium team tried to remain aloof from the complicated politics of the situation — they were there to do a job — but Wright recognized a hornet's nest when he stepped into one.

Preparing for the relocation was like marshalling troops for battle. Every contingency had to be identified, then prepared for; every possible mistake foreseen, then forestalled. The checklist of details was endless. Accommodations had to be secured for members of the crew as they arrived at Gold River. Scheduling had to be arranged with the veterinarians and scientists who were only free to be on site at the time of capture. Netpens had to be found, transported and installed. Because the First Nations had grievances against a local fish farm company, Grieg Seafood, Wright decided to obtain pens from the other side of Vancouver Island. He did not want Grieg to become a focus of discontent that might scuttle the whole operation. Pumps, cranes, boats, cameras—they all had to be obtained and moved on-site. Once again Six Flags Marine World in California donated the transport box in which to move Luna, and it was making its way north on the back of a truck. And there were always lots of media representatives wanting updates.

The unflappable Wright planned every step of the operation, then prepared backup plans and backup plans to the backup plans. The level of detail sometimes reached humorous proportions. At one point he decided that the ropes that were going to be used around the pens were too brightly coloured and might spook the whale. Every rope needed to be painted black. The owner of the local hardware store could only shake her head at the eccentricities of the out-of-towners as Aquarium staff kept coming into the store to buy another dozen cans of spray paint.

The plan was to haul Luna to Pedder Bay by truck. Wright was concerned about the steepness of hills and sharpness of curves along the route so he asked two of his colleagues from the Aquarium, Jeremy Fitz-Gibbon and Brian Sheehan, to make a test run using a transport box in the back of an Aquarium van. They filled the box with water and set off, Sheehan riding in the back of the van to keep an eye on the box. After a couple of kilometres, Fitz-Gibbon stopped to check on things and discovered Sheehan soaking wet from all the water that had slopped over the sides. They decided, however, that the sloshing would be less of a problem with a whale on board and baffles in the tank to calm the water. A bigger problem was the fact that the tank kept shifting from side to side as the van rounded corners. In Campbell River they found a tire shop and they obtained about thirty used tires, which they jammed in all around the tank to keep it from moving. It worked beautifully and the dry run was considered a great success, but when Fitz-Gibbon got back to the Aquarium he had thirty bald tires to get rid of. He hadn't realized there was a charge for disposing of them. No wonder the dealer in Campbell River had been so keen to have them take as many as they wanted!

Once again, Mark Miller from the Discovery Channel was authorized by the DFO to be the official videographer on the project. Wright was very comfortable with Miller, who had filmed the Springer release in Dong Chong Bay. From Wright's point of view, Miller was an experienced filmmaker who knew how to obtain good footage without getting in the way of the operation. However, as the situation became polarized, some of the animal activists suspected Miller of being overly partial to the government point of view, at one point even claiming that he was chosen because he had agreed to turn off his cameras if anything bad happened to Luna in the course of the capture.

The Aquarium team was based at the site of the former pulp mill at the mouth of the Gold River. It was a large area scattered with old buildings and rusting machinery, some of which was being dismantled by the site's new owner, Green Island Energy. Part of the site had reverted to meadow and the drive in was lined with apple trees, which presented a particular attraction to the local black bear population. To the south a high cliff overlooked the site. Members of the team stayed at an old bunkhouse, where they ate most of their meals. A chain-link fence with a locked gate surrounded the site, and the DFO restricted access to people in some way connected to the project. Members of the media remained at the public dock about a kilometre away and were rarely invited inside. When staff ventured outside the fence, they were set upon by the press, who wanted to find out what was going on. As events unfolded, it became clear that the locked compound contributed to an us-versus-them mentality both inside and outside the fence, and fuelled public suspicion that something furtive and clandestine was taking place.

A couple of days before the intended capture, the use of a tail rope emerged as a bone of contention. The hope was that a boat would lead Luna freely into the netpen. But if he balked, another option would be to capture him the same way Springer had been captured in Puget Sound, by placing a soft rope around his tail, holding him in the water and placing him in a sling to be hoisted onto a barge for transport to the pen. Springer had been a smaller animal than Luna, who by this time had grown to about 4.2 metres and weighed close to 1,590 kilograms. Paul Spong, for one, worried that the potential for injuring Luna was high if a tail rope was used. Given that Spong was dead set against keeping cetaceans in captivity, it was not surprising that he was suspicious of Jeff Foster's involvement in the capture. Foster was one of the original "killer whale cowboys." He had participated in the infamous corralling of whales at the head of Puget Sound in 1976, the brouhaha that had led to the banning of all killer whale captures in US waters. For anyone opposed to cetaceans in captivity, he was public enemy number one. But Foster had played a key role in the successful relocation of Springer, where the tail rope technique had been used with success, and Wright had every confidence that he was a skilled professional who cared deeply about the animals with which he worked.

Complicating matters was the fact that Marilyn Joyce and Spong had had a falling out some days previously. In her zeal to secure the operation, Joyce was being very strict about who could visit the compound, and Spong was furious to discover that he was denied access. During the Springer operation, OrcaLab had played a key partnership role with the Vancouver Aquarium and the DFO. It was, in fact, a remarkable reconciliation given the years of mistrust between Spong and the Aquarium. In the case of Luna, this rapprochement evaporated. Instead of being a partner, OrcaLab was left "outside the fence." Spong became antagonistic to the DFO, criticizing its secrecy and some of its methods.

Spong shared his reservations about the tail rope with Wright one evening when they ran into each other at the Gold

River pub. Wright was unaware of any recent instances where an animal had been injured using a rope but he told Spong that he was open to hearing evidence to the contrary. Spong referred Wright to an American scientist who had reported tail rope injuries. Wright contacted the scientist and learned that the injuries had resulted when he had used a tail rope to lift dolphins out of the water. Wright felt this precedent had little relevance to Luna since Foster's plan involved no lifting but took advantage of the fact that killer whales generally stop struggling when their tails are encumbered with a rope. But he agreed with Spong that leading the whale into the netpen was the best possible scenario. Still, the tail rope issue continued to be raised by Spong, by whale advocacy groups and by the First Nations, who did not think it was a respectful way to treat their former chief. Later, one of the things that the DFO held against Spong was that in his conversations with the Mowachaht/Muchalaht he had not conveyed to them that using the tail rope, if necessary, was a safe procedure. But Spong could not have said that because he never believed it himself. He consistently maintained that in the event a tail rope was used it could easily provoke Luna to bolt and break his back. He wanted the use of a rope removed from the list of options altogether. The media had a field day with this issue, sometimes making it sound like a public hanging was in store for Luna. In the event, a rope was never deployed.

By Tuesday, June 15, the team was assembling at Gold River. Everything was in readiness for Luna's capture. Wright, recalling how rapidly events had unfolded during Springer's release, thought the operation might go ahead as early as the next day, but he expected it would probably take at least another day to acclimatize Luna to the boats and equipment. The Mowachaht/Muchalaht issued a press release on the Tuesday making it quite clear that they opposed the relocation effort. They invited anyone who agreed with them to a "non-confrontational" demonstration at their former village site near the dock the next day. On Wednesday, two canoes, each paddled by nine members of the

Mowachaht/Muchalaht Nation, intercepted Luna and led him far down the inlet away from Gold River and the capture pen. Mike Maquinna characterized plans to capture Luna as a "theft," as taking something that belonged to his people away from them. "The number one priority was to keep him away from the pen," said Chief Maquinna. "Then somewhere along the way it dawned on us, my God, we're fighting for his freedom, for his very life." This view of the government operation was reflected in the page 1 headline in the *Vancouver Province* the next day, "Orca Lured Away from Trap."[64] From the beginning, the government was losing the propaganda war. What the DFO and the Aquarium viewed as a rescue, the rest of the world was quickly coming to see as an abduction.

At this point, Wright gauged opinion in Gold River itself to be fairly evenly divided between those who thought Luna was good for business and should be left alone, those who empathized with the First Nations, and those who thought the whale was a nuisance and wanted him gone. The *Times-Colonist* reported that there was talk in the community of leaving Luna alone and using the money earmarked for relocation to install effective monitoring and to allow the Mowachaht/Muchalaht to operate a whale-watching operation. Joyce reiterated that such an approach was impossible because Luna's behaviour around boats made him a threat to public safety.[65]

Late on the Thursday afternoon, Joyce met with Mike Maquinna in an attempt to defuse a situation that had the potential to develop into a confrontation. Mark Miller and Lance Barrett-Lennard ferried her and DFO public relations person Lara Sloan down the inlet to find Maquinna, who was in a power-boat that was resupplying the canoes. As they came alongside, the paddlers seemed sullen and unfriendly. Low on fuel, Miller shouted, "We'll trade these two women for a jerry can of gas." "Not enough," someone responded. Everyone laughed and the tension was broken. Joyce and Maquinna began talking, and after a few minutes they asked Miller to take them out to Yuquot to continue their conversation. It was a beautiful evening. While Barrett-Lennard and the others helped an elderly resident fix his boat at the dock, Joyce and Maquinna wandered off through the meadow to a bench overlooking the beach behind the village site and tried to find a solution to the impasse. By the time approaching darkness forced their return to Gold River, Joyce felt that she and the chief had achieved a meeting of minds. Before they parted, Joyce asked Maquinna to talk the matter over with his elders. As a gesture of goodwill, she said that she would postpone Luna's capture until after the weekend, giving the Mowachaht/Muchalaht time to conduct any ceremonial farewell they considered appropriate. She doubtless had in mind the Tlingit dancers in Puget Sound and the 'Namgis welcoming Springer back to Johnstone Strait.

On Friday most members of the team from the Aquarium headed back to Vancouver for the weekend and the capture site was deserted. Wright stayed on to take care of more details. The truck carrying the transport box would be arriving and a commercial fisherman was bringing in some live salmon that had to be transferred to one of the pens. In an interview with the press, Chief Maquinna revealed that he did not support the operation after all. He reiterated that the Mowachaht/Muchalaht opposed Luna's capture. They wanted to be given the opportunity to try leading the whale down the outside coast with their canoes, he said, an approach that they considered to be more "natural" than a hard capture. If that was not possible, they wanted Luna left where he was.[66] Since neither option was acceptable to the DFO, it looked as if the standoff would continue. When the operation geared up again on Monday afternoon (June 21), Joyce had not heard directly from Maquinna but she was hoping that he would not interfere with the capture, which looked likely to take place the next day. Increasingly, Joyce seemed to be in a no-win situation. Her job was to complete the capture without alienating the First Nations, but the First Nations were adamantly opposed to the capture.

The capture scenario was a straightforward one. There were four netpens set up near the concrete wharf that formerly had been used by the pulp mill. One was a standard fish farm pen, much like the one that had held Springer at Manchester. Two others held salmon for Luna. The fourth was a larger, hexagonal pen that consisted of six air-filled tubes that looked much like the pontoons on a Zodiac. The net hung down from these tubes, weighted with plastic-covered concrete "cannon balls" that kept the shape of the netting. One of the pontoons swung open like a gate. The plan was to lure Luna through this opening into the hex pen using a jet boat that he had grown particularly fond of following. About the size of a standard runabout, the jet boat had an engine that operated like a pump, sucking in water and expelling it out the back: it had no propeller to injure Luna or foul in the pen's netting. Once Luna was inside, another boat would push the gate closed behind him. At that point a crane, situated on the dock, would lift the jet boat out of the pen. Then the crane would lift one side of the net into the air, reducing the depth of water in the pen. Experience had shown that when killer whales are grounded or in shallow water, instead of flopping about like fish, they don't move around much and they don't threaten people who might be handling them. As a result, it was expected that Jeff Foster's team would be able to enter the pen and put Luna in a sling. The crane then would lift him out and deposit him in the other netpen, which was easier for people to work around and more suited to longer-term confinement. While this was going on, the veterinarians would take blood samples and carry out other tests of the animal's health. It was anticipated that Luna would be held for about a week awaiting results of the medical tests before relocation to Pedder Bay began.

■ Mowachaht-Muchalaht paddlers in Muchalat Inlet. *Lance Barrett-Lennard*

■

TUESDAY, JUNE 22 WAS CAPTURE DAY. Following an early-morning briefing, Ed Thorburn took three DFO Zodiacs down the inlet to find Luna, which he did at Mooyah Bay, playing beside one of the Mowachaht/Muchalaht canoes. Luna came to the boats but so did the canoe, which had a toddler on board. Clint Wright, who was being informed of these events by Thorburn, was very concerned at the potential for an accident and frustrated that the First Nations were interfering in the capture. By noon, nothing much had happened. Distracted by the different boats on the water, Luna shied away from following the DFO Zodiacs. Wright set out in another boat to see if he could do anything to speed things along. Michael Parfit was also on the water in his own small Zodiac. Parfit was an American journalist who, along with his wife Suzanne Chisholm, was in Gold River to write about Luna.[67] He was photographing what was going on, but as the wind picked up and the chop intensified he had to break off and head back to the dock. By the time Wright arrived on the scene, Thorburn's boats had succeeded in engaging Luna's attention and were making good time moving him along toward Gold River. Wright could not see the canoe at first but soon he spotted it, apparently looking for Luna. When they saw him, the paddlers thought that Wright was with the whale and began paddling toward him, struggling to make headway against the rising sea. A cat-and-mouse game ensued whereby Wright led the canoe to the west away from Gold River, then doubled back to the dock. By three o'clock Thorburn had managed to lure Luna to the vicinity of the pens without any more interference from the paddlers.

At this point the jet boat was deployed to lure Luna into the pen. Several times he followed the boat to the entrance but he was reluctant to venture all the way inside. He seemed to be of two minds what to do. Should he enter the pen or should he turn around and swim away? On a couple of occasions he did swim

■ Marilyn Joyce, the senior DFO official at Gold River, and Chief Mike Maquinna attempt to find a solution to the impasse. *CP/Richard Lam*

inside but Wright hesitated to give the signal, worried that in the time it took to close the gate and get the net in place Luna might easily swim out. Once spooked, the whale might never come in again.

Still, Wright was confident that days of meticulous planning would ultimately end in success, when all of a sudden word arrived that a plane had crashed nearby. Divers and emergency help were requested immediately. The capture was put on hold while members of the team hopped into boats and headed for the crash site. It turned out to be a float plane carrying Brad

Hanson, the biologist from the National Marine Mammal Laboratory in Seattle, who had been expected all day. Hanson had been at the site the previous week and was returning to take part in the capture. A brisk wind was still blowing in the inlet. The plane's pilot had made one attempt to set down, bounced off the waves, then managed to get airborne again. Instead of giving up, he decided to make another try, this time with the wind at his back. Once it touched down, the plane, a Cessna 185, could not decelerate fast enough. It skidded across the surface of the water and slammed into the shore, coming to rest on its nose. Within minutes, some Native paddlers arrived to offer help, followed by

■ Preparing the capture setup at the Gold River dock. As it turned out, Luna never did co-operate by swimming inside. *Lloyd Murrey*

the RCMP and the local paramedic team. Miraculously, the pilot, co-pilot and Hanson all tumbled from the wreck unhurt, and after his dramatic entrance Hanson was able to join the capture operation, which had started up again.

By this time Wright was wondering what could possibly go wrong next. Thinking that perhaps Luna was intimidated by the number of people who were in position on the pen, he asked everyone to move some distance away. In response, Luna seemed to relax and followed the boat inside the enclosure. Immediately the crew ran back to the water to prepare to slam the door. But after about a minute Luna swam out again. Observing the whale, Lance Barrett-Lennard had the impression that he was hungry and was going off to look for fish. As things turned out, he never returned. (Later it was discovered that the net had wrapped itself around one of the cannon balls. If they had attempted to close the pen, they would never have been able to do so in time.)

Shortly before Luna left the pen, the Mowachaht/Muchalaht canoes had arrived, along with a support vessel, and were maintaining a watchful position just outside the bay. Somehow they had found out what was going on. In the aftermath of the failed capture, this became another cause of heated disagreement between Paul Spong and Marilyn Joyce. During the days leading up to the capture, Spong's research assistant, Lisa Larsson, had continued her work from the observation post atop the cliff overlooking the Gold River dock. Larsson worked co-operatively with the DFO and shared the results of her research with the department, but over time she had grown to mistrust Ed Thorburn. She was convinced that the fisheries officer had passed on prejudicial information about her colleague David Howitt that had gotten him kicked out of the country. What's more, she resented the fact that Thorburn never showed any appreciation for the information about Luna that she was passing on. In her view, she was helping out the DFO by keeping an eye on the whale yet they began treating her as some kind of spy. Earlier she had moved one of her hydrophones down to the compound's dock, hoping to record Luna's vocalizations as he was taken into custody. Barrett-Lennard was checking it for her and keeping the batteries charged. On June 16 Thorburn had hauled this hydrophone out of the water, believing that Larsson was telling the Mowachaht/Muchalaht when the DFO boats were leaving the dock to search for Luna. Over the next few days there was a growing feeling on the part of Thorburn and Joyce that Larsson and Spong were providing a direct conduit to the Mowachaht/Muchalaht, passing on every detail of what the capture team was doing from the observation post on the cliff. In Joyce's view, Spong had turned against the operation. Initially he had said that Luna should be moved but then he altered his opinion in deference to the views of the First Nations. Joyce interpreted this as a flip-flop. She felt Spong had become an enemy of the capture. That was why she had earlier denied him access to the site and why she shared Thorburn's suspicions of Larsson.

Opponents of the relocation plan—the First Nations, Parfit and his wife Suzanne, Spong—believed the DFO was excluding witnesses because it wanted to keep people in the dark about what was happening. Joyce responded that she was merely trying to run a secure operation to ensure that no one, human or whale, got hurt. She didn't want unauthorized people wandering around the site. But in her zeal to run a tight ship, and in keeping with the DFO's tendency to try to control information, Joyce created the impression that the DFO had something to hide. Once the Mowachaht/Muchalaht mounted their interference on June 22, the department became even more secretive, hoping the Aquarium team could pull the capture off in a hurry before more concerted opposition had time to build. In this context, Joyce was very wary of anyone whom she suspected of undermining that effort. But the public started to think that perhaps the capture team, hidden away behind locked gates at the old pulp mill site, did have something to conceal.

For their part, Spong and Larsson denied emphatically that they were spying for the First Nations. Insulted and angry at being accused of sabotage, Larsson insisted that her only concern was the research that she was doing. She had been sharing her research findings with the Mowachaht/Muchalaht but that was all. Spong believed the DFO had to work within the reality of the situation and the reality was that the First Nations opposed the capture. Spong felt that this view had to be accommodated somehow, not rejected out of hand. This is why he was sympathetic to the proposal that the Mowachaht/Muchalaht lead Luna down the coast by canoe, even though the other scientific experts dismissed this option as unrealistic. But Spong denied the imputation that he had influenced Mike Maquinna in some way. In his view, his commitment to returning Luna to his pod never wavered. What changed was his understanding of the best way to accomplish it.

No matter how the First Nations had learned about Luna's location, the attempt to capture him ended with the arrival of their vessels. If Luna had been wary before, he was downright unco-operative now. The canoes remained outside the small bay containing the pens but the paddlers chanted and yelled and banged their paddles on the water and against the sides of the canoes and Luna could certainly hear them. Already a bit bored by the game with the jet boat, he was distracted by the commotion and looked as if he wanted to go foraging for fish. Clint Wright and Jeff Foster in the jet boat tried to hold his attention by giving him a salmon, which worked for a moment, but then Luna was gone, out of the bay and off to investigate the canoes.

The bizarre tug-of-war now resumed between the First Nations and the capture team, with Luna in the middle. The canoes paddled in one direction, trying to lead Luna away from the pens. DFO officers in their boats tried equally hard to draw him back into the bay. But without physically stopping the canoes, which they did not want to do, there was little the enforcement officers could do. As Wright, Foster, Barrett-Lennard and the others watched from the dock, Luna disappeared around the corner. The moment had passed. There would be no more attempts made to capture this whale. Every member of the team was disappointed, even angry, that the long day, with every prospect of success, had ended in failure.

The Mowachaht/Muchalaht celebrated the events of the day as a great victory. "Hopefully, Luna has made the choice to come with us rather than being led into a pen," Chief Maquinna told the press. "We have been blessed and honoured with his presence and that he has decided to come with us." On the DFO side, Joyce expressed her frustration. "The more interference, the more that there is this kind of tug-of-war, the more confused he [Luna] gets, the less likelihood that the lead into the pen will succeed," she said. "The Mowachaht/Muchalaht were not respecting the 'no go zone' around Luna as they had originally promised." But Maquinna denied that he had ever promised anything. Relations between the First Nations and the DFO soured swiftly. Wright felt that the Mowachaht/Muchalaht position was hardening and they were now prepared to do whatever they had to do to deny the government the whale. This meant that from the Vancouver Aquarium's point of view, the operation had changed from a straightforward animal rescue to a deeply polarized, politically fraught media event. "The whole thing was blowing up out of all proportion," thought Wright.

Wright still felt that the best thing for Luna was to move him away from a situation where he was a risk to the public and to himself, but the press reported that most townspeople in Gold River now wanted the whale left alone. Public opinion seemed to have swung decidedly behind the Mowachaht/Muchalaht and against the government. Barrett-Lennard observed the dramatic shift. A week earlier, when he had arrived in town, he felt like a conquering hero. "Everyone I met said they were glad the Aquarium was there to help with their problem whale. Seven or eight days later, the same people said in no uncertain terms that we should go away and leave 'their' whale in peace." During the next day, Wednesday, Thorburn and the Aquarium staff made further attempts to carry out the capture, with no success. The Native paddlers were back on the water running interference. Emotions were running high and there was too much boat traffic interfering with Luna to proceed with the operation. Technically, enforcement officials could have stepped in to charge people with harassing the whale, but no one really wanted to go down that road. While all this was going on, the capture team back at the dock was sitting on their hands, not knowing what might happen.

At 4:30 p.m., Chief Maquinna arrived at the site and met with Marilyn Joyce for about an hour. Maquinna was very unhappy with the way things had turned out. He made it clear that he believed Joyce had misrepresented earlier conversations they had had and he no longer wanted to deal with her. He showed Joyce a letter that he had written to senior DFO officials asking that she be removed from the operation. "Ms. Joyce has lost all credibility with the Mowachaht/Muchalaht First Nations and the Nuu-chah-nulth Tribal Council," he wrote. "We no longer have any faith in her ability to properly consult with us and communicate with us on a regular basis."[68] Joyce felt betrayed by Maquinna's actions. She thought they had an agreement. But Maquinna was a chief, the leader of his people, who may have thought that it was time he started talking to senior government officials. Although she was visibly upset to have been attacked personally, Joyce maintained some hope after the meeting that there remained a chance to get the capture done.

The next day, Thursday, the capture team felt they had one more opportunity. However, once again the situation on the water became dangerous. There were media representatives, Native paddlers, police and DFO personnel in boats, all chasing the whale. When the police or fisheries officers intervened to warn boats away from Luna, they were ignored, sometimes abused. "It was anarchy out there," said Wright, "and certainly not the situation you want to be in if you are trying to rescue a whale."

In the middle of this uncertainty, Larsson again became a lightning rod for the suspicion and ill will that had accumulated around the project. At about noon, Thorburn sent word to Larsson that she had to come down from the cliff. Apparently the owners of the mill site wanted her to leave and Thorburn was passing on their request. But he had his own reasons for wanting her gone. He was increasingly worried about the security of the operation and he was convinced that she was communicating with the Mowachaht/Muchalaht, by radio or by some sort of signal. The message conveyed to Larsson was that she had to be off the cliff by three o'clock or she would be arrested. Surprised at being so summarily evicted from her perch, she had no choice but to comply. Spong and Helena Symonds were furious and concerned for Larsson's safety. They felt that Thorburn's ultimatum was abusive and threatening. They denied emphatically that Larsson was engaged in a conspiracy to sabotage the capture. From her home on Hanson Island, Symonds phoned Barrett-Lennard, who was at the capture site, to ask him to "rescue" Larsson. Barrett-Lennard, who had pressing matters of his own to attend to, spoke with Thorburn, who assured him that no one was going to arrest Larsson or seize her hydrophones and that she would be helped with her equipment. When Barrett-Lennard relayed this information to Symonds, she told him that she had heard from Mike Maquinna and that he wanted Larsson to remain on the cliff as an observer. Barrett-Lennard was flabbergasted. For the past two weeks he had been telling anyone who would listen that Larsson was not spying for the First Nations. Now Symonds seemed to be confirming that the researcher had been monitoring the DFO boats for Chief Maquinna. Like other members of the operation, Barrett-Lennard concluded that Spong and Symonds, motivated by their sympathy for the First Nations' cause, had not been playing straight with the DFO and the team from the Vancouver Aquarium.

While the Larsson episode was a sideshow to the main event, it illustrated how antagonistic relations had become between the major players, all of whom claimed to have the best interests of the whale at heart. That afternoon, a hastily convened conference call took place involving Chief Maquinna, senior DFO officials in Ottawa and representatives from the BC First Nations Summit and the Nuu-chah-nulth Tribal Council. Shortly afterwards the DFO announced that it was suspending the attempt to capture Luna "in the interests of public safety and the well-being of the whale," pending further discussions with the Mowachaht/Muchalaht. "Tsu-xiit is free," announced a jubilant Chief Maquinna, "and we have helped him stay free. We are not going to let anyone buy him, prod him, tag him or do anything unnatural."[69] Among members of the capture team there was sadness and frustration. Not one of them doubted that Luna needed to be moved. An operation that was justified by science and by public safety seemed to have been sabotaged by politics and it left behind a sour taste.

Those who had been involved in Springer's return, as most of the team had, could not help reflecting on the profound differences between the two outcomes. Springer had brought people together in a united effort that left only good feelings in its wake. Her relocation had provided a blueprint for future interventions. Old enemies had worked together as friends. Even Spong, with his history of antagonism toward the Vancouver Aquarium, had co-operated with the Aquarium for the good of the animal.

Yet the case of Luna turned out to be the precise opposite. An attempt to do the right thing for the whale had left people disillusioned and divided. The First Nations and the government were further apart than ever. Friendships were broken. In the eyes of the public, the government looked inept and insensitive. During the Springer release, the press had been universally positive, presenting it as a feel-good story. In Gold River, the media took a more critical position. Instead of a story about a whale, it became a story about government imposing its authority on a First Nation that refused to accept it. There could not have been two more different outcomes: one a fairytale, the other a horror story.

With the operation on hold, at least for the foreseeable future, the television satellite trucks left town and members of the capture team dispersed for home. Wright and a couple of others remained in Gold River to tidy up loose ends. Left on his own to reflect, Wright was extremely discouraged at the outcome. "I remember just sitting out on the dock by myself and wondering, 'what's going to happen to this whale?' Everyone had left and it was all quiet and it was almost as if it hadn't happened." Wright recognized that if the capture had not succeeded when everything was planned and in place, the chances of it happening again were slim indeed. Even if capture was feasible, with feelings running as high as they were, there was no reason to believe that a truck carrying Luna would be allowed to leave Gold River. Wright had heard rumours that the Mowachaht/Muchalaht and their sympathizers had plans to blockade the site or even to break in and free the whale. Thorburn had heard that the local band might call in militants from Port Alberni to spark a physical confrontation. Whether or not these rumours were true, it would be asking for trouble for the DFO to try again in such a confrontational atmosphere.

In the aftermath of the debacle, there were a lot of theories about what had gone wrong. Ed John, Grand Chief of the BC First Nations Summit, circulated the story that the DFO wanted to move Luna because he threatened the fish farms. "The local chiefs are convinced absolutely that the only reason that DFO is moving with any haste is because of that," said Chief John, lending credence to the suspicion that resentment against the department's fish farm policies contributed to the Mowachaht/Muchalaht's views on Luna.[70] Another important factor was the fear that Luna would end up in permanent captivity. In their conversations, Chief Maquinna had asked for a guarantee that this would not happen, but Marilyn Joyce could not give such a guarantee because if relocation failed for some reason, permanent captivity might have been the only option left. And this was an outcome the Mowachaht/Muchalaht and some NGOs would not tolerate. To Aquarium representatives, this "better dead than fed" philosophy was selfish and misguided. "The fear of animals going into an aquarium blinds these people to common sense," Wright said bluntly. Yet if some of the Mowachaht/Muchalaht did believe that Luna embodied the spirit of their late chief, it was understandable that they would not want the whale penned up for the rest of its life.

People who wanted Luna moved had their own conspiracy theories. Spong and his team were accused of "stirring up things" with the First Nations, feeding them information and trying to stay on their good side for reasons of political correctness, accusations that Spong vehemently denied. Some said the Mowachaht/Muchalaht did not want Luna to leave Nootka Sound because they saw the whale as a tourist attraction and therefore a cash cow. Others argued that Chief Maquinna was simply picking a fight with the DFO to strengthen his own position in the band.

It was clear that whatever goodwill had existed at the beginning of the operation had hardened into mutual suspicion and recrimination by the end. It was hard to identify a middle ground on which reconciliation could take place, leaving Wright's question unanswered. What was going to happen to the whale?

■

DURING THE STRUGGLE OVER LUNA, the Mowachaht/Muchalaht and, to some extent, the townspeople of Gold River, had asserted their ownership of the whale. "There was a feeling of 'it's our whale, leave it alone,'" one resident told a newspaper reporter.[71] Much to the chagrin of the scientists and officials from the DFO and the Vancouver Aquarium, the capture became a David-and-Goliath story pitting a small coastal First Nation against the outside world, a tiny whale against the giant federal bureaucracy that sought to take away his freedom. Local people, Native and non-Native, ended up cheering for the underdog and were jubilant when David—that is, the Mowachaht/Muchalaht—won. The fact that this interpretation of events was a distortion of the DFO's motives didn't stop it from being widely accepted. The scientists and animal trainers had arrived in Gold River wearing their white hats, flush with their success with Springer, greeted as saviours by the locals. Two weeks later they were handed black hats and shown the door, their plans dashed by a group of determined Native paddlers and the complicated calculus of Aboriginal politics.

With the media whirlwind gone and the tension easing, both sides in the Gold River standoff had a chance to catch their breath, to reflect on what had gone wrong and what to do next. Over the summer, representatives of the DFO met with the Mowachaht/Muchalaht to discuss Luna. The government remained convinced that he posed a threat to the public and belonged back with his family in the south. The Mowachaht/Muchalaht remained equally convinced that "nature should take its course." Whatever that ambiguous phrase meant, it apparently did not mean an active intervention like the one attempted by the Vancouver Aquarium in June. That option was off the table.

Meanwhile, Luna's playful nature continued to get him into trouble with boaters. The most notorious incident took place in mid-August, when he approached a sailboat, the *Cat's Paw*, belonging to retired Vancouver crime reporter Greg Middleton, who was on a cruise around Vancouver Island. According to Middleton, Luna appeared "out of nowhere" as the boat was cruising up Muchalat Inlet near Mooyah Bay and disabled the steering by ramming the rudder. Middleton was rescued by a worker from the fish farm in the bay and towed to shore, where he managed to rig up a temporary rudder. However, Luna returned, broke the steering again and proceeded to entertain himself by "slamming" the 9.7-metre boat around at the dock. "This was thirty-six hours of hell," Middleton told CBC radio. "We thought it [the boat] was going to sink." Eventually Luna went away and Middleton got a tow into Gold River. From there he trucked the boat to Comox for repairs. While some people speculated that Middleton had come into the sound looking for some sort of an encounter with Luna that he could write about, he clearly got more than he could have bargained for. "This inlet is no longer safe to bring a boat that does less than fifteen knots and can outrun this thing," he said. To the public, the incident came across as an "attack," conjuring up the bad old days when killer whales were considered dangerous predators. In an article that he wrote about the incident for *Pacific Yachting*, a popular pleasure boating magazine, Middleton reported hearing many stories about boats being damaged by the whale and complained that the DFO, hamstrung by politics, was powerless to do anything about the situation.[72]

By September the First Nations and the DFO had worked out a stewardship plan for Luna, partly funded by a grant of ten thousand dollars from the DFO. A brochure was produced explaining to boaters how to behave around the five-year-old whale, and new warning signs were posted at the Gold River dock. The Mowachaht/Muchalaht agreed to make regular marine patrols to control interactions between Luna and the public. The Kakawin Guardians would warn boats away, prevent Luna from making a nuisance of himself and record his daily activities. They would also be at the Gold River dock in a stepped-up campaign to raise public awareness. This program continued for the duration of the boating season. At the same time the DFO reconvened its scientific panel to discuss some of the issues surrounding Luna. Although members of the panel warned that more interactions with boats would occur as the whale reached adolescence, no plans were made to pursue relocation.

For the next year and a half, Luna continued to treat Nootka Sound as his own private swimming pool full of toys. He followed along after the *Uchuck III*, nestled up next to fishing boats, played in the wake of tugs, hung around the log sorts and investigated the fish farms. Every once in a while his behaviour frightened some unsuspecting kayaker or sport fisherman, the press picked up the story and the government was urged to "do something" about the whale. As opposed to the negative events that got reported in the press, however, most of Luna's everyday encounters were playful and non-threatening and local people came to accept him a part of the scenery, an awkward, inquisitive child who didn't mean anyone any harm.

During 2005, the possibility of a "natural relocation" was raised once again. Lisa Larsson, the OrcaLab researcher, had returned to the sound and was moving into a lodge on Nootka Island, where she took a job as a caretaker. Deploying her hydrophones to listen for Luna, she unexpectedly picked up calls one day belonging to some northern resident whales, members of G clan, which had arrived in the neighbourhood. Larsson heard Luna respond with his own calls and there was a few minutes of back and forth before the newcomers fell silent and were not heard again. It was never known whether Luna made an attempt to join or follow these whales. In the normal course of events, northern residents do not mix socially with southern residents, of which Luna was one. Still, the incident raised Larsson's hopes. "The fact that he made calls after hearing the other whales feels encouraging for a natural reunification," she told a reporter. "If the northern resident orcas pass through at times it is just as likely that the southern resident orcas do too."[73] Later in the summer the Kakawin Guardians managed to lead Luna in their boat right out to the entrance of Nootka Sound, where he remained for more than an hour foraging for salmon before swimming back into the sound, another indication that natural relocation might work.

The American writers Michael Parfit and Suzanne Chisholm, who had stayed on in Nootka Sound following the abortive capture attempt, made their own proposal to the DFO. They had gathered anecdotal evidence that local fishermen were getting angry with Luna's antics and were threatening to shoot him. One sports fisherman who had his boat pushed around by Luna told Parfit, "next time I come here, I will have a gun."[74] Gail Laurie from the ReuniteLuna website confirmed that many people were threatening to harm the whale. Even though she realized that in most cases people were merely blowing off steam, she still feared that one day someone would get angry or frightened enough to pull the trigger. After all, it was not that long ago that people on the coast thought nothing of shooting at killer whales.

Parfit and Chisholm thought a whole new approach was needed to protect Luna from boaters and boaters from Luna. They proposed the creation of a surrogate family, a "foster pod," to which Luna could attach himself. A select group of people, including the Mowachaht/Muchalaht, would be authorized to associate with Luna, keeping him out of trouble but also teaching him to follow along beside them. Eventually, Parfit hoped, Luna would be encouraged to swim to the outer reaches of Nootka Sound, where he might encounter his own family and be reunited with them. Meanwhile, Parfit had come to believe that Luna craved and needed human contact and that it was wrong to deny it. Luna had a deep emotional impact on people. While knowing not to anthropomorphize the animal, Parfit, Ed Thorburn, the Kakawin Guardians and others who came into regular contact with him could not help feeling that Luna's insistent interactions with people showed that he was desperately lonely. They were caught in a conundrum. Luna needed to be kept wild, which meant that interactions with him had to be kept to a minimum. But he was an intensely social animal. How could that sociability be appeased in the absence of other whales?

The downside of Parfit's proposal was that it would further habituate Luna to human interaction and lessen the chance that he might ever reintegrate with his family group. When Parfit's plan got no official response, he more or less initiated it himself. During the winter of 2005–2006 he and Chisholm began operating their own stewardship program, spending time in their Zodiac watching Luna and from time to time leading him away from troublesome encounters with fish farms or other boats. Where this would have led eventually is anyone's guess. Parfit was hopeful that it might be a prelude to leading Luna back into the bosom of his family. But before that could happen, disaster struck.

■

THE END FOR LUNA CAME on the morning of Friday, March 10, 2006. The skies over Nootka Sound were partly cloudy and a moderate wind blew as a large tugboat, the *General Jackson*, with a log barge in tow idled slowly in Muchalat Inlet near Mooyah Bay (where Luna had first been sighted in 2001). While the crew waved at the whale and took photographs, the captain had to adjust his engine speed periodically to control the orientation of the vessel. Luna was playing around the stern, as he had done with so many other vessels, when he was sucked into the blades of the propeller and killed instantly. The tug's crew felt the impact, then saw parts of the mangled carcass floating in the wash. Fisheries officers who retrieved some of these pieces confirmed that it was a killer whale.

On the one hand, Luna's death was a surprise. During his five years in Nootka Sound he had shown a remarkable ability to avoid the lethal propellers around which he loved to play. "He knew every nook and cranny" of Nootka Sound, wrote Paul Spong, "and every vessel that plied its waters, and everyone knew him."[75] He had been around for so long that everyone had gotten used to having him there. But it had been clear from the

day of his appearance in the sound that he was an accident waiting to happen. His fearless interactions with boats of all types
and sizes were a pleasure to many but a threat to some, and it
was long feared that he would make a mistake and be struck by
a boat or propeller or that an angry or frightened boater would
shoot him. In the end, his death was no less tragic for being so
expected.

Many people who had been involved in the attempts to rescue
Luna were angry at his death. For them, the failure to "save" this
one whale was symptomatic of a larger failure of community and
humanity. They thought that Luna died because the interested parties had not been able to put aside their personal agendas to work
for the good of the animal. "That tugboat did not kill him, the politics did," remarked a distraught Gail Laurie.

Ellen Hartlmeier was equally distressed. Thrilled at the
successful return of Springer, she had become equally pas-
sionate about Luna's plight, even setting up an online peti-
tion to gather signatures from people urging the government
to return the young whale to his family. She had volunteered
with Spong's research project and spent many hours listening
to Luna vocalize in Nootka Sound. On March 10, when a friend
telephoned to give her the sad news, Hartlmeier immediately
went online to the Luna website, where she discovered a vast
outpouring of grief and anger. Feeling extremely sad, she left
her home in Steveston and walked to her favourite spot in
Garry Point Park, where she sat looking out at the ocean thinking about the meaning of Luna's life. Then she used a stick to
engrave Luna's name in the sand as a final tribute to the whale
who had had such an emotional impact on people around the
world.

"Can we, collectively as a community with all our disparate
parts, opinions, attitudes and agendas, sort through the wreckage
of this tragedy and find enough common ground to ensure that
next time the ending is different, a rejoicing instead of a dirge?"
asked Spong and Helena Symonds in a letter announcing Luna's

passing.[76] As part of this process, Michael Parfit helped to organize a "reconciliation cruise" aboard the *Uchuck III* from Gold River to Mooyah Bay in June, when passengers shared memories of the whale and set flowers adrift on the water. The purpose of the cruise was to commemorate Luna's life and heal the wounds opened by the controversy over his fate. In the meantime, condolences had flooded in from around the world. It was astonishing how much attention a single small animal could generate and proof, if any was still needed, that killer whales had become a potent symbol of the wild, their survival linked in the public mind to the survival of the marine environment as a whole.

9 ▪ CONCLUSION

BY THE SUMMER AND FALL OF 2001, when the two wayward calves, Springer and Luna, appeared where they didn't belong, the Vancouver Aquarium had been involved with killer whales for thirty-seven years. During that time the species had experienced a complete transformation in the public imagination. In 1964, when Sam Burich and Joe Bauer fired their harpoon into Moby Doll off Saturna Island, the Aquarium accidentally acquired its first whale for exhibit. In retrospect, Moby's brief stay on the Vancouver waterfront can be seen as the beginning of a major shift in public attitude. Gradually the killer whale went from being a pariah of the deep to a poster animal for the Pacific Northwest. As people were exposed to these animals in aquariums and oceanariums, fear and suspicion gave way to fascination, even affection. This change in public attitude strengthened as research conducted along the coast beginning in the 1970s revealed more and more about the whales. The public learned that they are peaceable, intelligent creatures that communicate using complex, group-specific dialects and have stronger family ties than humans. At one time they were targeted for sport, killed for animal food by fox farmers, and shot at by fishermen who feared them or wanted to eliminate the competition for salmon. With the change in attitude, it became illegal to so much as touch one. Tourists and boaters now smother killer whales with so much attention in the wild that they run a greater risk of drowning in affection than dying from abuse.

Nothing illustrates this shift in public attitude better than the stories of Springer and Luna. The fate of these two solitary animals, separated from their families, attracted worldwide attention from a concerned public that demanded that they be "saved." It would have been easy to do nothing. Killer whales die of natural causes all the time. Two more deaths would not have had much impact on the survival of their populations. But because the killer whale has become such an iconic animal in the Pacific Northwest, the public in these two cases cried out for something to be done. Of course, what it meant to save the whales was not always clear. For some it meant returning them to their families. For others it meant keeping them alive in the wild whether they rejoined their families or not. Others felt that saving their lives was the first priority, even if they ended up living in a netted-off inlet or an oceanarium. What everyone agreed on was that killer whales had to be protected.

Eventually, major operations were launched to capture the two calves and transport them back to their home territories. The Vancouver Aquarium was chosen to play a leading role in both initiatives. It was an opportunity for the experts at the Aquarium to put into practice everything they had learned from years of research into the lives of killer whales, both in captivity and in nature. After all the criticism they had taken for keeping whales on display, they could now use their expertise actually to preserve the lives of two animals in the wild.

The Vancouver Aquarium was first called in to save a killer whale in the wild in mid-December 1996. This incident was short-lived and offered none of the complexity of the Springer and Luna episodes, but it had far-reaching implications nonetheless. Two prawn fishermen noticed a lone whale in difficulty in Saltery Bay, south of Powell River. John Ford, then on staff at the Aquarium, was alerted. He flew to the scene with the DFO's Graeme Ellis and identified the animal as Kelkpa (A57), a five-year-old female. Later that day, the animal died. Veterinarian

Ron Lewis from the Animal Health Centre in Abbotsford and Skip Young from the Aquarium came to Saltery Bay to perform a necropsy. As they hauled the carcass up onto the beach with a tractor, members of Kelkpa's family milled about offshore, spy-hopping and vocalizing loudly. The two men found the situation so heart-wrenching that they thought of trying to shield Kelkpa's body from her pod.

The necropsy revealed that the young whale had died of erysipelas, a bacterial infection, the source of which was traced to the fish she had been eating. Erysipelas in marine mammals is a serious concern for marine parks and aquariums that own killer whales. It had been assumed that the source of infection had to do with the preparation or handling of the dead fish that were fed to the captive animals. In 1997, Skip Young presented the findings from Kelkpa's necropsy to a meeting of the International Association for Aquatic Animal Medicine. It was a revelation for the scientists to discover that erysipelas could be contracted from live fish in the wild.

This incident illustrates one reason why Canadian veterinarians were so cautious about giving Springer a clean bill of health before allowing her back into Canadian waters. It also reveals the importance of much of the research that goes on with the Vancouver Aquarium's marine mammal program and in collaboration with other whale researchers and veterinary scientists. In the captive environment, a great deal of information is collected that can usefully be applied to the wild population. It was this legacy of research that put the Aquarium in a position to take the lead role in relocating Springer.

The glare of publicity that accompanied the Springer and Luna incidents was intense and double-edged. It brought enormous positive publicity to the Aquarium, to the cause of animal rescue and to the animal itself. Public awareness about killer whales was higher than ever. The animal conservation message could not have been stronger. For weeks the dramatic stories were front-page news not just in the Pacific Northwest but around the world. On the television news, images of Springer and Luna cavorting in the water took precedence over wars and natural disasters. The episode provided an opportunity to teach people around the globe about the complex lives of whales. As well, it showed the Vancouver Aquarium out in the wild rescuing animals, validating the research that had been carried out by a generation of scientists. The entire incident created enormous public goodwill for the institution.

But the constant attention of the media placed extreme pressure on the decision-makers as they tried to determine what to do about Springer and Luna. Officials on both sides of the border were so frightened of making a mistake that they hesitated to do anything at all. Even if the chances of failure were small, with the whole world watching, the consequences would be enormous. Experience with other animals had shown that when wild cetaceans allow themselves to be caught, it usually means they are very ill. At the back of everyone's mind was the real possibility that the whales might die from whatever it was that had put them in such an anomalous position to begin with. It had happened before with other marine mammals—but never in front of boatloads of journalists and television cameras carrying instant images around the world.

The fear of a public relations disaster contributed to the inability of government officials to make a firm decision. In the case of Springer, it nearly resulted in tragedy. The delay stretched to a few months and most of the experts involved believed that the animal was close to death by the time it was taken into custody and rehabilitated. In the case of Luna, delay probably was fatal. The longer the decision to move him was put off, the more familiar he became with boats and humans and the more difficult it became to reintegrate him into his family group. In the end, the attempt was scuttled by politics but the deck was probably already stacked against Luna's successful re-entry. He had lost his ability to be a wild whale. In the end, the consequences cost him his life. If there was a lesson to be learned, it was that

■ In the summer of 2007 some of the people who were involved in the Springer operation held a reunion in Johnstone Strait, and who should show up but the guest of honour herself. This photograph shows Springer (l.) with her great aunt Yakat. *Lance Barrett-Lennard*

time was an important factor. There was not a lot of it to waste. Should a similar circumstance arise again, governments will have to work faster to achieve the desired outcome.

Springer's relocation represented the first time that a wild whale had ever been captured, transported back to its home range and successfully released. It was the most ambitious animal rescue effort ever mounted on the Pacific coast. A variety of government agencies, non-governmental organizations and private individuals in the US and Canada worked together to make sure it was a success. It was reminiscent of another dramatic rescue that occurred in 1988 during the waning months of the Cold War.

Three young gray whales became entrapped in the ice in the US western Arctic off Barrow, Alaska. Trying to leave the Beaufort Sea at the beginning of their fall migration southward, they would have drowned had it not been for the intervention of a Soviet icebreaker. Again, the world media were riveted by the plight of the whales, two of whom survived, and it was argued that co-operation with the Soviets to save the whales helped a generation of Americans believe in the essential humanity of the Russian people. Is it far-fetched to think that wild animals can sometimes have a positive effect in the affairs of humankind? In the case of Springer, antagonists from all sides of the animal rights movement put aside their usual quarrels and worked together to effect a rescue. It was an unprecedented collaboration, epitomized for many at the Vancouver Aquarium by the involvement of their long-time critic, Paul Spong.

Unhappily, for many reasons the *entente cordiale* that had been established around Springer broke down when the scene shifted to Nootka Sound. The collaborative atmosphere was absent in Luna's case. In its concern for security and secrecy, the Canadian government created an us-and-them atmosphere in which many of the old suspicions resurfaced. The NGOs, again symbolized by Spong, were excluded from the process and became critics instead of partners. First Nations were not adequately consulted and attempts to manage the news provoked an adversarial media. The whole episode collapsed in an embarrassing and very public setback for the Department of Fisheries and Oceans.

However, the failure to rescue Luna should not overshadow the fact that efforts to rescue marine mammals at risk in the wild can succeed. Before Springer there was no reason to believe it could be done. Now there is. During Springer's relocation, thousands of person-hours were expended, many by volunteers, while vast amounts of equipment and supplies were donated or loaned and hundreds of thousands of dollars were spent. Not so long ago Springer would have been shot as a nuisance. It may seem strange that we are now willing to spare no effort or expense to preserve a whale's life. But it is difficult to put a price on what was accomplished. Techniques have been tested and lessons learned that will allow scientists to intervene in the future to assist other endangered animals or populations. Scientists gained new insight into killer whale behaviour. For example, they were fascinated to discover that while Springer was very motivated to rejoin her natal group, it was the group that seemed uncertain about whether to take her back. One of the most remarkable things about resident killer whales is their social cohesion. No other creature stays together in a family unit for its entire life. Why aren't stray whales absorbed into other groups? The individual's motivation when it finds itself alone is to re-enter a social group, and if it is isolated for a prolonged period it will probably not be too choosy about which one. But the group is. It has no incentive to invite newcomers or prodigal children to join it. As a result, Springer's group initially exhibited mild curiosity toward her but made no welcoming gesture. It was only her persistence that eventually opened the door and she swam through. By observing this phenomenon, scientists gained deeper insight into the social life of these complex animals.

Springer's relocation also validated the extensive amount of research compiled over the years about the coastal population of killer whales, starting with Mike Bigg's trailblazing studies of the 1970s. Without this research, it would not have been possible to identify Springer (or later, Luna), to know where she belonged and with whom, and to know right away that if she was left alone she would not be able to integrate with the local population. The experts knew what to do because they knew who she was, and they knew who she was because of the exhaustive database—photographic, acoustic, genetic—that now exists on the whales of the Northwest. In the event of some catastrophic incident along the coast—an oil spill, for example—this same data will allow responders to intervene with a significant background of knowledge.

In the end, whatever scientific or institutional benefits accrued from the relocation of Springer and the attempt to relocate Luna, these were, in the main, humanitarian gestures. People reached out to save a life. Empathy need not be species-specific. Humans, social animals themselves, relate to other social animals, especially ones with the iconic status of the killer whale. We instinctively care about other creatures in dire circumstances. We will do what we can to help them.

If there was any lingering doubt about the kinds of animals killer whales are, the strength of their social bonds and the complexities of their behaviour, the episodes of Springer and Luna and the publicity surrounding them dispelled these doubts forever. "We think that that message was accepted some time ago in North America," observes Lance Barrett-Lennard. "But this story got huge publicity all around the world and it could be that it had more of an impact changing attitudes in Norway or South America or other places where killer whales exist but remain poorly understood."

The poet T.S. Eliot wrote in "Little Gidding," the fourth of his *Four Quartets*: "We shall not cease from exploration, and the end of all our exploring will be to arrive where we started and know the place for the first time." After the huge shift in public attitude that has taken place since the 1960s, to be involved in rescuing a whale from the wild, confirming its health and letting it go again, felt very much like arriving back at the beginning and understanding it for the first time.

▪ AFTERWORD

WHILE IT IS BEST KNOWN as an educational facility that displays animals for viewing by the general public, the Vancouver Aquarium also sponsors a variety of outreach programs that deal with marine mammals in the wild.

Marine Mammal Rescue Centre

During the 1960s the Aquarium began caring for stranded marine mammals—animals that were ill, orphaned, abandoned or injured and required human assistance to survive, animals in predicaments similar to Springer and Luna. Initially, rescued animals were cared for behind the scenes at the Aquarium in Stanley Park. As more animals were admitted each year, the program outgrew the space available. In 1994 the marine mammal rescue program (MMR) was relocated to the old seal pool in the Stanley Park Zoo, and in 1996 it moved again to a facility in East Vancouver. In 2004 the rescue centre settled into its current site on the Vancouver harbourfront, where the facility contains outdoor areas for animals in various stages of rehabilitation and indoor areas for food preparation, administration and diagnostic testing.

Initially, patients are accommodated individually while their presenting conditions are treated. Once they are stabilized, they are housed with other animals of the same species in larger enclosures or pools. They are fed a specialized diet depending on their physiological needs. Young animals are given electrolyte solutions or fish-based formulas, while older animals are fed high-quality fishes like herring and pilchard. Their medical conditions are treated with medications, surgery or other therapies deemed necessary by the veterinarian and the rescue team. As well, the program offers information to educate beach walkers and boaters on how to respond to distressed or stranded animals.

Over the years, the Aquarium has cared for a variety of marine mammals. Northern fur seals undertake a long migration each year from their breeding grounds in the Bering Sea to southern Oregon and California. They usually stay far offshore until they near the northern tip of Vancouver Island, staying closer to the coast for the rest of their journey. The Aquarium received its first northern fur seal in 1964, when a sport fisherman in Campbell River accidentally hooked a young animal. The pup was sent to the Aquarium, where he was named Nippy, for obvious reasons. Nippy recovered and lived for twenty years. He was the first of several stranded northern fur seal pups assisted by the Aquarium, most of them males.

In the early 1970s a commercial fisherman brought in two Steller sea lion pups, a female and a male. While fishing near Triangle Island off the north end of Vancouver Island, he saw other fishers shooting into the sea lion rookery. He counted seventy-five animals killed before he stopped keeping track. When he went ashore, he found the two pups and decided to save them by bringing them to the Aquarium. Although in those days it was thought that Steller sea lions could not be raised, these two, Sam and Jose, thrived. Once they grew larger they were sent to the Mystic Aquarium in Connecticut.

Since 1980 the population of Steller sea lions has plunged from 300,000 to less than 50,000. Over eighty-five percent of the world's Stellers have vanished and no one knows why. The Vancouver Aquarium has joined researchers at the University of British Columbia in an effort to find out what's behind this mysterious disappearance. The research at the Aquarium concentrates on the theory that the animals are not getting enough healthy food, but there is likely no single reason for the decline of the Stellers.

Sea otters were eradicated from the BC coast during the heyday of the commercial fur trade in the late eighteenth and early nineteenth centuries. A remnant population survived in Alaska, however, and in the 1960s a few individuals were relocated to the west coast of Vancouver Island at the Bunsby Islands. Since that time, the sea otter population has expanded steadily. By the early 1980s, MMR was dealing with its first imperilled sea otters from Kyuquot Sound. Then, in March 1989, the oil tanker *Exxon Valdez* struck a reef in Prince William Sound, spilling eleven million gallons of oil into the Gulf of Alaska. The Aquarium's Jeremy Fitz-Gibbon was called in to help treat the oil-soaked sea otters. He arrived a few days after the spill to find dying sea otters everywhere. To his horror, Fitz-Gibbon discovered that well-meaning rescuers were holding the otters in cages at a local gymnasium. But sea otters, with their dense fur, overheat very quickly. Fitz-Gibbon could see that the animals were comatose in their cages and were in the process of dying right in front of his eyes. He ordered them taken outside immediately and within minutes they began to revive. Because of his experience at the Aquarium, Fitz-Gibbon was able to show the volunteers in Valdez the correct food to feed the animals and how to handle them. He also introduced them to the specially designed sea otter transport cage that he and Gil Hewlett had designed several years earlier. Today this cage design is used by most institutions housing and transporting sea otters. Six sea otters were brought back from Alaska to the Aquarium to determine the long-term effects of oil exposure. Like many of the otters affected by the spill, five did not survive long-term but one young female, called Nyac, recovered and is still alive eighteen years later.

Northern elephant seals are very rare visitors to the Marine Mammal Rescue facility. Only three have ever been admitted for treatment. The first was in early May 1993. Clint Wright, then the senior marine mammal trainer at the Aquarium, took a call from Vancouver Island about a stranded female harbour seal and her pup that were going to need some help. Typically, Clint was not the person to respond to these calls, but it was toward the end of the day and he was the only person around. He agreed to come out to the Horseshoe Bay ferry terminal that evening, thinking he was going to be picking up a couple of harbour seals. Instead, when the back of the truck opened, he found a juvenile harbour seal, the supposed "mother," and a giant Northern elephant seal that was covered in oozing sores and excrement. The stench was intolerable. They drove him back to the Aquarium, where the veterinarian Dave Huff went to work on him. Later that same spring a second specimen was found at Race Rocks with a broken jaw. Both these animals recovered their health and were released back into the wild. The third elephant seal, a one-year-old female juvenile, appeared on the beach at Horseshoe Bay in April 2002. Given the name Ella, she was treated for a skin infection and released near Sooke two months later.

The MMR program is also involved in cetacean strandings and rescues. Among the first of these was a lone white-sided dolphin swimming aimlessly around the floats in Fishermans Cove in the late 1970s. It ended up beaching itself in Coal Harbour in Stanley Park, where it was rescued, brought to the Aquarium and named Arion. Despite the medical care it received, it never flourished. It had a nervous tic to its head movements and only survived about a year. The necropsy revealed that its brain was filled with parasites. Arion was the only white-sided dolphin the Aquarium has ever treated, but over the years several harbour porpoises have been rescued. It is often the case that by the time cetaceans are discovered in distress it is already too late to save them.

On April 25, 2005, the Marine Mammal Rescue division was called to Boundary Bay, where a juvenile gray whale was stranded. It was beached but still alive, despite the warm temperature. It had been discovered early that morning by passersby, including a couple of local firefighters, who erected a tent over the whale to keep the sun off and organized firehoses to keep her cool and wet. She was kept hydrated and cool all day until blood test results confirmed she was healthy. When the tide came in, the rescue staff refloated her and ushered her out into the Strait of Georgia, where she appeared to reunite with several other whales. Three months later, she was sighted around Telegraph Cove and Alert Bay.

Sea otters, Steller sea lions, northern elephant seals, northern fur seals, porpoises and whales have all been assisted by the Marine Mammal Rescue division. However, the most frequently admitted patient by far is the Pacific harbour seal pup. These animals generally arrive during the summer months, rehabilitate for several months, then are released back into the Strait of Georgia. On average, about ninety harbour seals come through the gates each season.

The need for facilities such as the Aquarium's MMRC was highlighted in dramatic fashion on August 20, 2007, just as *Operation Orca* was going to press. In Johnstone Strait, close to the rubbing beaches at Robson Bight, a passing barge under tow tipped its load of heavy equipment into three hundred metres of water. Among the vehicles spilling into the ocean was a tanker truck containing ten thousand litres of diesel fuel, some of which leaked out into the water, creating a fuel slick on the surface about two kilometres long and fifty metres wide. About sixty killer whales were in the vicinity of the spill, including Springer, and witnesses verified that at least some of the animals swam through the slick. Unlike oil, diesel fuel evaporates fairly quickly. Still, the whales could have breathed in fumes, which can create carcinogenic toxins in the animals' lungs. Scientists will probably never be able to determine what damage, if any, resulted from this incident. But it provides a warning as to just how fragile are the coastal environment and the animals that inhabit it.

Killer Whale Adoption Program

The Vancouver Aquarium has sponsored a Killer Whale Adoption Program since 1993. Members of the public have the opportunity actually to "adopt" an individual whale from among the coastal resident or transient populations. For a fee, participants in the program receive adoption papers for a year for a particular whale of their own choosing, along with a biography of the whale and a copy of the program's newsletter, *The Blackfish Sounder.* Proceeds from the adoption program fund continuing research on wild killer whales. To learn more about the adoption program, visit its website at **www.killerwhale.org**.

British Columbia Cetacean Sightings Network

Established in 1999 and operated in co-operation with Fisheries and Oceans Canada, the BC Cetacean Sightings Network is the place to call if you have spotted a wild whale, porpoise or dolphin in coastal waters. The network also monitors sightings of sea turtles. The central clearing house for sightings in the province, it collects information on cetacean activity that researchers would not be able to obtain on their own. The network receives sightings from whale watchers, tour guide operators, lighthouse keepers, tugboat crews, pleasure boaters and anyone else lucky enough to spot an animal. During the summer it logs between fifty and one hundred sightings a week. Each one is entered into a database, which is available to researchers and scientists. To report a sighting, telephone **1-866-I SAW ONE** or email **sightings@vanaqua.org**.

■ ENDNOTES

1 Alexandra Morton, *Listening to Whales* (New York: Ballantine Books, 2002), p. 230.
2 Peter Knudtson, *Orca: Visions of the Killer Whale* (Vancouver: Douglas & McIntyre, 1996), p. 39.
3 The best introduction to killer whales of the North Pacific Coast: John K.B. Ford, Graeme M. Ellis and Kenneth C. Balcomb, *Killer Whales*, 2nd ed. (Vancouver: UBC Press, 2000); John K.B. Ford and Graeme M. Ellis, *Transients: Mammal-Hunting Killer Whales* (Vancouver: UBC Press, 1999); and Craig Matkin, Graeme Ellis, Eva Saulitis, Lance Barrett-Lennard and Dena Matkin, *Killer Whales of Southern Alaska* (Homer AK: North Gulf Oceanic Society, 1999).
4 *Vancouver Sun*, March 2, 2002.
5 This account is based mainly on Kenneth Brower, *Freeing Keiko: The Journey of a Killer Whale from Free Willy to the Wild* (New York: Gotham Books, 2005), and Susan Orlean, "Where's Willy?", *The New Yorker*, Sept. 23, 2002, pp. 57–63.
6 *Vancouver Province*, March 6, 2002.
7 *Seattle Times*, May 7, 2002.
8 Ibid., May 17, 2002.
9 Murray Newman, *Life in a Fishbowl: Confessions of an Aquarium Director* (Vancouver: Douglas & McIntyre, 1994), p. 81.
10 Morton, *Listening to the Whales*, p. 205.
11 For the story of the basking shark, see Scott Wallace and Brian Gisborne, *Basking Sharks: The Slaughter of BC's Gentle Giants* (Vancouver: New Star Books, 2006).
12 *Vancouver Sun*, May 16, 1956.
13 Erich Hoyt, *Orca: The Whale Called Killer* (Camden East ON: Camden House, 1984), pp. 18–19; originally published 1981.
14 The following account is based on Newman, *Life in a Fishbowl*, pp. 80ff.
15 *Vancouver Sun*, June 3, 1964.
16 Newman, p. 93.
17 The following account is based on Ted Griffin, *Namu: Quest for a Killer Whale* (Seattle: Gryphon West Publishers, 1982); Sylvia Fraser, "The Wild Saga of Namu the Whale." *Star Weekly* (Aug. 28, 1965); Gil Hewlett, "Unpublished notes taken during observation of whale Namu, July 1–29, 1965", 58 pp.; and Newman, pp. 104–106.
18 Newman, pp. 106–8.
19 Hoyt, p. 43.
20 Newman, p. 112.
21 This episode is described in Newman, pp. 112–16.
22 This incident is described in Hoyt, pp. 115–19.

23 David A. E. Spalding, *Whales of the West Coast* (Madeira Park: Harbour Publishing, 1998), p. 136.

24 Newman, pp. 157–58.

25 Ford, et.al., *Killer Whales*, p. 13.

26 John K.B. Ford, "Obituary for Mike Bigg," *Marine Mammal Science*, 7(3) (July 1991), pp. 326–28.

27 Hoyt, pp. 203–4.

28 This account relies, in part, on Paul Jeune, *Miracle: The Story of a Baby Killer Whale* (Victoria: Sealand of the Pacific, 1978).

29 Morton, p. 147.

30 Transcript of National Public Radio program, June 11, 2002.

31 John Swanton, "Contributions to the Ethnology of the Haida," Vol. V, *The Jessup North Pacific Expedition* (New York: Memoir of the American Museum of Natural History, 1905), p. 17.

32 Franz Boas, "Kwakiutl Culture as Reflected in Mythology," *Memoirs of the American Folk-Lore Society*, Vol. XXVIII (New York, 1935), p. 158.

33 Robert Galois, *Kwakwaka'wakw Settlements, 1775–1920: A Geographical Analysis and Gazetteer* (Vancouver: UBC Press, 1994), p. 8.

34 Ibid., p. 317.

35 Lance Barrett-Lennard, John Ford and K.A. Heise, "The mixed blessing of echolocation: differences in sonar use by fish-eating and mammal-eating killer whales," *Animal Behaviour*, 51 (1996), pp. 553–65.

36 John Ford, "Vocal Traditions among Resident Killer Whales (*Orcinus orca*) in Coastal Waters of British Columbia," *Canadian Journal of Zoology*, 69 (1990), p. 1476.

37 Alexandra Morton and Helena Symonds, "Displacement of *Orcinus orca* (L.) by high amplitude sound in British Columbia, Canada." *ICES Journal of Marine Science*, 59 (2002), pp. 76–78.

38 Andrew D. Foote, Richard W. Osborne and A. Rus Hoelzel, "Environment: Whale-call response to masking boat noise," *Nature* 428 (April 29, 2004), p. 910.

39 *Victoria Times-Colonist*, Nov. 12, 2002.

40 Ibid , May 16, 2003.

41 J.C. Beaglehole, ed., *The Journals of Captain James Cook,* vol. 3, part II (Cambridge: Cambridge University Press: 1967), p. 1088.

42 James R. Gibson, *Otter Skins, Boston Ships, and China Goods: The Maritime Fur Trade of the Northwest Coast, 1785–1841* (Montreal: McGill-Queen's University Press, 1992), pp. 300–307.

43 Martha Black, *Out of the Mist: Treasures of the Nuu-chah-nulth Chiefs* (Victoria: Royal British Columbia Museum, 1999), p. 33. For more on the Nuu-chah-nulth, see also E.Y. Arima, *The West Coast (Nootka) People* (Victoria: British Columbia Provincial

Museum, 1983) and Alan L. Hoover, ed., *Nuu-chah-nulth Voices, Histories, Objects and Journeys* (Victoria: Royal British Columbia Museum, 2000).

44 Hilary Stewart, ed. *The Adventures and Sufferings of John R. Jewitt, Captive of Maquinna* (Vancouver: Douglas & McIntyre, 1987), orig. pub. 1815, p. 92.

45 The story of the shrine is told in Aldona Jonaitis, *The Yuquot Whalers' Shrine* (Seattle: University of Washington Press, 1999).

46 Philip Drucker, *The Northern and Central Nootkan Tribes* (Washington: The Smithsonian Institution, 1951), p. 49.

47 Chief Earl Maquinna George, *Living on the Edge: Nuu-chah-nulth History from an Ahousaht Chief's Perspective* (Winlaw BC: Sono Nis Press, 2003), p. 54.

48 "Luna journal," Aug. 15, 2002, **www.salishsea.ca**.

49 Ibid., Sept. 12, 2002.

50 "Letter from Marilyn Joyce to Orca Network," Oct. 11, 2002, **www.salishsea.ca/m3/luna/ luna_articles**.

51 Ibid.

52 *National Post*, Feb. 13, 2003.

53 Ibid.

54 *Blackfish Sounder*, no. 11, 2003.

55 Bjorn Carey, "How killer whales trap gullible gulls," **www. msnbc.msn.com/id/11163990/ from/RS.4**.

56 Vancouver Aquarium press release, May 29, 2003.

57 *Victoria Times-Colonist*, July 24, 2003.

58 *Victoria Times-Colonist*, June 12, 2003.

59 Ibid., July 6, 2003.

60 *Ha-Shilth-Sa* newspaper, Oct. 6, 2005.

61 *Victoria Times-Colonist*, April 3, 2004.

62 Reports from OrcaLab's Luna research project, June 2, 2004, **www.reuniteluna.com/luna_ research-project**.

63 *Vancouver Province*, Oct. 8, 2003.

64 *Vancouver Province*, June 17, 2004.

65 *Victoria Times-Colonist*, June 22, 2004.

66 *Victoria Times-Colonist*, June 19, 2004.

67 See Michael Parfit, "Whale of a Tale," *Smithsonian Magazine* (Nov. 2004).

68 *Victoria Times-Colonist*, June 24, 2004.

69 Ibid., June 25, 2004.

70 *Nanaimo Daily News*, June 26, 2004.

71 *Victoria Times-Colonist*, July 19, 2004.

72 *Pacific Yachting*, December 2004.

73 *Ha-shilth-Sa* newspaper, March 24, 2005.

74 Michael Parfit and Suzanne Chisholm, "Luna Behaviour Updates," July 29, 2005, **www.reuniteluna.com**.

75 Paul Spong and Helena Symonds, "OrcaLab: Luna Dies," March 20, 2006, **www.reuniteluna.com**.

76 Ibid.

■ SOURCES

INTERVIEWS

Most of the research for this book consists of recorded interviews with the following individuals. The interviews took place between 2002 and early 2007.

Kelly Anderson, Washington State Ferries, Seattle, WA

Chris Angus, Totem Oysters, Egmont, BC

Clare Backman, Stolt Sea Farm Inc., Campbell River, BC

David Bain, University of Washington, Seattle, WA

Kenneth Balcomb, Center for Whale Research, Friday Harbor, WA

Lance Barrett-Lennard, Vancouver Aquarium

Joe Bauer, commercial fisher

Keith Bell, Nootka Sound boater, Gold River, BC

Diana Best, widow of Alan Best, mother of Robin Best

Joseph Bettis, retired professor of religious studies and recreational boater, Friday Harbor, WA

Jim Borrowman, whale-watch operator, Telegraph Cove, BC

Richard Buchanan, Agrimarine Industries, Vancouver, BC

Helen Burich, widow of Sam Burich, Vancouver, BC

Margaret Butschler, Vancouver Aquarium

Barbara Cranmer, Umista Cultural Centre, Alert Bay, BC

Bill Cranmer, 'Namgis First Nation, Alert Bay, BC

Marilyn Dalheim, National Marine Mammal Laboratory, Seattle, WA

Nic Dedeluk, Straitwatch coordinator, Telegraph Cove, BC

Volker Deeke, research associate, Vancouver Aquarium

Mike Downey, Nichols Brothers Boat Builders, Whidbey Island, WA

Vick Edwards, Hanson Lumber, Seattle, WA

Graeme Ellis, Department of Fisheries and Oceans, Nanaimo, BC

Jeremy Fitz-Gibbon, Vancouver Aquarium

John Ford, Department of Fisheries and Oceans, Nanaimo, BC

Jeff Foster, marine mammal capture specialist, Auburn, WA

Floyd Fulmer, Washington State Ferries, Seattle, WA

Fred Fulmer, Tlingit carver, Seattle, WA

Gerry Furney, Mayor, Port McNeill, BC

Brad Hanson, National Marine Mammal Laboratory, Seattle, WA

Ellen Hartlmeier, Vancouver Aquarium volunteer, Steveston, BC

David Howitt, OrcaLab, Hanson Island, BC

David Huff, Vancouver Aquarium

Marilyn Joyce, Department of Fisheries and Oceans, Vancouver, BC

Jim Kershaw, Vancouver Aquarium board director

Brian Konrad, tug deckhand, Nootka
Sound, BC
Michael Kundu, Project Sea Wolf,
Marysville, WA
Lisa Lamb, whale watch operator,
San Juan Island, WA
Janet Landucci, Vancouver
Aquarium
Lisa Larsson, OrcaLab, Nootka
Sound, BC
Gail Laurie, reuniteluna website,
Campbell River, BC
Darlene Lazuk, charter operator,
Gold River, BC
Ian McAskie, Pacific Biological
Station, Nanaimo, BC
Jim McBain, Sea World, San Diego,
CA
Pat McGeer, University of British
Columbia, Vancouver, BC
Bill Mackay, whale watch operator,
Port McNeill, BC
Bob McLaughlin, Project Sea Wolf,
Seattle, WA
Tom McMillen, charter boat
operator, Roche Harbor, WA
Peter Macnair, ethnologist, Victoria,
BC
Ian McTaggart-Cowan, zoologist,
Victoria, BC
Peter Miles, Vancouver Aquarium
board director, Vancouver, BC
Mark Miller, filmmaker, Vancouver,
BC
Sue Murray, Vancouver Aquarium
Angela Neilson, Vancouver
Aquarium
Matt Nichols, Nichols Brothers Boat
Builders, Whidbey Island, WA
John Nightingale, Vancouver
Aquarium
Brent Norberg, National Marine
Fisheries Service, Seattle, WA

Brian O'Neill, Springer rescue team,
Colorado
Michael Parfit, writer and filmmaker,
Sidney, BC
Stan Patty, *Seattle Times,* Seattle, WA
Dan Peiser, Vancouver Aquarium
Keith Petrie, Stolt Sea Farms,
Campbell River, BC
Bets Rasmussen, Oregon Graduate
Institute, Beaverton, Oregon
Stephen Raverty, BC Animal Health
Centre, Abbotsford, BC
Donny Reid, Vancouver Aquarium
Brian Richman, retired fisheries
officer, Port Coquitlam, BC
Christine Sakhrani, Vancouver
Aquarium
Celia Schorr, Washington State
Ferries, Seattle, WA
Peter Schroeder, veterinarian,
Sequim, WA
Rob Scott, Canadian Coast Guard,
Victoria, BC
Mark Sears, Parks Department,
Seattle, WA
Brian Sheehan, Vancouver
Aquarium
Jen Shore, Springer rescue team,
Seattle, WA
Kim Shride, Washington State
Ferries, Seattle, WA
Janine Siemens, Stolt Sea Farm Inc.,
Campbell River, BC
Paul Spong, OrcaLab, Hanson
Island, BC
Sandra Stone, recreational boater,
Cincinnati, OH
Helena Symonds, OrcaLab, Hanson
Island, BC
David Taylor, veterinarian,
International Zoo Veterinary
Group, West Yorkshire, UK

Ed Thorburn, Department of Fisheries and Oceans, Gold River, BC

Hilary Vallance, Children and Women's Health Centre of British Columbia, Vancouver, BC

Valeria Vergara, University of British Columbia, Vancouver, BC

Janice Waite, National Marine Mammal Laboratory, Seattle, WA,

Chris White, Nootka Sound logger, Gold River, BC

Bob Wood, Project Sea Wolf, Seattle, WA

Clint Wright, Vancouver Aquarium

Harald, Yurk, Department of Zoology, University of British Columbia, Vancouver, BC

UNPUBLISHED MATERIAL

Hewlett, Gil. Unpublished notes taken during observation of whale Namu, July 1–29, 1965, 58 pp.

National Public Radio. Selected program transcripts, 2001–2003

Pacific Biological Station, Nanaimo, BC, Minutes of meetings, July 16 and 27, 1960.

Vancouver Aquarium. Board of Directors. Minutes of meetings, March–July 2002.

Vancouver Aquarium. Press releases, 2002–2004.

NEWSPAPERS AND PERIODICALS

Blackfish Sounder
Ha-Shilth-sa newspaper
Nanaimo Daily News
Nanaimo Free Press
National Post
The Oregonian
Seattle Times
Vancouver Sun
Vancouver *Province*
Victoria Times-Colonist

WEBSITES

www.lunastewardship.com
www.reuniteluna.com
www.salishsea.ca
www.westcoastaquatic.ca

FILMS

Kaka'win, a documentary film by Leah Nelson, 2006. 16:38 min.

Tale of Two Whales, a film by Mark Miller, Discovery Channel, 43 min.

BOOKS AND ARTICLES

Arima, E.Y. *The West Coast People: The Nootka of Vancouver Island and Cape Flattery*. Victoria: BC Provincial Museum, Special Publication #6, 1983.

Barrett-Lennard, Lance, John K.B. Ford and K.A. Heise. "The mixed blessing of echolocation: differences in sonar use by fish-eating and mammal-eating killer whales."

Animal Behaviour 51 (1996): 553–65.

Beaglehole, J.C., ed. *The Journals of Captain James Cook.* Cambridge: Cambridge University Press, 1967.

Bigg, M.A., P.F. Olesiuk, G.M. Ellis, John K.B. Ford and Kenneth Balcolm, III. "Social organization and geneology of resident killer whales (*Orcinus orca*) in the coastal waters of British Columbia and Washington State." *Report of the International Whaling Commission,* Special Issue 12 (1990): 383–405.

Black, Martha. *Out of the Mist: Treasures of the Nuu-Chah-Nulth Chiefs.* Victoria: Royal British Columbia Museum, 1999.

Boas, Franz. "Kwakiutl Culture as Reflected in Mythology." *Memoirs of the American Folk-Lore Society,* vol. XXVIII. New York, 1935.

Brower, Kenneth. *Freeing Keiko: The Journey of a Killer Whale from Free Willy to the Wild.* New York: Gotham Books, 2005.

Carl, G. Clifford. "Albinistic Killer Whales in British Columbia," *British Columbia Provincial Museum of Natural History Anthropological Report* (1959): 29–36.

Drucker, Philip. *The Northern and Central Nootkan Tribes.* Washington: Smithsonian Institution, 1951.

Foote, Andrew D., Richard W. Osborne and A. Rus Hoelzel. "Environment: Whale-call response to masking boat noise." *Nature,* 428 (April 29, 2004): 910.

Ford, John K.B. "Vocal Traditions among Resident Killer Whales (*Orcinus orca*) in Coastal Waters of British Columbia." *Canadian Journal of Zoology,* 69 (1990): 1454–1483.

Ford, John K.B., G.M. Ellis, Lance Barrett-Lennard, Alexandra Morton, R.S. Palm, and Kenneth Balcolm, III. "Dietary Specialization in two sympatric populations of killer whales (*Orcinus orca*) in coastal British Columbia and adjacent waters." *Canadian Journal of Zoology,* 76 (1998): 1456–71.

Ford, John K.B., Graeme M. Ellis and Kenneth C. Balcomb. *Killer Whales,* 2nd ed. Vancouver: UBC Press, 2000.

Ford, John K.B. and Graeme M. Ellis. *Transients: Mammal-Hunting Killer Whales.* Vancouver: UBC Press, 1999.

Fraser, Sylvia. "The Wild Saga of Namu the Whale." *Star Weekly* (August 28, 1965).

Galois, Robert. *Kwakwaka'wakw Settlements, 1775–1920: A Geographical Analysis and Gazetteer.* Vancouver: UBC Press, 1994.

George, Chief Earl Maquinna. *Living on the Edge: Nuu-chah-nulth History from an Ahousaht Chief's Perspective.* Winlaw BC: Sono Nis Press, 2003.

Gibson, James R. *Otter Skins, Boston Ships, and China Goods: The*

Maritime Fur Trade of the Northwest Coast, 1785–1841. Montreal: McGill-Queen's University Press, 1992.

Griffin, Ted. *Namu: Quest for a Killer Whale.* Seattle: Gryphon West Publishers, 1982.

Haley D. "Albino Killer Whale." *Sea Frontiers* (Mar/April 1973), vol. 19, no. 2: 66–71.

Hoover, Alan L., ed. *Nuu-Chah-Nulth Voices, Histories, Objects & Journeys.* Victoria: Royal British Columbia Museum, 2000.

Hoyt, Erich. *Orca, The Whale Called Killer.* Toronto: Camden House, 1984; orig. publ. 1981.

Jeune, Paul. *Miracle: the Story of a Baby Killer Whale.* Victoria: Sealand of the Pacific, 1978. Jonaitis, Aldona. *The Yuquot Whalers' Shrine.* Seattle: University of Washington Press, 1999.

Jones, Laurie. *Nootka Sound Explored: A Westcoast History.* Campbell River: Ptarmigan Press, 1991.

Kennedy, Liv. *Coastal Villages.* Madeira Park, BC: Harbour Publishing, 1991.

Knudtson, Peter. *Orca: Visions of the Killer Whale.* Vancouver: Douglas & McIntyre, 1996.

Matkin, Craig, Graeme Ellis, Eva Saulitis, Lance Barrett-Lennard and Dena Matkin. *Killer Whales of Southern Alaska.* Homer AK: North Gulf Oceanic Society, 1999.

Morton, Alexandra. *Listening to Whales: What the Orcas Have Taught Us.* New York: Ballantine Books, 2002.

_____ and H.K. Symonds, "Displacement of *Orcinus orca* (L.) by high amplitude sound in British Columbia, Canada." *ICES Journal of Marine Science,* 59 (2002): 71–80.

Newman, Murray. "Making Friends with a Killer Whale." *National Geographic* (March 1966), pp.

_____. *Life in a Fishbowl: Confessions of an Aquarium Director.* Vancouver: Douglas & McIntyre, 1994.

Newman, Murray A. and Patrick L McGeer. "The Capture and Care of a Killer Whale, *Orcinus orca*, in British Columbia." *Zoologica,* vol. 51, no. 2 (Summer, 1966): 59–75.

Newman, Murray A., with John Nightingale. *People, Fish and Whales: The Vancouver Aquarium Story.* Madeira Park: Harbour Publishing, 2006.

Norris, Kenneth. *The Porpoise Watcher: A Naturalist's Experiences with Porpoises and Whales.* New York: W.W. Norton & Co., 1974.

Orlean, Susan. "Where's Willy?" *The New Yorker* (Sept. 23, 2002): 57–63.

Parfit, Michael. "Whale of a Tale." *Smithsonian Magazine* (Nov. 2004).

Spalding, David A.E. *Whales of the West Coast.* Madeira Park: Harbour Publishing, 1998.

Stewart, Hilary, ed. *The Adventures and Sufferings of John R. Jewitt, Captive of Maquinna.*

Vancouver: Douglas & McIntyre, 1987; orig. publ. 1815.

Swanton, John R. "Contributions to the Ethnology of the Haida." Vol. V. *The Jessup North Pacific Expedition*. New York: Memoir of the American Museum of Natural History, 1905.

Wallace, Scott and Brian Gisborne. *Basking Sharks: The Slaughter of BC's Gentle Giants*. Vancouver: New Star Books, 2006.

Wallas, Chief James. *Kwakiutl Legends*. North Vancouver: Hancock House, 1981.

■ INDEX